Camping
Southern
California

Richard McMahon

FALCONGUIDE®

GUILFORD, CONNECTICUT
HELENA, MONTANA
AN IMPRINT OF THE GLOBE PEQUOT PRESS

A FALCON GUIDE ®

All photos by Richard McMahon unless otherwise noted.
Cover photo © Cheyenne Rouse.

Cataloging-in-Publication Data is on record at the Library of Congress
McMahon, Richard, 1928–
    Camping Southern California / by Richard McMahon,
       p. cm. — (A Falcon Guide)
    Includes index.
    ISBN-13: 978-1-56044-711-5
    ISBN-10: 1-56044-711-7
       1. Camp sites, facilities, etc.—California, Southern—Guidebooks. 2.
Camp sites, facilities, etc.—California, Southern—Guidebooks. 3. California,
Southern—Guidebooks.
I. Title. II. Series.

GV191.42.C2M346 1998
796.54'09794'9—dc21
                                                  98-49848
                                                     CIP

Text pages printed on recycled paper
Manufactured in the United States of America
First Edition/Fourth Printing

To Ann, for a lifetime of love and support,
and to Rick, Geoffrey, Carol, and Chris,
for being all any parent could ask for.

Contents

Acknowledgments

Many people assisted me in the writing of this book. They are too numerous to mention individually, but I would be remiss if I did not at least acknowledge the organizations they represented. I am indebted to the many rangers and administrative personnel of the national, state, and county parks of California who provided information and offered me assistance.

As I began my travels, I was aware, like most people, of the minor controversy regarding public versus private use of land managed by the USDA Forest Service. I am happy to say that, wherever I went, I found Forest Service employees friendly, knowledgeable, and deeply committed to the recreational use of our national forests.

Whatever tax dollars are spent on the Division of Tourism of the California Trade and Commerce Agency, taxpayers are clearly getting their money's worth. Tourism employees cheerfully answered a flood of questions; provided brochures, maps, and other publications; returned long distance calls; and generally worked to insure that the wonderful features of their state were made known to me.

Two people were particularly helpful and deserve special mention. Ranger Cathy Johnson, at Lake San Antonio County Park, took much time to give me a guided tour of one of the best waterfront campgrounds in the state and provided much detailed information. Paul Kaleth, general manager of Parks Management Company, Morro Bay, came to my assistance when rock slides threatened to maroon me on the Big Sur Coast.

Finally, I would like to tip my hat to the many volunteers who donate their time and energy to our national, state, and county parks and forests. Staffing information desks, assisting with outdoor programs, building and maintaining trails, serving as campground hosts, and performing other tasks, these dedicated folks, many of them senior citizens, provide services and perform jobs that would not otherwise get done.

Introduction

Welcome to California, the Golden State, the most populous state in the Union and the third largest in area. By far the richest state in terms of gross product, California is more appropriately compared to nations than to other states. In this context, California is the sixth largest "nation" in the world, its gross product exceeded only by those of the United States, the United Kingdom, Russia, Germany, France, and Japan.

Driving this economic dynamo is agriculture; California's output far exceeds that of any other state. If the Midwest is the breadbasket of the United States, California is the nation's fruit and vegetable basket, leading the nation in production of grapes, tomatoes, lettuce, and a host of other orchard and vegetable crops. And in manufacturing, mineral extraction, and fishing, California ranks among the top four states.

Geographically, the state resembles a giant water trough. The Coast Ranges to the west and the Sierra Nevada to the east line the Central Valley, the bottom of the trough, which runs north to south. Both the highest and the lowest points in the contiguous 48 states can be found in California, less than 100 miles apart: Mount Whitney soars to 14,495 feet, while Death Valley plunges 282 feet below sea level.

The climate of California is as diverse as its landscape. Frigid winter temperatures are common in the high reaches of the Sierra Nevada, while searing summer heat bakes the southeastern deserts. In the main, the state features dry summers and rainy winters, with regional variations. The coast from the Oregon

Visitors to the deserts of California will find a unique and dramatic landscape embellished with snowcapped mountains, golden sand dunes, and colorful wildflowers.

border to just north of Los Angeles boasts cool summers and mild winters; south of Los Angeles, coastal residents enjoy some of the most pleasant year-round temperatures found anywhere. In the Central Valley, a continental climate prevails, with hot summers and cool winters, and the mountainous regions are noted for short summers and cold winters.

The first sighting of California by Europeans was made in 1542 by the Spanish navigator Juan Rodriguez Cabrillo. But it was not until 1769 that Franciscan friar Junipero Serra established the first mission at San Diego. Additional missions and the opening of an overland supply route from Mexico spurred colonization from the south, and following Mexico's independence from Spain in 1821, American settlers began to arrive. In 1846, a group of American settlers proclaimed the establishment of the California Republic, and in May of that year the United States declared war on Mexico. In the peace treaty drafted following the war, Mexico ceded California to the United States, and in 1850 California became the 31st state of the Union.

With its diverse landscape, its relatively mild climate, and its magnificent scenery, California is a paradise for outdoor enthusiasts and sportsmen. The state contains eight national parks, five national monuments, nearly 400 state and county parks, 20 million acres of national forest, and numerous other recreational lands under federal, state, and local jurisdiction. There are more than 1,500 public and private campgrounds, most of them accessible by car. Stretching from the northern mountains to the southern deserts, they range from primitive sites for tents or self-contained RVs to plush resorts with pools, spas, tennis courts, and even golf courses. What they have in common is their ability to provide a memorable outdoor experience.

Camping in Southern California

Southern California has a campground for everyone and every kind of outdoor activity. In addition to the hundreds of standard family campgrounds, there are campgrounds designed for hikers, equestrians, boaters, anglers, and even off-road-vehicle drivers. Dozens of group campgrounds are set aside for organizations or other private groups.

This book features descriptions of more than 400 campgrounds managed by public agencies in Southern California. Together, the following agencies administer more than 95 percent of all the campgrounds in the state.

The National Park Service manages campgrounds in Sequoia, Kings Canyon, Death Valley, and Joshua Tree National Parks, Pinnacles National Monument, and Mojave National Preserve. *Sunset: The Magazine of Western Living* lists two campgrounds administered by the NPS among its top 100 campgrounds in the western United States: Wildrose in Death Valley, and Hole-in-the-Wall in Mojave Preserve. Most NPS campgrounds are available only on a first-come, first-served basis, but a few accept reservations. These are noted in the campground descriptions. NPS campgrounds do not have hookups. A fee is charged at most, but some of the more remote sites with minimum facilities are free.

The Forest Service, a branch of the U.S. Department of Agriculture, oversees by far the largest number of campgrounds of any organization in Southern California. These campgrounds can be found in all seven national forests: Los Padres, Angeles, San Bernardino, Cleveland, Inyo, Sierra, and Sequoia. *Sunset* has listed one Forest Service campground, Kirk Creek, among the ten best campgrounds in the western United States; three, Burnt Rancheria, Quaking Aspen, and Lion, are listed in the top 100. Although most Forest Service campsites are available on a first-come, first-served basis, reservations are accepted at the more popular locations, some of which have hookups. Most charge a fee, and many of these are operated by concessionaires. At some undeveloped sites, no fee is charged.

In the national forests, it is not necessary to stay only at established campgrounds. It is permissible to camp anywhere unless regulations specifically prohibit it. It is best to check with the nearest Forest Service office or ranger station, where personnel can recommend the best areas for such open camping. A campfire permit is required outside developed campgrounds, even to cook with a camp stove or charcoal brazier. The permit is free at Forest Service facilities.

At four national forests (Los Padres, Angeles, San Bernardino, and Cleveland) an Adventure Pass is now required for day use of the forest. The fee is $5 a day or $30 a year; holders of Golden Age Passports get a 50 percent discount. The pass is not required for those driving through the forest, stopping at visitor centers, seeking information at ranger stations or other Forest Service offices, or parking at any location where a site-specific fee is already charged, such as a campground. This fee is likely to be extended to other national forests in the future.

California State Parks and Recreation Areas provide campgrounds in some of the most scenic and recreation-oriented areas in the state. *Sunset* includes five of these campgrounds among the top 100 in the West: Pfeiffer Big Sur, Montana de Oro, Cuyamaca Ranchos, and Doheny and El Capitan State Beaches. Many state-park campgrounds accept reservations, and during the summer months it is often impossible to stay at the more popular sites without one, especially on weekends or holidays. Many state-park campgrounds offer hookups. Many of those that do not have flush toilets and hot showers. All state-park campgrounds charge a fee.

County campgrounds often offer the opportunity to stay at first-rate sites in scenic areas that are off the beaten path and sometimes overlooked by the traveling hordes of summer. For those who might be inclined to overlook county campgrounds, two of them, William Heise and Jalama Beach Parks, made *Sunset's* list of the top 100 in the West. About half of all county campgrounds accept reservations, and about half (not necessarily the same ones) have hookups. All except one (Palo Verde) charge a fee.

The Bureau of Land Management administers campgrounds in the eastern Sierra and the southeastern desert, including three within the Imperial Sand Dunes. BLM campgrounds do not accept reservations, and none have hookups. Fees are charged at about half the campgrounds; undeveloped campgrounds are usually free.

The agency has also established the California Long-Term Visitor Areas Program for the benefit of campers who wish to spend all or part of the winter season in the desert areas of California and Arizona. Participants can purchase a weekly or seasonal permit that entitles them to camp at any of eight campgrounds in California and two in Arizona and to move around freely among them for the duration of the permit. Cost of a seasonal permit, good from September 15 to April 15, is $100. The weekly permit, good for seven consecutive days, is $20. Golden Age Pass discounts do not apply. Permits may be obtained by contacting the Bureau of Land Management, Palm Springs Resource Area, 63-500 Garnet Avenue, PO Box 2000, North Palm Springs, CA 92258; phone: 760-251-4800.

The U.S. Army Corps of Engineers has constructed a series of dams throughout California, and many of the reservoirs created by these dams offer a full range of water sports. The corps has constructed campgrounds at most of them. Although none have hookups, they do offer most other amenities, including flush toilets and showers. Corps campgrounds do not accept reservations and are available on a first-come, first-served basis. Fees are charged at all locations.

Special districts and municipalities also manage campgrounds throughout the state. Special district facilities are similar to Corps of Engineer sites in that they are usually associated with water reclamation projects, such as lakes. Cities and townships also offer campgrounds, usually in connection with a nearby point of interest or within a park. Most have hookups and accept reservations, and all charge fees.

4

Travel Tips

Maps. Although it is possible to find many of the campgrounds listed in this book by using the maps and directions furnished with the entries, it is still a good idea to carry a California road map to get an idea of the big picture and to help locate nearby points of interest. For those who want more detail, I recommend the DeLorme Mapping Company's *Southern & Central California Atlas & Gazetteer*, available in most large bookstores.

If you plan to camp in the national forests, the appropriate Forest Service map is an invaluable guide, particularly if you intend to hike or explore by car, horseback, or bicycle. Maps are available at Forest Service visitor centers and most ranger stations and can also be ordered by mail. There is a map for each of the seven national forests in Southern California—two for the Los Padres. Cost per map is $4. A word of warning, though: campground information on Forest Service maps is not always up to date. This is particularly true in the case of fee status and the availability of water. Some district offices have published separate pamphlets that update campground information.

Pets. In almost all campgrounds where pets are permitted, they must be confined or leashed. In county, state, and national parks, pets are usually not permitted on hiking trails or on beaches. In national forests, pets are prohibited on some trails. Many public campgrounds charge fees for pets, ranging from $1 to $3 a night.

Wheelchair access. Many public campgrounds have wheelchair-accessible facilities, including restrooms, and this is indicated in the campground quick-reference tables. Some feature wheelchair-accessible trails and nature loops. Because many public jurisdictions are making efforts to upgrade the accessibility of their existing facilities, prospective users should contact individual campgrounds for the latest information.

Fishing and hunting licenses. Licenses are required in California for both salt- and freshwater fishing. The annual cost is $27.05 for residents. There are three types of license available to nonresidents: annual ($73.50), 10-day ($27.05), and one-day ($9.70). Annual licenses are available at a reduced cost of $4.25 for people over 65 who live on reduced incomes or receive financial aid and to military veterans with a 70 percent or higher disability rating.

To be eligible for a hunting license in California, an individual must take an approved hunter safety course, present a hunter safety certificate from another state or Canadian province, or present a valid hunting license from another state or province. Licenses cost $26.25 for residents and $92.25 for nonresidents.

Rules of the road. The speed limit on rural interstate highways is 65 miles an hour unless otherwise posted. Elsewhere, speed limits are as posted. Right turns at red lights are permitted after stopping, unless posted otherwise. At least two people must occupy a vehicle in order to use car-pool lanes. Seat belts must be worn by the driver and all passengers. Children up to 4 years of age or under 40 pounds must be restrained in a child safety seat. Automobile liability insurance is mandatory.

Rules for RVs. Passengers are not permitted to ride in trailers, but they may ride in fifth-wheelers if there is a way to communicate with the driver. Trailer brakes and safety chains are required for trailers weighing more than 1,500 pounds; power-brake systems require breakaway switches. The maximum width for RVs driving on California roads is 102 inches, and the maximum length, including towed vehicles, is 65 feet. Propane cylinders must be turned off when a vehicle is in motion. RVs are required to carry a fire extinguisher.

Reservations. If you are traveling in summer, on holidays, or on weekends, it is a good idea to make reservations wherever it is possible to do so—especially for longer stays. Beach, national park, state park, and many other campgrounds fill quickly during these periods, and campers who arrive late may find no vacancies.

Off-season travel. One of the best times to travel in Southern California is in the fall. After Labor Day, students and teachers go back to school and campgrounds are less crowded, as are beaches, hiking trails, and other points of interest. Travel is more enjoyable without the hassle of bucking large crowds on the road and at tourist attractions. A wonderful time to visit the desert is in the spring, when hundreds of thousands of wildflowers burst into bloom, and the temperature is cooler than in the summer.

Avoiding the crowds. Unless you simply must have your TV or microwave, visit the more remote campgrounds—those without hookups and with a minimum of amenities. You will have more privacy, a better view of the scenery, more room between sites, and a better chance to see wildlife. This is particularly true for self-contained RVers, who do not need to rely on hookups.

How to Use This Guide

For the purposes of this book, I have defined Southern California as extending from the Mexican border in the south to the northern borders of Monterey, San Benito, Fresno, and Inyo Counties (see overview map). Although some maps divide this area into Central and Southern California, the number of campgrounds within this area does not justify the publication of two books. My apologies, therefore, to those living in cities such as Monterey and Fresno who may not consider themselves residents of Southern California.

For purposes of tourism and travel, the California Division of Tourism has divided the state into 12 tour regions. Of these, six fall completely within the borders of Southern California and two lie partially inside its boundary. This book groups campgrounds by these same tour regions, usually in the order of their location along or near major highways.

This book was written primarily for campers who want to drive to campgrounds in conventional, two-wheel-drive vehicles. There are hundreds of additional backcountry and trailside campgrounds that can be reached only by hiking and backpacking; many of the campgrounds described here serve as excellent base camps to reach them. For information about these more remote sites, consult offices and publications of the Forest Service, national and state parks, Bureau of Land Management, and similar organizations.

For each of the eight tour regions described in *Camping Southern California*, the following information is provided:

- A map of the tour region, as well as maps of any areas within it.
- A table listing all the campgrounds in the region and their most important attributes.
- A brief overview of the region and, in some cases, of areas within the region.
- A description of each of the public campgrounds within the region.

Maps of the tour regions. With the exception of Orange County, each of the eight tour regions covered in this book has been divided into smaller areas. Each regional map (excluding Orange County) indicates the boundaries of these areas. Each area map shows the location of the campgrounds located within it, with the number on the map corresponding to the number of the campground description within the text.

The maps in this book are not drawn precisely to scale, and campground locations are approximate. However, by using the map and the instructions in the "Finding the campground" section, travelers should have no difficulty reaching many of the sites. Additional maps may be needed to find some of the more remote campgrounds.

Quick-reference tables. For quick reference, a table at the beginning of each section lists all the campgrounds in the area and highlights their most important attributes. Travelers looking for specific amenities, such as fishing access, can use these to narrow their selection of campgrounds.

Overview. Highlights and points of interest in the tour region are discussed briefly here. Overviews of smaller areas within the region are also included.

CALIFORNIA TOUR REGIONS

Campground descriptions. Each campground description is numbered to correspond with the campground's location on the map. For each campground, the following information is provided:

Location. This is the name of a city or town near the campground, the distance in miles from that city to the campground, and the general direction of travel to reach it.

Sites. This section explains the number of campsites available and whether tents, RVs, or both are allowed. When possible, it also indicates whether hookups are available. An increasing number of public campgrounds are remodeling at least some of their sites to offer hookups. This is especially true of state and county parks.

Facilities. This section describes the facilities and amenities provided, including any recreational opportunities available at the campground.

Water. Some public campgrounds do not provide drinking water, and this fact is noted in the campground description. But a "no drinking water" notation does not necessarily mean there is no water at the site. Nonpotable water may be available at the campground or from a nearby stream or lake. In either case, the water should be filtered, boiled, or otherwise treated before use.

Fee per night. This is usually given as a price range for individual sites, allowing for differences between summer and winter rates, hookup and no-hookup sites, and premium (such as waterfront) and average campsites. The fees shown here are current as of the date of this writing, but they are subject to change.

Pets. Some campgrounds charge a daily fee for pets, and this is indicated where applicable.

Discounts. Many public campgrounds offer discounts to senior citizens. The National Park Service, Forest Service, Bureau of Land Management, and U.S. Army Corps of Engineers offer 50 percent discounts to campers holding Golden Age Passports, and California state parks and recreation areas offer a $2 discount to campers 62 years of age and older.

Reservations. Most public campgrounds do not accept reservations. For those that do, information about obtaining them is provided. If the "Fee per night" section does not mention reservations, they are not accepted by the campground.

Agency. The agency or organization managing the campground is shown here, along with a phone contact. As indicated earlier, more than 95 percent of the public campgrounds in this book are controlled by one of the following entities: National, state, or county parks; Forest Service; Bureau of Land Management; U.S. Army Corps of Engineers; and various municipal and regional water authorities. See "Camping in Southern California" (page 3) for a description of these agencies and the campgrounds they manage.

Activities. Recreational activities that can take place at or from the campground are listed here. For example, swimming may be possible from the shore of a lakeside campground, hiking trails may begin at or within a reasonable walking distance of a campground, boats may be launched from a campground boat launch, etc.

Finding the campground. Here, detailed instructions are furnished for driving to the campground from the nearest city, town, or major highway. Although it is possible to find the campgrounds by using the directions in this section along with the corresponding map, the task will be made easier with the help of a good California road map.

About the campground. This is information that differentiates this particular campground from others or is of special interest. If the campground is located on the water (ocean, lake, river, or stream), that fact is noted.

Elevation. This is provided if it is a significant factor, such as high altitudes in mountainous areas and locations below sea level, such as Death Valley and the Salton Sea.

Stay limits. Most public campgrounds limit the number of days a camper may stay on site.

Season. Many campgrounds are open year-round, while others are seasonal. The opening and closing dates of certain campgrounds is approximate, depending upon snow and other weather conditions.

(AUTHOR'S NOTE: *Despite the best efforts of author and publisher to be up-to-date, a camping guide begins to grow obsolete as soon as it is published. Established campgrounds close, new ones open, fees go up or (rarely) down, and phone numbers change. Readers may thus encounter some unavoidable differences between the information provided in this book and what they actually encounter on the road. These differences should be few and minor, and some information will remain useful despite changes that may occur. For example, prices usually rise by only a small percentage and can still be compared against other campgrounds when cost is a factor in deciding where to stay.)*

KEY TO ABBREVIATIONS

I have tried to minimize the use of abbreviations in this book. The few that have crept in are shown below, as well as some that may be encountered on maps or other travel references.

AAA	American Automobile Association
AARP	American Association of Retired Persons
ATV	All-Terrain Vehicle
BLM	Bureau of Land Management
CSP	California State Park(s)
FR	Forest Service Road. These letters precede numbers (such as FR 18S03) and designate roads in national forests that are maintained by the Forest Service. They always appear on Forest Service maps but are not always posted along the road.
LTVA	Long-Term Visitor Area, a camping program sponsored by the Bureau of Land Management. See page 4 for an explanation.
NPS	National Park Service
OHV	Off-Highway Vehicle. This usually refers to a campground or a trail for the primary use of those who wish to drive trail motorcycles, all-terrain vehicles, four-wheel-drive vehicles, and snowmobiles. It does not include mountain bicycles. In some publications, the abbreviation ORV (Off-Road Vehicle) may be used instead.
SRA	State Recreation Area
SVRA	State Vehicle Recreation Area, for use of off-highway vehicles.

MAP LEGEND

Interstate Highway		Public Campgrounds	▲ 89
U.S. Highway		Cities, Towns	• Burbank • El Centro
State or County Road			
Lake		Compass	N
National Park, Monument, Recreation Area	Death Valley National Park		
		Scale	0 25 50
			Miles
National, State Forest	SEQUOIA NATIONAL FOREST		

CENTRAL COAST

Three hundred and fifty miles of dramatic seacoast, 2 million acres of national forest, Spanish missions, first-rate wineries, rolling hills, bucolic valleys, and rugged mountains all characterize this marvelously diverse and magnificently scenic region which Spanish explorer Juan Rodriguez Cabrillo called "the land of endless summers." Even the names on the land conjure up enchanting images and whet the appetite for travel: Monterey, Pebble Beach, Cannery Row, Big Sur, Hearst Castle, Morro Bay, Solvang—and the list goes on.

Coastal mountain ranges, such as the Santa Lucia and Santa Ynez, help give the shoreline its rugged beauty, while coastal forests enhance its wild character. Inland ranges—the La Panza, San Rafael, and Sierra Madre—team up with the Los Padres National Forest to create a 220-mile-long wilderness recreation area reaching from Carmel Valley to the western edge of Los Angeles County. The foothills of these mountains host vineyards that produce excellent wines.

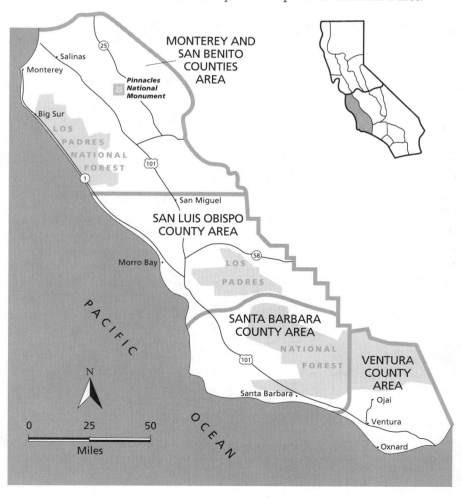

One of the outdoor jewels of this tour region is the Los Padres National Forest, which encompasses nearly 2 million acres of beautiful coastal mountains, 75 vehicle-accessible campgrounds, and more than 1,500 miles of trails for hiking, horseback riding, mountain biking, and off-highway driving.

Although the region's climate is somewhat cooler than the "endless summer" described by Cabrillo, it is moderate year-round with little seasonal variation. Average winter temperatures range from 39 to 64 degrees F, spring 45 to 66 degrees F, summer 52 to 71 degrees F, and fall 47 to 73 degrees F. The percentage of sunny days reaches a high of 92 percent in summer, drops to 82 percent in the fall and 66 percent in winter, and rises to 74 percent in the spring. For touring and camping, the best weather occurs in the late summer and fall. Fog is common in the coastal areas from June to mid-August.

The Central Coast region is divided into four areas here: Monterey & San Benito Counties, San Luis Obispo County, Santa Barbara County, and Ventura County.

MONTEREY & SAN BENITO COUNTIES

		Group sites	RV sites	Max. RV length	Hookups	Toilets	Showers	Drinking water	Dump station	Pets	Wheelchair	Recreation	Fee ($)	Season	Can reserve
1	Fremont Peak State Park		•	26		P		•		•		H	7		
2	Hollister Hills SVRA		•	26		F	•			•		O	8		
3	Laguna Seca Rec Area		•		WE	F	•	•	•	•	•		16–20		•
4	Bottcher's Gap		•			V				•		H	10		
5	Pfeiffer Big Sur State Park		•	32		F	•	•		•	•	HS	14–20		•
6	White Oaks					V				•		H			
7	China Camp		•	30		V				•		H			
8	Arroyo Seco	•	•	30		V		•		•	•	HFS	10		
9	Escondido					V				•		HF	8	Apr–Oct	
10	Memorial Park					V				•		H	8		
11	Limekiln State Park		•	21		F	•	•	•	•	•	HSF	12–23		•
12	Kirk Creek		•			F		•		•	•	HSF	17		
13	Nacimiento		•			V				•		HF	5		
14	Ponderosa		•	30		V		•		•		HF	10		
15	Plaskett Creek	•	•			F		•		•	•	HF	17		
16	Pinnacles National Monument					P	•		•			H	10		
17	San Lorenzo Rec Area		•		WES	F	•	•	•	•	•	HSF	14–19		•
18	Lake San Antonio North		•		WES	F	•	•	•	•	•	HSFBL	14–21		
19	Lake San Antonio South		•		WES	F	•	•	•	•	•	HSFBL	14–21		

Hookups: W = Water E = Electric S = Sewer
Toilets: F = Flush V = Vault P = Pit C = Chemical
Recreation: H = Hiking S = Swimming F = Fishing B = Boating L = Boat Launch O = Off-highway Driving R = Horseback Riding
Maximum Trailer/RV Length given in feet. **Stay Limit** given in days. **Fee** given in dollars.
If no entry under **Season**, campground is open all year. If no entry under **Fee**, camping is free.

Monterey & San Benito Counties Area Map

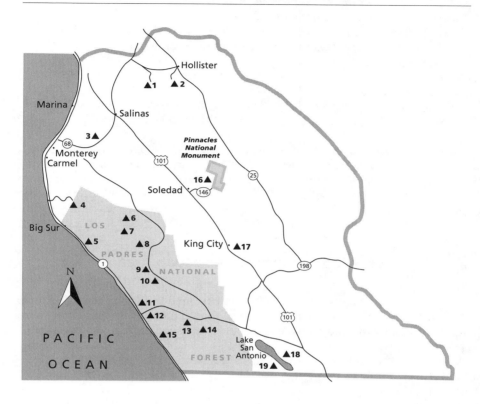

Some of the most magnificent scenery in Southern California unfolds along the coastline of Monterey County. From Carmel south to Big Sur, Gorda, and beyond, the Pacific Coast Highway snakes its way from one postcard-worthy scene to another. Nearly 300 turnouts allow motorists to stop and enjoy the spectacular views. More vehicles drive this stretch of road annually than visit Yosemite, the most crowded of our national parks. On the other hand, inland in San Benito County, the striking spires, crags, and trails of Pinnacles National Monument are rarely crowded.

Monterey was California's first capital, a distinction it held from 1770 until just after the Gold Rush of 1849. Its Old Town is well worth a walking tour. Also worth visiting are Fisherman's Wharf and the world-class Monterey Bay Aquarium. On the other hand, Cannery Row and the 17-Mile Drive at Pebble Beach are both overrated tourist traps. Despite glowing travel literature, Cannery Row is just a collection of shops and booths trading on the name of the novel by John Steinbeck, and 17-Mile Drive, which leads you through an upscale golf community, is nothing more than an uninspiring drive for which a hefty fee is charged. Instead, take the 90-mile drive through Big Sur, which is infinitely more spectacular—and free.

1   Fremont Peak State Park

Location: 11 miles south of San Juan Bautista.
Sites: 25 sites for tents, RVs up to 26 feet long, and trailers up to 18 feet long.
Facilities: Picnic tables, fire rings, drinking water, pit toilets.
Fee per night: $7, pets $1.
Agency: California Department of Parks and Recreation, 408-623-4255.
Activities: Hiking.
Finding the campground: From San Juan Bautista, drive south on San Juan Canyon Road (County Road 61) for 11 miles. The road ends at the campground.

About the campground: Situated at an elevation of 2,900 feet, the campground affords a sweeping view over Monterey Bay and the surrounding area. Hiking opportunities include a nature trail and a 0.6-mile trail to the summit of Fremont Peak (3,169 feet). An astronomical observatory on the mountain is open to the public from April to October on Saturday evenings occurring near a new moon. Stay limit 7 days. Open all year.

2   Hollister Hills State Vehicle Recreation Area

Location: 8 miles south of Hollister.
Sites: 125 sites for tents, RVs up to 26 feet long, and trailers up to 18 feet long.
Facilities: Picnic tables, grills, flush toilets, showers, store, and snack bar. Water at the campground is not potable and should be boiled or treated before use.
Fee per night: $8.
Agency: California Department of Parks and Recreation, 408-637-3874.
Activities: Off-highway driving.
Finding the campground: From the town of Hollister, follow California 25 to the southeast part of town. At Cienega Road, turn right (south) and proceed 8 miles to the campground.

About the campground: Designed for off-highway vehicles, this 6,700-acre park ranges in elevation from 800 to 2,900 feet. It contains 80 miles of trails and six practice tracks for motorcycles and ATVs, as well as 40 miles of trails and an obstacle course for four-wheel-drive vehicles. The park also features hiking and nature trails. The campground is located in an area lightly wooded with sycamore, oak, and madrone trees. Stay limit 30 days. Open all year.

3   Laguna Seca Recreation Area

Location: 9 miles east of Monterey.
Sites: 170 sites for tents and RVs, many with water and electrical hookups.
Facilities: Picnic tables, barbecue grills, drinking water, flush toilets, showers, dump station, playground, ball field, horseshoe pits, store.
Fee per night: $16-$20, pets $1. For reservations, call 888-588-CAMP. Reservation fee, $3.50.
Agency: Monterey County Parks Department, 408-758-3504.
Activities: Exploring Monterey Bay area.

Finding the campground: The campground lies about 9 miles east of Monterey and 8 miles west of Salinas on the north side of California 68.

About the campground: The campground is situated in a stand of small oaks on a hillside above the Laguna Seca Raceway. Stay limit 14 days. Open all year.

4 Bottcher's Gap

Location: 19 miles southeast of Carmel.
Sites: 9 sites for tents and small RVs.
Facilities: Picnic tables, fire rings, vault toilets. No drinking water.
Fee per night: $10.
Agency: Los Padres National Forest, Monterey Ranger District, 408-385-5434.
Activities: Hiking.
Finding the campground: From Carmel, drive south on California 1 for about 10 miles. Turn left onto Palo Colorado Road and continue for 9 more miles. Palo Colorado Road becomes FR 18S05 before it reaches the campground.

About the campground: Situated in a mixed oak and madrone forest, the campground provides a fine view of the Ventana Double Cones and the Santa Lucia Mountains. A trail at the camp leads to a series of trails and hike-in campsites in the Ventana Wilderness. Stay limit 14 days. Open all year.

5 Pfeiffer Big Sur State Park

Location: 26 miles south of Carmel.
Sites: 218 sites for tents, RVs up to 32 feet long, and trailers up to 27 feet long.
Facilities: Picnic tables, grills, drinking water, flush toilets, showers, store, restaurant, ball field, laundry, cabins.
Fee per night: $14-$20, pets $1. For reservations, call Parknet, 800-444-7275. One-time $7.50 reservation fee.
Agency: California Department of Parks and Recreation, 408-667-2315.
Activities: Hiking, swimming.
Finding the campground: From Carmel, drive 26 miles south on California 1.

About the campground: Right in the center of the magnificent scenery of the Big Sur area, this 821-acre park provides dramatic shoreline vistas and shaded trails through coastal redwood forests. *Sunset* lists this as one of the 100 best campgrounds in the western United States. The 1.8-mile Pfeiffer Falls/Valley View Loop leads to a redwood grove and a 60-foot waterfall. A sea-otter game refuge begins just south of the park, and the Los Padres National Forest offers miles of trails to the west and south. Stay limit 7 days from June through September, 15 days from October through May. Open all year.

6 White Oaks

Location: 30 miles southeast of Carmel.
Sites: 7 sites for tents.

Facilities: Picnic tables, fire grills, vault toilets. No drinking water.
Fee per night: None.
Agency: Los Padres National Forest, Monterey Ranger District, 408-385-5434.
Activities: Hiking.
Finding the campground: From California 1 in Carmel, turn east onto G16 (Carmel Valley Road). Proceed about 22 miles, turn right onto Tassajara Road (Route 5007), and drive about 8 more miles. The road is not paved about 3 miles after leaving Carmel Valley Road and is not recommended for trailers or large RVs during periods of inclement weather.

About the campground: Elevation 4,200 feet. Stay limit 14 days. Open all year.

7 China Camp

Location: 32 miles southeast of Carmel.
Sites: 8 sites, 5 of which can be used by RVs up to 30 feet long.
Facilities: Picnic tables, fire grills, vault toilets. No drinking water.
Fee per night: None.
Agency: Los Padres National Forest, Monterey Ranger District, 408-385-5434.
Activities: Hiking.
Finding the campground: Drive 2.2 miles south of White Oaks Campground (see above) on Tassajara Road.

About the campground: Elevation 4,300 feet. Stay limit 14 days. Open all year.

8 Arroyo Seco

Location: 19 miles west of Greenfield.
Sites: 50 sites for tents and RVs up to 30 feet long; 1 group site.
Facilities: Picnic tables, fire rings, drinking water, vault toilets.
Fee per night: $10, group site $50.
Agency: Los Padres National Forest, Monterey Ranger District, 408-385-5434.
Activities: Hiking, swimming, fishing.
Finding the campground: From the town of Greenfield, turn west off U.S. Highway 101 onto Route G16 (Elm Avenue, which becomes Arroyo Seco Road). Continue for 19 miles, bearing left at the junction with Carmel Valley Road, staying on Arroyo Seco Road.

About the campground: The Arroyo Seco River runs through the campground, which is situated in a stand of oak trees. Canoeing and fishing can also be enjoyed at nearby Abbot Lakes. A hiking trail leads from the camp into the Ventana Wilderness. Stay limit 14 days. Open all year.

9 Escondido

Location: 26 miles southwest of Greenfield.
Sites: 9 tent sites.

Facilities: Picnic tables, fire rings, vault toilets. No drinking water.
Fee per night: $8.
Agency: Los Padres National Forest, Monterey Ranger District, 408-385-5434.
Activities: Hiking, fishing.
Finding the campground: From Arroyo Seco Campground (see above), continue south on Arroyo Seco Road for about 7 miles. The road is narrow and winding and is not recommended for trailers or large RVs. A better approach is to drive 2.5 miles north from Memorial Park Campground (see below).

About the campground: Escondido sprawls across a grassy meadow and through a stand of oaks. Fishing is available in nearby Arroyo Seco River. The campground is the trailhead for the Lost Valley Trail into the Ventana Wilderness. Stay limit 14 days. Open April through October.

10 Memorial Park

Location: 22 miles northwest of Jolon.
Sites: 8 tent sites.
Facilities: Picnic tables, fire rings, vault toilets. No drinking water.
Fee per night: $8.
Agency: Los Padres National Forest, Monterey Ranger District, 408-385-5434.
Activities: Hiking.
Finding the campground: From the town of Jolon, drive northwest on Mission Road for 6 miles through Fort Hunter Liggett. Turn left onto Del Venturi-Milpas Road and drive 16 miles.

About the campground: Memorial Park is the trailhead for the Arroyo Seco Trail. Stay limit 14 days. Open all year.

11 Limekiln State Park

Location: 23 miles southeast of Big Sur.
Sites: 43 sites for tents, RVs up to 21 feet long, and trailers up to 15 feet long.
Facilities: Picnic tables, barbecue grills, drinking water, flush toilets, showers, dump station, grocery store.
Fee per night: $12-$23. For reservations, call Parknet, 800-444-7275. One-time $7.50 reservation fee.
Agency: California Department of Parks and Recreation, 408-667-2315.
Activities: Hiking, swimming, fishing.
Finding the campground: From the town of Lucia (about 21 miles southeast of Big Sur), drive 2 miles southeast on California 1.

About the campground: Limekiln State Park contains a coastal redwood grove, a small, sheltered beach, and a trail to a waterfall, as well as the historic limekilns for which the park is named. Stay limit 7 days from June through September, 15 days from October through May. Open all year.

12 Kirk Creek

Location: 25 miles southeast of Big Sur.
Sites: 33 sites for tents and RVs.
Facilities: Picnic tables, fire grills, drinking water, flush toilets.
Fee per night: $17; $5 for cyclists.
Agency: Los Padres National Forest, Monterey Ranger District, 408-385-5434.
Activities: Hiking, swimming, fishing.
Finding the campground: From the town of Lucia (about 21 miles southeast of Big Sur), drive southeast on California 1 for 4 miles.

About the campground: On a bluff overlooking the Pacific Ocean yet boasting easy beach access, Kirk Creek is listed by *Sunset* as one of the ten best campgrounds in the West. The campground lies alongside Kirk Creek at a point just before the stream plunges into the sea. Stay limit 14 days. Open all year.

13 Nacimiento

Location: 15 miles southeast of Lucia.
Sites: 8 sites for tents and small RVs.
Facilities: Picnic tables, fire rings, vault toilets. No drinking water.
Fee per night: $5.
Agency: Los Padres National Forest, Monterey Ranger District, 408-385-5434.
Activities: Hiking, fishing.
Finding the campground: Drive 4 miles southeast of Lucia on California 1 to the Nacimiento-Fergusson Road (Route 4004), near Mill Creek Picnic Area. Turn east onto this road and go 11 miles to the campground. This is a steep, narrow, winding road, not suitable for trailers or large RVs. A better approach for such vehicles is to drive west from Jolon on Route 4004 through Fort Hunter Ligget. Even this route is narrow and winding and has limited visibility.

About the campground: Situated on the bank of the Nacimiento River, the campground affords fishing and hiking in the Ventana Wilderness. The entry road to the campground is difficult to negotiate and is not suited for vehicles larger than pickup campers. Stay limit 14 days. Open all year.

14 Ponderosa

Location: 17 miles southeast of Lucia.
Sites: 23 sites for tents and RVs up to 30 feet long.
Facilities: Picnic tables, fire grills, drinking water, vault toilets.
Fee per night: $10.
Agency: Los Padres National Forest, Monterey Ranger District, 408-385-5434.
Activities: Hiking, fishing.
Finding the campground: Drive 2 miles east of Nacimiento Campground (see above) on Route 4004. See the warning about road conditions, above.

About the campground: Situated in a mixed oak and madrone forest, Ponderosa provides access to fishing in the Nacimiento River. Campsites are small and not suited for large vehicles. A hiking trail leads south from the campground along Negro Fork. Stay limit 14 days. Open all year, but occasional closures of upper campsites precludes use by RVs at those times.

15 Plaskett Creek

Location: 9.5 miles southeast of Lucia.
Sites: 45 sites for tents and RVs, plus 3 group sites.
Facilities: Picnic tables, fire grills, drinking water, flush toilets.
Fee per night: $17, $5 cyclists, $55 groups. For reservations, call 800-280-CAMP. One-time fee of $8.65 for individual reservations and $17.35 for group.
Agency: Los Padres National Forest, Monterey Ranger District, 408-385-5434.
Activities: Hiking, fishing.
Finding the campground: From the town of Lucia, drive 9.5 miles southeast on CA 1.

About the campground: Plaskett Creek is on the east side of California 1, with beach access across the highway at Sand Dollar, the largest public beach on the southern Big Sur coast. A trail descends a bluff to the beach. Swimming is dangerous due to rip tides and currents, but surf fishing and beachcombing are popular. Stay limit 14 days. Open all year.

Surf fishing and beachcombing are popular with campers at Plaskett Creek Campground southeast of Big Sur.

16 Pinnacles National Monument: Chaparral

Location: 11 miles east of Soledad.
Sites: 24 sites for tents.
Facilities: Picnic tables, fire grills, drinking water, pit toilets.
Fee per night: $10.
Agency: National Park Service, 408-389-4578.
Activities: Hiking.
Finding the campground: From the junction of U.S. Highway 101 and California 146 in Soledad, drive east on CA 146 for about 11 miles to the entry to the campground. The road is steep and narrow and is not suited for large RVs or trailers.

About the campground: Pinnacles National Monument is divided into east and west districts, with no road connecting the two. Chaparral Campground is in the west district. Spectacular trails weave through jagged rock spires and connect the two sections of the monument. The west district is the main section of the park, and the entrance and visitor center are located there, on CA 146. Pinnacles Campground, commercially operated, is located half a mile from the park entrance (phone: 408-389-4462). Stay limit 14 days. Open all year; from President's Day in February through Memorial Day in May, camping is only permitted Monday through Thursday.

17 San Lorenzo Recreation Area

Location: In King City.
Sites: 19 sites for tents, 99 for RVs.
Facilities: Picnic tables, barbecue grills, drinking water, flush toilets, showers, dump station, store, playground, horseshoe pits, softball field, and courts for volleyball and badminton.
Fee per night: $14-$19, pets $1. For reservations, call 888-588-CAMP. One-time $3.50 reservation fee.
Agency: Monterey County Parks Department, 408-755-4899.
Activities: Hiking, swimming, fishing.
Finding the campground: From U.S. Highway 101 at King City, take Broadway exit to campground entrance at 1160 Broadway.

About the campground: The campground is situated on the Salinas River by the Salinas Valley Agricultural and Rural Life Museum. Stay limit 14 days, longer if space is available. Open all year.

18 Lake San Antonio: North Shore

Location: 34 miles northwest of Paso Robles.
Sites: More than 250 open, grassy sites for tents and RVs, most with lake frontage. Some have full hookups; some have water and electrical hookups.
Facilities: Picnic tables, barbecue grills, drinking water, showers, flush toilets, dump stations, store, restaurant, boat launch and dock, fishing dock, playground,

North Shore Campground on Lake San Antonio swarms with water-sports enthusiasts on busy summer weekends. PHOTO BY CATHY JOHNSON

horseshoe pits, equestrian camp, and courts for volleyball and shuffleboard.
Fee per night: $14-$21, pets $1.
Agency: Monterey County Parks Department, 805-472-2311.
Activities: Swimming, fishing, boating, waterskiing, sailboarding, hiking.
Finding the campground: From Paso Robles, drive north on U.S. Highway 101 for 22 miles. Exit onto County Road G18 (Jolon Road) and drive west 9 miles. Turn left onto New Pleyto Road and drive 2.5 miles.

About the campground: The unique thing about Lake San Antonio North Shore is the large number of waterfront sites made possible by ten peninsula-like points of land reaching out into the lake. Campers may set up anywhere on these points, as close to the water as they like, and put boats directly into the lake next to their tents or RVs. A boat launch is available for large boats. Many of the hookup sites have striking views of the lake and surrounding mountains. Trophy-sized bass can be caught here, as well as bluegill and catfish. The campground's extensive facilities combined with the scenic, 16-mile-long lake make this an excellent vacation spot for water-sport enthusiasts. Stay limit 14 days, negotiable if space is available. Open all year.

19 Lake San Antonio: South Shore

Location: 41 miles northwest of Paso Robles.
Sites: 489 sites for tents and RVs, many with full or partial hookups. Sites are divided into 3 separate campgrounds (Harris Creek, Redondo Vista, and Lynch), all within a 1-mile radius.

Facilities: Picnic tables, barbecue grills, drinking water, showers, flush toilets, dump station, store, restaurant, boat launch and dock, playground, volleyball court, horseshoe pits, visitor information center.

Fee per night: $14-$21, pets $1.

Agency: Monterey County Parks Department, 805-472-2311.

Activities: Swimming, fishing, boating, waterskiing, sailboarding, hiking.

Finding the campground: From Paso Robles, drive north on U.S. Highway 101 for 22 miles. Exit onto County Road G18 (Jolon Road) and turn left almost immediately onto CR G19 (Nacimiento Lake Drive). Drive 9 miles and turn right onto CR G14. Drive 7 miles, turn right onto San Antonio Road, and drive about 3 miles farther.

About the campground: Although none of the three campgrounds at South Shore are directly on the water, some campsites are within 100 feet of the shoreline. More than a dozen wineries are located within a 10-mile radius of Paso Robles, less than 20 miles from the campground. Most offer tours, sales, and wine tasting. Stay limit 14 days. Open all year.

SAN LUIS OBISPO COUNTY

An entirely different coastline greets the traveler who leaves the rugged Big Sur landscape and enters San Luis Obispo County—but it is no less beautiful. High, precipitous cliffs give way to rolling green hills, and the beaches become more accessible. The area is more densely settled and towns are larger, but there is still ample space to enjoy the surf and the hills beyond the beaches.

High above San Simeon, overlooking California Highway 1 and the Pacific

SAN LUIS OBISPO COUNTY AREA MAP

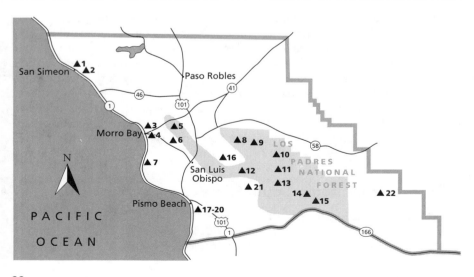

	Group sites	RV sites	Max. RV length	Hookups	Toilets	Showers	Drinking water	Dump station	Pets	Wheelchair	Recreation	Fee ($)	Season	Can reserve
1 San Simeon Creek		•	35		F	•	•	•	•	•	HF	14–17		•
2 Washburn		•	31		C		•		•	•	HF	7–10		•
3 Morro Strand State Beach		•	24		F	•	•		•	•	SF	14–18		•
4 Morro Bay State Park		•	31	WE	F	•	•	•	•	•	HSFB	14–24		•
5 Cerro Alto		•	30		V		•		•		H	16		
6 El Chorro Regional Park		•		WES	F	•	•		•	•		18–21		
7 Montana de Oro State Park		•	24		P		•		•		HFR	7–11		
8 Navajo					V		•		•		HO			
9 Friis		•	21		V		•		•		HO			
10 La Panza		•			V		•		•		O			
11 American Canyon		•	30		V				•		H			
12 Hi Mountain		•	23		V				•		H			
13 Stony Creek					V				•		H			
14 Buck Spring		•			P				•		H			
15 Baja		•			P				•		HO			
16 Santa Margarita Lake	•	•	30		V	•	•		•		HSFB	13		•
17 North Beach		•	31		F		•	•	•	•	HFS	14–18		•
18 Oceano		•		WE	F	•	•		•	•	HFS	14–24		•
19 Oceano Dunes SVRA		•			C				•	•	HFOS	8		
20 Oceano Memorial Park		•		WES	F	•	•		•	•	FB	20		
21 Lopez Lake Rec Area		•		WES	F	•	•		•	•	HSFBL	12–20		•
22 Carrizo Plain/Soda Lake		•			C				•					

Hookups: W = Water E = Electric S = Sewer
Toilets: F = Flush V = Vault P = Pit C = Chemical
Recreation: H = Hiking S = Swimming F = Fishing B = Boating L = Boat Launch O = Off-highway Driving R = Horseback Riding
Maximum Trailer/RV Length given in feet. **Stay Limit** given in days. **Fee** given in dollars.
If no entry under **Season,** campground is open all year. If no entry under **Fee,** camping is free.

Ocean, stands the opulent mansion built by newspaper baron William Randolph Hearst. Now a state historical monument, the buildings and grounds attract more than a million visitors a year who come to admire the art, architecture, and gardens of "Hearst Castle." Farther south along the coast, famed Morro Rock looms over the picturesque town of Morro Bay. From Pismo Beach, Nipomo Dunes Preserve stretches south more than 20 miles, well into Santa Barbara County. It is the largest expanse of coastal dunes remaining in the state.

Inland, the mountains of the Los Padres National Forest and the alkaline flats of the Carrizo Plain offer a stark contrast in landscape. Missions such as San Miguel and San Luis Obispo are reminders of the area's Spanish heritage. A dozen of the more than 30 wineries located in San Luis Obispo County lie within a 12-mile radius of the town of Paso Robles. Many offer picnic sites, wine tasting, and retail sales.

1 San Simeon State Park: San Simeon Creek

Location: 3 miles north of Cambria.
Sites: 132 sites for tents and RVs up to 35 feet long.
Facilities: Picnic tables, barbecue grills, flush toilets, showers, drinking water, dump station.
Fee per night: $14-$17, pets $1. For reservations, call Parknet, 800-444-7275. Reservation fee, $7.50.
Agency: California Department of Parks and Recreation, 805-927-2035.
Activities: Hiking, fishing, wildlife watching.
Finding the campground: From Cambria, drive 3 miles north on California 1.

About the campground: One of two campgrounds at San Simeon State Park, San Simeon Creek is located across the highway from the ocean. However, safe access to the beach is provided through a passageway beneath the road. Shoreline fishing is popular from the beach. A 2.2-mile coastal trail and the 3.5-mile inland Whittaker Ranch Trail provide hiking opportunities. Wildlife-viewing opportunities abound for shorebirds, sea otters, and gray whales, which migrate in the winter. San Simeon Creek flows through the campground. Stay limit 14 days from June through September, 30 days from October through May. Open all year.

2 San Simeon State Park: Washburn

Location: 3 miles north of Cambria.
Sites: 70 sites for tents, RVs up to 31 feet long, and trailers up to 21 feet long.
Facilities: Picnic tables, barbecue grills, drinking water, chemical toilets.
Fee per night: $7-$10, pets $1. For reservations, call Parknet, 800-444-7275. Reservation fee, $7.50.
Agency: California Department of Parks and Recreation, 805-927-2035.
Activities: Hiking, fishing, wildlife watching.
Finding the campground: From Cambria, drive 3 miles north on California 1. Washburn is situated on a hill just beyond San Simeon Creek Campground (see above).

About the campground: Washburn serves primarily as an overflow area if San Simeon Creek (see above) is full, but it has a view of the ocean. Hearst Castle is 5 miles to the north. Stay limit 14 days from June through September, 30 days from October through May. Open all year.

3 Morro Strand State Beach

Location: 3 miles north of Morro Bay.
Sites: 104 sites for tents and RVs up to 24 feet long.
Facilities: Picnic tables, fire rings, drinking water, outdoor showers, flush toilets.
Fee per night: $14-$18, pets $1. For reservations, call Parknet, 800-444-7275. Reservation fee, $7.50.
Agency: California Department of Parks and Recreation, 805-772-2560.

Activities: Swimming, fishing, sailboarding, beach walking.
Finding the campground: From Morro Bay, drive 3 miles north on California 1. Take the Yerba Buena exit.

About the campground: Morro Strand resembles a parking lot more than a campground, with planted dividers between campsites, but it is right on the beach. The 3-mile-long beach is lined with homes, although the southern end is less crowded and more accessible. Stay limit 7 days from Memorial Day to Labor Day, 14 days thereafter. Open all year.

4 Morro Bay State Park

Location: Morro Bay.
Sites: 115 sites for tents and RVs up to 31 feet long, including 20 sites with water and electrical hookups.
Facilities: Picnic tables, barbecue grills, drinking water, flush toilets, showers, dump station, cafe/restaurant, marina, golf course.
Fee per night: $14-$24, pets $1. For reservations, call Parknet, 800-444-7275. Reservation fee, $7.50.
Agency: California Department of Parks and Recreation, 805-772-2560.
Activities: Swimming, fishing, boating, hiking, golf, bird watching.
Finding the campground: From Main Street in the city of Morro Bay, take State Park Road to the campground entrance.

About the campground: Lots of tall, mature trees shade the campground, which is situated close to, but not on, the shoreline of Morro Bay. Morro Bay is probably the most developed park in the California state park network. Although its borders encompass a marina and an 18-hole golf course, its natural features include tidal flats, hiking trails, and three prime bird-nesting areas. The famed landmark, Morro Rock, is nearby. The park encompasses 2,749 acres from the lagoon shoreline to hills behind the beach, and it offers guided nature walks and interpretive programs. The Museum of Natural History provides exhibits and displays on geology, oceanography, plants and animals of the area, and Native American life. Stay limit 14 days. Open all year.

5 Cerro Alto

Location: 11 miles northeast of Morro Bay.
Sites: 15 sites for tents and RVs up to 30 feet long, plus 7 walk-in sites.
Facilities: Picnic tables, fire rings, drinking water, vault toilets.
Fee per night: $16. For reservations, call 800-280-CAMP. Reservation fee, $8.65.
Agency: Los Padres National Forest, Santa Lucia Ranger District, 805-772-4399.
Activities: Hiking.
Finding the campground: From Morro Bay, drive 10 miles northeast on California 41. Turn right (southeast) on FR 29S11 for 1 mile.

About the campground: Cerro Alto is situated amid chaparral and young oak trees. A short trail leads from the camp to the summit of Cerro Alto (elevation

2,624 feet), from which there are excellent views of Morro Bay and the Santa Lucia Mountains. Stay limit 14 days. Open all year.

6 El Chorro Regional Park

Location: 4 miles northwest of San Luis Obispo.
Sites: 46 sites for tents and RVs, with full hookups, plus an overflow area.
Facilities: Picnic tables, barbecue grills, drinking water, showers, flush toilets, playground, ball field, horseshoe pits.
Fee per night: $18-$21, pets $2.
Agency: San Luis Obispo County Parks, 805-781-5219.
Activities: Golf, hiking.
Finding the campground: From the intersection of U.S. Highway 101 and California 1 in San Luis Obispo, drive 4 miles northwest to the park, which is on the right.

About the campground: For campers who want to golf, El Chorro is ideal. A public course adjoins the campground, and some sites are almost on the fairway. A self-guided nature trail and a botanical garden are also part of the park. Stay limit 14 days. Open all year.

7 Montana de Oro State Park

Location: 10 miles south of Morro Bay.
Sites: 50 sites for tents and RVs up to 24 feet long, plus 6 equestrian sites with pipe corrals and parking for horse trailers.
Facilities: Picnic tables, barbecue grills, pit toilets. Drinking water is usually available from a tanker truck.
Fee per night: $7-$11, horse camp $14-$18. For reservations, call Parknet, 800-444-7275. Reservation fee, $7.50.
Agency: California Department of Parks and Recreation, 805-528-0513.
Activities: Hiking, fishing, mountain biking, horseback riding.
Finding the campground: From Morro Bay, drive east on California 1 for 2 miles, then turn right on South Bay Boulevard and drive 3 miles to Los Osos. Turn right on Pecho Valley Road and proceed another 5 miles.

About the campground: This relatively secluded park of 8,400 acres includes 7 miles of wild and rugged coastline, groves of coastal oak, Bishop pine, and chaparral, and wooded creeks. *Sunset* has included the campground in its list of the 100 best in the western United States. Hiking trails explore a remote sand spit, skirt the edge of a sea bluff, follow Islay Creek, and scale Valencia Peak, the area's most dominant feature. Some of the finest tide pools on the California coast are found at Corallina Cove. Stay limit 14 days. Open all year.

8 Navajo

Location: 34 miles east of San Luis Obispo.
Sites: 3 tent sites.

Facilities: Picnic tables, fire rings, vault toilets. No water.
Fee per night: None.
Agency: Los Padres National Forest, Santa Lucia Ranger District, 805-925-9538.
Activities: Hiking, off-highway driving.
Finding the campground: From its intersection with California 1 in San Luis Obispo, take U.S. Highway 101 north for 8.5 miles to CA 58. Turn right (east). After 3.3 miles, turn right again in Santa Margarita and continue for 16 miles to Pozo. From there, go 1.3 miles, bear left (north) at an intersection, and continue for about 5 miles on a road which becomes FR 29S02.

About the campground: Situated in an oak forest at 2,200 feet, Navajo is close to hiking and off-highway-vehicle trails. Stay limit 14 days. Open all year.

9 Friis

Location: 35 miles east of San Luis Obispo.
Sites: 3 sites for tents and RVs up to 21 feet long.
Facilities: Picnic tables, fire rings, vault toilets. No drinking water.
Fee per night: None.
Agency: Los Padres National Forest, Santa Lucia Ranger District, 805-925-9538.
Activities: Hiking, off-highway driving.
Finding the campground: Follow the directions to Navajo (see above) and continue 1.2 miles beyond Navajo on FR 29S02.

About the campground: Friis, elevation of 2,600 feet, is of interest mainly to hikers and off-highway-vehicle enthusiasts. Stay limit 14 days. Open all year.

10 La Panza

Location: 38 miles east of San Luis Obispo.
Sites: 16 sites for tents and RVs.
Facilities: Picnic tables, fire rings, vault toilets. No drinking water.
Fee per night: None.
Agency: Los Padres National Forest, Santa Lucia Ranger District, 805-925-9538.
Activities: Off-highway driving.
Finding the campground: Follow the directions to Navajo (see above) until reaching Pozo. At the intersection 1.3 miles past Pozo, turn right, staying on Pozo Road. The road soon becomes unsurfaced, then winding and narrow. It is not suited for large trailers or RVs. An easier but longer approach route is to remain on California 58 past Santa Margarita until reaching the eastern end of Pozo Road. Then turn west and drive about 7 miles to the campground. This road is also unsurfaced for the last 3 miles.

About the campground: Its proximity to the Black Mountain OHV driving area is La Panza's main attraction. Stay limit 14 days. Open all year.

11 American Canyon

Location: 26 miles east of Santa Margarita.
Sites: 14 sites for tents and RVs up to 30 feet long.
Facilities: Picnic tables, fire rings, vault toilets. No drinking water.
Fee per night: None.
Agency: Los Padres National Forest, Santa Lucia Ranger District, 805-925-9538.
Activities: Hiking.
Finding the campground: From Santa Margarita, drive 16 miles southeast to Pozo. Continue east on Pozo Road for another 3.2 miles to the end of the pavement and a Y junction. Bear right, drive another 5 miles, and turn left for 2 more miles to the campground.

About the campground: American Canyon provides access to the trails of the Machesna Mountain Wilderness. Stay limit 14 days. Open all year.

12 Hi Mountain

Location: 20 miles southeast of Santa Margarita.
Sites: 11 sites for tents and RVs up to 23 feet long.
Facilities: Picnic tables, fire rings, vault toilets. No water.
Fee per night: None.
Agency: Los Padres National Forest, Santa Lucia Ranger District, 805-925-9538.
Activities: Hiking.
Finding the campground: From Santa Margarita, drive 16 miles southeast to Pozo on Pozo Road. Turn right (south) onto Hi Mountain Road and drive 4 miles to the campground.

About the campground: A narrow, winding road leads from the campground to the Big Falls Trailhead. Stay limit 14 days. Open all year.

13 Stony Creek

Location: 25 miles east of Arroyo Grande.
Sites: 6 sites for tents.
Facilities: Picnic tables, fire rings, vault toilets. No drinking water.
Fee per night: None.
Agency: Los Padres National Forest, Santa Lucia Ranger District, 805-925-9538.
Activities: Hiking.
Finding the campground: From U.S. Highway 101 in Arroyo Grande, drive east on Grand Avenue to Lopez Drive, about 1 mile. Bear right on Lopez, proceed another mile, and turn east onto Huasna Road. After the small settlement of Huasna, the road becomes unpaved and is designated FR 32S07 to its end at the campground.

About the campground: Stony Creek serves as a base camp for hikers entering the Garcia Wilderness. Stay limit 14 days. Open all year.

14 Buck Spring

Location: 38 miles east of Guadalupe.
Sites: 1 primitive campsite for either tent or RV.
Facilities: Picnic table, fire ring, open-air pit toilet. No drinking water.
Fee per night: None.
Agency: Los Padres National Forest, Santa Lucia Ranger District, 805-925-9538.
Activities: Hiking.
Finding the campground: From its intersection with California 1 in Guadalupe, take CA 166 east for about 36 miles. Turn north (left) onto unpaved FR 30S02 and drive 2 more miles.

About the campground: Solitude is the main offering here. Stay limit 14 days. Open all year.

15 Baja

Location: 39 miles east of Guadalupe.
Sites: 1 primitive campsite for either tent or RV.
Facilities: Picnic table, fire ring, open-air pit toilet. No drinking water.
Fee per night: None.
Agency: Los Padres National Forest, Santa Lucia Ranger District, 805-925-9538.
Activities: Hiking, hunting, off-highway driving.
Finding the campground: From Buck Spring Campground (see above), continue on FR 30S02 for 1.2 more miles.

About the campground: Stay limit 14 days. Open all year.

16 Santa Margarita Lake

Location: 11 miles east of Santa Margarita.
Sites: 50 sites for tents and RVs up to 30 feet long, plus group sites.
Facilities: Picnic tables, fire rings, grills, drinking water, showers, vault toilets, store, playground, pool, boat ramp and dock, boat rentals, horseshoe pits, public phone.
Fee per night: $13, pets $2. For reservations, call 805-489-8019.
Agency: San Luis Obispo County Parks, 805-438-5485.
Activities: Hiking, mountain biking, boating, fishing, swimming (pool only).
Finding the campground: From Santa Margarita, drive southeast on Pozo Road for 10 miles, turn left onto Santa Margarita Lake Road, and drive 1 mile.

About the campground: All water activities involving body contact in the reservoir are prohibited, as it supplies drinking water for the city of San Luis Obispo. In addition to the water activities in the developed area of the park, several thousand acres have been set aside as a Natural Area, with miles of trails for hikers, mountain bikers, and equestrians. Stay limit 14 days. Open all year.

17 Pismo State Beach: North Beach

Location: 1 mile south of the city of Pismo Beach.
Sites: 103 sites for tents and RVs up to 31 feet long.
Facilities: Picnic tables, barbecue grills, drinking water, flush toilets, dump station.
Fee per night: $14-$18, pets $1. For reservations, call Parknet, 800-444-7275. Reservation fee, $7.50.
Agency: California Department of Parks and Recreation, 805-489-2684.
Activities: Fishing, clamming, swimming, hiking.
Finding the campground: From Pismo Beach, drive 1 mile south on California 1. The entrance to the state beach is well marked.

About the campground: Stretching 7 miles from the city of Pismo Beach to Oso Flaco Creek and backed by extensive sand dunes, Pismo State Beach draws large numbers of visitors every year. The park's 3,500 acres include the Oceano Dunes Natural Preserve and a state vehicular recreation area (see below). The natural preserve is closed to vehicles, but hikers are free to roam its shifting sands. Other hiking opportunities are a trail circling Oceano Lagoon and the mile-long Oso Flaco Beach Trail. To reach the latter, drive 10 miles south of Oceano Dunes Campground (see below), turn right onto Oso Flaco Road and go 3 miles. It is still possible to dig for the famous Pismo clams, although their numbers have been severely depleted in recent years. A state fishing license is required, and specific regulations apply. Stay limit 7 days from June through September, 15 days from October through May. Open all year.

18 Pismo State Beach: Oceano

Location: 2 miles south of the city of Pismo Beach.
Sites: 82 sites for tents and RVs, including 42 with water and electrical hookups.
Facilities: Picnic tables, barbecue grills, drinking water, showers, flush toilets.
Fee per night: $14-$24, pets $1. For reservations, call Parknet, 800-444-7275. Reservation fee, $7.50.
Agency: California Department of Parks and Recreation, 805-489-2684.
Activities: Fishing, clamming, swimming, hiking.
Finding the campground: From the intersection of California 1 and Pier Avenue, 2 miles south of Pismo Beach, turn west onto Pier Avenue and drive about 1 block to the campground entrance on the right.

About the campground: Oceano is one of two campgrounds in Pismo State Beach. For a description of the area and its attractions, see North Beach (above). Stay limit 7 days from June through September, 15 days from October through May. Open all year.

19 Oceano Dunes State Vehicular Recreation Area

Location: 1–2 miles south of the city of Pismo Beach.
Sites: 1,000 undesignated primitive sites.

Facilities: Picnic tables and barbecue grills at some but not all locations, chemical toilets. No drinking water.
Fee per night: $8. For reservations, call Parknet, 800-444-7275. Reservation fee, $7.50.
Agency: California Department of Parks and Recreation, 805-473-7230.
Activities: Off-highway driving, swimming, hiking, fishing.
Finding the campground: There are two entrances to the recreation area: at the beach end of Grand Avenue, 1 mile south of Pismo Beach, and at the beach end of Pier Avenue, 2 miles south of Pismo Beach.

About the campground: The recreation area consists of 2,500 acres of sand dunes for off-highway driving. Camping is permitted along a 3-mile stretch of beach beginning 1 mile south of the Pier Avenue entrance and extending to Oso Flaco Lake. The area is subject to soft sands and high tides and is recommended for four-wheel-drive vehicles only. There is no limit to the size and type of vehicles. Conventional vehicles may sometimes drive with caution on the compacted sand close to the water's edge at the north end of the recreation area. Stay limit 15 days. Open all year.

20 Oceano Memorial County Park

Location: 4 miles south of the city of Pismo Beach.
Sites: 24 sites with full hookups for RVs.
Facilities: Picnic tables, barbecue grills, drinking water, showers, flush toilets, playground, ball field, basketball, horseshoe pits.
Fee per night: $20, pets $2.
Agency: San Luis Obispo County Parks, 805-549-5200.
Activities: Fishing, canoeing.
Finding the campground: From Pismo Beach, drive south on California 1 about 4 miles to Airpark Drive. Turn right, and the campground is at 414 Airpark Drive.

About the campground: The park is 1 block from the ocean and has its own private lagoon for fishing or small boating. Stay limit 14 days. Open all year.

21 Lopez Lake Recreation Area

Location: 10 miles east of Arroyo Grande.
Sites: 356 sites for tents and RVs, with a choice of dry, partial, or full hookups.
Facilities: Picnic tables, barbecue grills, flush toilets, showers, laundry, playground, store, snack bar, and boat dock, ramp, and rentals.
Fee per night: $12-$20, pets $1.50. For reservations, call 805-489-8019. For group campsite reservations, call 805-781-5219. Reservation fee, $5.
Agency: San Luis Obispo County Parks, 805-489-2895.
Activities: Hiking, swimming, fishing, boating, waterskiing, sailboarding, bird watching.
Finding the campground: From U.S. Highway 101 in Arroyo Grande, take the

Grand Avenue exit and drive east on Grand Avenue for about 1 mile to Lopez Drive. Bear right on Lopez and continue for 9 miles to the lake.

About the campground: A large, resort-type campground, Lopez Lake offers 1,000 acres of water surface and 22 miles of shoreline. Many campsites overlook the lake or are located in the shade of oak trees. Oak-covered hills surround the lake, and wildflowers bloom profusely in the spring. Fishing is year-round, and catches include trout, crappie, and largemouth and smallmouth bass. Stay limit 14 days. Open all year.

22 Carrizo Plain\Soda Lake

Location: 70 miles southwest of Bakersfield.
Sites: 2 primitive campgrounds, Selby and KCL, both with open camping for tents and RVs; no designated sites.
Facilities: Picnic tables, fire rings, chemical toilets. No drinking water.
Fee per night: None.
Agency: Bureau of Land Management, 805-391-6000.
Activities: Bird watching, hunting.
Finding the campgrounds: From the intersection of California 99 and CA 58 in Bakersfield, take CA 58 west for 63 miles, turn left onto Soda Lake Road, and drive 7 miles to Selby or 8 miles farther to KCL.

About the campgrounds: Selby and KCL are on the scenic Carrizo Plain, on the southeast side of Soda Lake, and almost directly on the San Andreas Rift Zone. Summer temperatures reach an average high of 100 to 115 degrees F. The lake is famous as a major stop on the Pacific Flyway for migratory birds, including large congregations of sandhill cranes. A profusion of wildflowers carpets the area in the spring, and Painted Rock provides excellent examples of Native American pictographs. A small visitor center, open May to October, is located on Soda Lake Road, about 1.5 miles south of its junction with CA 58. Stay limit 14 days. Open all year.

SANTA BARBARA COUNTY

Many people consider Santa Barbara the most livable city in the United States. The blue ocean, sparkling beaches, green mountain backdrop, mild, sunny weather, and Spanish architecture all combine to provide the ingredients for a near-perfect lifestyle. The rest of the county is equally attractive to visitors and outdoor enthusiasts. Beaches such as Carpinteria, El Capitan, and Refugio are among the best in the state, and inland, the Sierra Madre and San Rafael Mountains join with the Los Padres National Forest to provide a prime wilderness experience. Lake Cachuma offers one of the largest waterfront campgrounds in the state, and nearby Solvang is a replica of a small Danish town, complete with authentic food and architecture.

The Santa Ynez Mountains are the only coastal range on the west coast of

North America that runs east-west. This allows ocean breezes and moisture to flow inland, creating an ideal climate for producing all the classic varieties of grapes. Consequently, more than 35 wineries are located north of Santa Barbara, mostly clustered around the small town of Los Olivos. Many are open for tours, wine tastings, and retail sales.

	Group sites	RV sites	Max. RV length	Hookups	Toilets	Showers	Drinking water	Dump station	Pets	Wheelchair	Recreation	Fee ($)	Season	Can reserve
1 Miranda Pine					V				•		H			
2 Horseshoe Spring		•			V				•		O			
3 Brookshire Spring					V				•		HO			
4 Colson					V				•		H			
5 Barrel Spring					V				•		H			
6 Wagon Flat					V				•		HO			
7 Bates Canyon		•	19		V				•		H			
8 Aliso Park		•	23		V				•		H			
9 Figueroa		•			V		•		•	•	H			
10 Davy Brown		•	19		V				•	•	HF			
11 Nira		•	19		V				•	•	HFR			
12 Cachuma		•	19		V				•		HS			
13 Jalama Beach Park	•	•		WE	F	•	•	•	•	•	SF	14–18		
14 Gaviota State Park		•	27		F	•				•	HSFBR	17–19		
15 Cachuma Lake Rec Area		•		WES	F	•	•	•	•	•	SFBR	14–18		
16 Live Oak Group Camp	•	•			C	•	•		•		HFR	192–720		•
17 River Park		•		WES	F	•	•	•	•	•	HF	15		•
18 Refugio State Beach		•	30		F	•	•		•	•	HSF	14–18		•
19 El Capitan State Beach		•			F	•	•	•	•	•	HSF	14–22		•
20 Fremont		•	19		F		•		•	•	SF	8		
21 Paradise		•	19		F		•		•	•	HSF	8		
22 Los Prietos		•	23		F		•		•		SF	8		
23 Sage Hill	•	•			F		•		•	•	HSFR	35		•
24 Upper Oso		•	27		F		•		•	•	HSR	8		
25 Juncal					V				•		HF			
26 Middle Santa Ynez					V				•		HF			
27 P-Bar Flat					V				•		HF			
28 Mono					V				•		HF			
29 Carpinteria State Beach		•	35	WES	F	•	•	•	•	•	SF	14–29		•

Hookups: W = Water   E = Electric   S = Sewer
Toilets: F = Flush   V = Vault   P = Pit   C = Chemical
Recreation: H = Hiking   S = Swimming   F = Fishing   B = Boating   L = Boat Launch   O = Off-highway Driving   R = Horseback Riding
Maximum Trailer/RV Length given in feet. **Stay Limit** given in days. **Fee** given in dollars.
If no entry under **Season,** campground is open all year. If no entry under **Fee,** camping is free.

SANTA BARBARA COUNTY AREA MAP

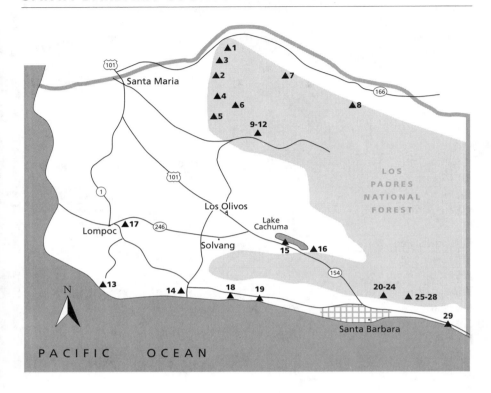

1 | Miranda Pine

Location: 40 miles east of Santa Maria.
Sites: 3 tent sites.
Facilities: Picnic tables, fire rings, vault toilet. No drinking water.
Fee per night: None.
Agency: Los Padres National Forest, Santa Lucia Ranger District, 805-925-9538.
Activities: Hiking, hunting.
Finding the campground: From the junction of U.S. Highway 101 and California 166 just north of Santa Maria, drive east 28 miles on CA 166 to Sierra Madre Road, which is unpaved. Turn right and drive 12 miles to the campground.

About the campground: Miranda Pine is situated at an elevation of 4,000 feet at the base of Miranda Pine Mountain. Stay limit 14 days. Open all year.

2 | Horseshoe Spring

Location: 21 miles east of Santa Maria.
Sites: 3 primitive sites for tents and RVs.

Facilities: Picnic tables, fire rings, vault toilet. No drinking water.
Fee per night: None.
Agency: Los Padres National Forest, Santa Lucia Ranger District, 805-925-9538.
Activities: Off-highway driving, hunting.
Finding the campground: From the intersection of U.S. Highway 101 and California 166 just north of Santa Maria, drive east on CA 166 for 16 miles to unpaved Pine Canyon Road. Turn right and drive 5 miles.

About the campground: This campground sits amid low chaparral at an elevation of 1,500 feet. Stay limit 14 days. Open all year.

3 Brookshire Spring

Location: 22 miles east of Santa Maria.
Sites: 2 tent sites.
Facilities: Picnic tables, fire rings, vault toilet. No drinking water.
Fee per night: None.
Agency: Los Padres National Forest, Santa Lucia Ranger District, 805-925-9538.
Activities: Hiking, off-highway driving.
Finding the campground: From the intersection of U.S. Highway 101 and California 166 just north of Santa Maria, drive east on CA 166 for 16 miles to unpaved Pine Canyon Road and turn right. Just before reaching Horseshoe Spring Campground (see above), turn left onto FR 11N04A and drive 1.6 miles.

About the campground: The Lake Ridge Trail and the Indian Trail through Kerry Canyon begin nearby. Stay limit 14 days. Open all year.

4 Colson

Location: 20 miles east of Santa Maria.
Sites: 6 tent sites.
Facilities: Picnic tables, fire rings, vault toilets. No drinking water.
Fee per night: None.
Agency: Los Padres National Forest, Santa Lucia Ranger District, 805-925-9538.
Activities: Hiking, hunting.
Finding the campground: From the intersection of U.S. Highway 101 and Betteravia Road in Santa Maria, follow Betteravia Road east for 12 miles to Tepusquet Canyon Road. Drive 5 miles north to Colson Canyon Road, turn right, and drive 3.5 miles to the campground. The road is unpaved and may be impassable by conventional vehicles when wet.

About the campground: Trails lead from the campground to Peach Tree Spring and Alejandro Canyon. The Byron Winery (tasting, sales, picnicking) is located about a mile after the turnoff onto Tepusquet Canyon Road. Stay limit 14 days. Open all year.

5   Barrel Spring

Location: 24 miles east of Santa Maria.
Sites: 6 tent sites.
Facilities: Picnic tables, fire rings, vault toilets. No drinking water.
Fee per night: None.
Agency: Los Padres National Forest, Santa Lucia Ranger District, 805-925-9538.
Activities: Hiking.
Finding the campground: From Colson Campground (see No. 4 above), continue on Colson Canyon Road (FR 11N04) southeast for 2 miles. When FR 11N04 turns north, continue southeast on unmarked road for 2 more miles. This road may be closed in wet weather.

About the campground: Stay limit 14 days. Open all year.

6   Wagon Flat

Location: 26 miles east of Santa Maria.
Sites: 4 tent sites.
Facilities: Picnic tables, fire rings, vault toilet. No drinking water.
Fee per night: None.
Agency: Los Padres National Forest, Santa Lucia Ranger District, 805-925-9538.
Activities: Hiking, off-highway driving.
Finding the campground: From Colson Campground (see No. 4 above), drive 2 miles southeast, then 4 miles northeast on Colson Canyon Road (FR 11N04).

About the campground: A trail for both hikers and off-road drivers leads from the campground to Kerry Canyon. Another trail leads east to the abandoned White Elephant Mine. Stay limit 14 days. Open all year.

7   Bates Canyon

Location: 57 miles east of Santa Maria.
Sites: 6 sites for tents and RVs up to 19 feet long.
Facilities: Picnic tables, fire rings, vault toilets. No drinking water.
Fee per night: None.
Agency: Los Padres National Forest, Santa Lucia Ranger District, 805-925-9538.
Activities: Hiking, hunting.
Finding the campground: From the intersection of U.S. Highway 101 and California 166 in Santa Maria, drive east 50 miles on CA 166 to Cottonwood Canyon Road (FR 11N01). Turn right and drive 7.5 miles southwest.

About the campground: Situated at 2,900 feet, the campground provides access to the Sierra Madre and the northern portion of the San Rafael Wilderness. A Forest Service lookout tower at nearby White Oaks affords a panoramic view of the surrounding area. Stay limit 14 days. Open all year.

8 Aliso Park

Location: 66 miles east of Santa Maria.
Sites: 11 sites for tents and RVs up to 23 feet long.
Facilities: Picnic tables, fire rings, vault toilets. No drinking water.
Fee per night: None.
Agency: Los Padres National Forest, Santa Lucia Ranger District, 805-925-9538.
Activities: Hiking.
Finding the campground: From the intersection of U.S. Highway 101 and California 166 in Santa Maria, drive 61 miles east on CA 166 to Aliso Canyon Road (FR 10N04). Turn right and drive 5.2 miles south to the campground.

About the campground: Two hiking trails lead from the campground (elevation 3,200 feet) into the San Rafael Wilderness. Stay limit 14 days. Open all year.

9 Figueroa Mountain Recreation Area: Figueroa

Location: 12 miles northeast of Los Olivos.
Sites: 33 sites for tents and RVs; not all sites can accommodate RVs.
Facilities: Picnic tables, fire rings, drinking water, vault toilets.
Fee per night: None.
Agency: Los Padres National Forest, Santa Lucia Ranger District, 805-925-9538.
Activities: Hiking.
Finding the campground: From Los Olivos (about 30 miles southeast of Santa Maria), drive north on Figueroa Mountain Road (FR 7N07) for 12 miles. The campground and recreation area can also be reached via Happy Canyon Road from Santa Ynez, but this road is not recommended for trailers or large RVs.

About the campground: Overnight camping in this attractive recreation area is permitted only in this and the following three campgrounds. The area also offers four picnic areas, two stocked fishing streams, and 14 hiking trails, some of which permit mountain biking. Most of the terrain is covered by heavy chaparral, but large big-cone fir, Ponderosa pine, and Jeffery pine can be found at the higher elevations. Fir Canyon and two streams, Davy Brown and Manzana, have lush vegetation and diverse wildlife. Both streams are stocked with legal-sized trout in early spring.

At an elevation of 3,500 feet, Figueroa offers a good view of the surrounding area during the day and of the lights of Santa Ynez at night. The glow from Santa Barbara can be seen in the night sky. Several hiking trails are close to the campground. Stay limit 14 days. Open all year.

10 Figueroa Mountain Recreation Area: Davy Brown

Location: 20 miles northeast of Los Olivos.
Sites: 11 sites for tents and RVs up to 19 feet long; not all sites can accommodate RVs.
Facilities: Picnic tables, fire rings, vault toilets. No drinking water.
Fee per night: None.

Agency: Los Padres National Forest, Santa Lucia Ranger District, 805-925-9538.
Activities: Hiking, fishing.
Finding the campground: From Los Olivos (about 30 miles southeast of Santa Maria), drive north 12 miles on Figueroa Mountain Road (FR 7N07) to Figueroa Campground (see No. 9 above). Continue east on Figueroa Mountain Road and then north on Sunset Valley Road (FR 8N09) for a total of about 8 more miles.

About the campground: Trout fishing is popular in Davy Brown Creek during the spring. Several hiking trails are accessible from the campground, which sits at an elevation of 2,100 feet. See Figueroa Campground (No. 9 above) for a further description of the attractions of this recreation area. Stay limit 14 days. Open all year.

11 Figueroa Mountain Recreation Area: Nira

Location: 21 miles northeast of Los Olivos.
Sites: 11 sites for tents and RVs up to 19 feet long.
Facilities: Picnic tables, fire rings, vault toilets, hitching posts for horses. No drinking water.
Fee per night: None.
Agency: Los Padres National Forest, Santa Lucia Ranger District, 805-925-9538.
Activities: Hiking, fishing, horseback riding.
Finding the campground: From Davy Brown Campground (see No. 10 above), continue north for 1.2 miles to the end of the road.

About the campground: Nira, elevation 2,000 feet, is a major trailhead for hikes and horseback trips into the San Rafael Wilderness. Trout fishing is popular in the spring in Manzana Creek, which flows beside the campground. See Figueroa Campground (No. 9 above) for a further description of the attractions of this recreation area. Stay limit 14 days. Open all year.

12 Figueroa Mountain Recreation Area: Cachuma

Location: 21 miles northeast of Los Olivos.
Sites: 7 sites for tents and RVs up to 19 feet long.
Facilities: Picnic tables, fire rings, vault toilets. No drinking water.
Fee per night: None.
Agency: Los Padres National Forest, Santa Lucia Ranger District, 805-925-9538.
Activities: Hiking, swimming, surfing.
Finding the campground: From Los Olivos (about 30 miles southeast of Santa Maria), drive north on Figueroa Mountain Road (FR 7N07) for 12 miles to Figueroa Campground (see above). Continue east on Figueroa Mountain Road to Happy Canyon Road, about 6.5 miles. Turn right and proceed another 2.2 miles.

About the campground: Cachuma, elevation 2,100 feet, is located in an attractive, narrow canyon shaded by large oak trees. Nearby Cachuma Creek is often deep enough for swimming. For a further description of the attractions of this recreation area, see Figueroa Campground (No. 9 above). Stay limit 14 days. Open all year.

13 Jalama Beach County Park

Location: 20 miles south of Lompoc.
Sites: 100 sites for tents and RVs, some with water and electrical hookups, plus 3 group sites.
Facilities: Picnic tables, barbecue grills, drinking water, flush toilets, showers, laundry, store, dump station.
Fee per night: $14-$18, groups $96, pets $1. For group reservations only, call 805-934-6211.
Agency: Santa Barbara County Parks Department, 805-736-3504.
Activities: Swimming, fishing, surfing, sailboarding, bird watching.
Finding the campground: From Lompoc, take California 1 south 5 miles to Jalama Road. Turn right (southwest) and drive an additional 15 miles.

About the campground: *Sunset* has listed Jalama as one of the 100 best campgrounds in the western United States. Although the beach is less than half a mile long, the campground is set in a 28-acre stand of trees. Gray whales migrate along the coastline of the park, moving north from February through March and south from September through November. They can be seen spouting just outside the surf line. Stay limit 14 days. Open all year.

14 Gaviota State Park

Location: 27 miles west of Santa Barbara.
Sites: 52 sites for tents, RVs up to 27 feet long, and trailers up to 25 feet long.
Facilities: Picnic tables, barbecue grills, flush toilets, showers, snack bar, store. Water in the park is not potable; boil or treat before use.
Fee per night: $17-$19, pets $1.
Agency: California Department of Parks and Recreation, 805-968-3294.
Activities: Hiking, swimming, fishing, boating, mountain biking, horseback riding.
Finding the campground: From the intersection of California 154 and U.S. Highway 101 in Santa Barbara, drive west on US 101 for 27 miles.

About the campground: A small, sandy cove and a 600-foot-long pier provide ocean access in this 2,900-acre park, which is composed mainly of rugged, chaparral wilderness. Fire roads and trails through the coastal mountains, such as the 3-mile round-trip Overlook Trail, provide sweeping vistas. Hot Springs Trail leads to two small warm-water pools. Stay limit 14 days. Open all year.

(AUTHOR'S NOTE: *Gaviota was severely damaged by storms and runoff in February 1998. At the time of this writing, the park was still closed, and it may not reopen. Check with the California Department of Parks and Recreation for its current status.*)

A windmill reflects the Old World heritage of Solvang, a quaint Danish settlement less than a half-hour drive from Cachuma Lake Campground.

15 Cachuma Lake Recreation Area

Location: 22 miles northwest of Santa Barbara.
Sites: 500 sites without hookups for tents and RVs, plus 90 with full hookups, 38 with water and electricity, and 6 with corrals for horses.
Facilities: Picnic tables, barbecue grills, flush toilets, showers, drinking water, playgrounds, swimming pools, marina (boat mooring, launch, and rental), store, laundry, dump station, fish cleaning station, snack bar.
Fee per night: $14-$18, pets $1.
Agency: Santa Barbara County Parks Department, 805-688-8780.
Activities: Hiking, swimming (pool only), fishing, boating, cycling, horseback riding.
Finding the campground: From Santa Barbara, take California 154 north for 22 miles.

About the campground: Cachuma is situated on a small peninsula jutting out into the lake for which it is named. It is a very large campground but is well scattered across many separated camping areas. Swimming, waterskiing, and sailboarding in the lake are prohibited, as the lake is a water reservoir. Boats on the lake must be 10 feet or longer. The lake is stocked annually with 150,000 rainbow trout, and other catches include bass, catfish, bluegill, crappie, and red-ear perch. From November through February, cruises are offered to view bald eagles that migrate to the lake for the winter. During summer months, wildlife-viewing cruises are substituted. A dozen wineries lie just west of the lake, most within a radius of 12 miles. The quaint Danish settlement of Solvang is less than a half-hour drive away. Stay limit 14 days. Open all year.

16 Live Oak Group Camp

Location: 14 miles northwest of Santa Barbara.
Sites: Group sites that accommodate a total of up to 1,000 people and 30 vehicles.
Facilities: Drinking water, showers, chemical toilets. A large covered pavilion houses picnic tables, stoves, and grills.
Fee per night: $192-$720 for a 2-night minimum (3-night minimum on holidays). For reservations, call 805-688-4658. Reservation fee, $25.
Agency: Santa Barbara County Parks Department, 805-688-8780.
Activities: Hiking, fishing, cycling, horseback riding.
Finding the campground: From Santa Barbara, take California 154 north for 14 miles.

About the campground: Live Oak is situated along the oak-lined bank of the Santa Ynez River, just over 8 miles south of Cachuma Lake Recreation Area (see No. 15 above). The river only flows seasonally, usually January through March, and no body contact with the water is permitted. Stay limit 14 days. Open all year.

17 River Park

Location: 1 mile east of Lompoc.
Sites: 41 sites for tents and RVs, including 35 with full hookups.

Facilities: Picnic tables, grills, fire rings, drinking water, showers, flush toilets, dump station, playground, ball field, volleyball, horseshoe pits.
Fee per night: $15. Reservations accepted.
Agency: City of Lompoc, 805-736-6565.
Activities: Hiking, pond fishing.
Finding the campground: From the junction of California 1 and CA 246 in Lompoc, drive half a mile east on CA 246.

About the campground: A small pond in the park is regularly stocked with trout. Stay limit 14 days. Open all year.

18 Refugio State Beach

Location: 15 miles west of Santa Barbara.
Sites: 85 sites for tents, RVs up to 30 feet long, and trailers up to 27 feet long.
Facilities: Picnic tables, barbecue grills, drinking water, flush toilets, showers, grocery store, snack bar.
Fee per night: $14-$18, pets $1. For reservations, call Parknet, 800-444-7275. Reservation fee, $7.50.
Agency: California Department of Parks and Recreation, 805-968-3294.
Activities: Hiking, cycling, swimming, fishing, surfing, snorkeling, scuba diving.
Finding the campground: From the intersection of California 217 and U.S. Highway 101 in Santa Barbara, drive west on US 101 for 15 miles.

About the campground: Refugio is a beautiful, crescent-shaped, sandy beach

Palm trees line the sandy beach at Refugio State Beach Campground, only a stroll away from Refugio Point and good views of the Channel Islands.

dotted by palms. A short path leads up to Refugio Point, from which there are good views of the Channel Islands. Trains pass nearby. Stay limit 7 days from June through September, 15 days from October through May. Open all year.

19 El Capitan State Beach

Location: 13 miles west of Santa Barbara.
Sites: 140 sites for tents and RVs.
Facilities: Picnic tables, barbecue grills, drinking water, flush toilets, showers, dump station, store, snack bar.
Fee per night: $14-$22, pets $1. For reservations, call Parknet, 800-444-7275. Reservation fee, $7.50.
Agency: California Department of Parks and Recreation, 805-968-3294.
Activities: Hiking, swimming, fishing, surfing, cycling.
Finding the campground: From the intersection of California 217 and U.S. Highway 101 in Santa Barbara, drive west on US 101 for 13 miles.

About the campground: El Capitan is listed by *Sunset* as one of the 100 best campgrounds in the West. Campsites are located on a wooded bluff above the beach, and stairways descend to the water. There is a good view of the Channel Islands. Trains pass nearby. A 2-mile bike path connects El Capitan and Refugio State Beach (see No. 18 above). Refugio is more scenic and has a better beach, but El Capitan does offer the better campground. Stay limit 7 days from June through September, 15 days from October through May. Open all year.

20 Lower Santa Ynez Recreation Area: Fremont

Location: 13 miles north of Santa Barbara.
Sites: 15 sites for tents and RVs up to 19 feet long.
Facilities: Picnic tables, fire rings, drinking water, flush toilets.
Fee per night: $8.
Agency: Los Padres National Forest, Santa Barbara Ranger District, 805-967-3481.
Activities: Swimming, fishing.
Finding the campground: From the intersection of U.S. Highway 101 and California 154 in Santa Barbara, drive northwest on CA 154 for 10 miles to Paradise Road. Turn right and proceed 2.6 more miles.

About the campground: Santa Ynez Recreation Area is just north of Santa Barbara in the Santa Ynez Mountains and along the Santa Ynez River, the longest stretch of free-flowing river with public access in Southern California. The recreation area is divided into upper and lower sections. The lower, west of Gibraltar Reservoir, contains Fremont and four other campgrounds (see below), as well as five picnic areas. All are accessible by a paved road that is subject to occasional seasonal flooding.

This is primarily chaparral country, with oak, cottonwood, and sycamore trees along the river, where most of the campgrounds are located. Hiking, fishing, swimming, and limited off-highway driving are the most popular activities. Stay limit 14 days. Open all year.

21 Lower Santa Ynez Recreation Area: Paradise

Location: 13 miles north of Santa Barbara.
Sites: 15 sites for tents and RVs up to 19 feet long.
Facilities: Picnic tables, fire rings, drinking water, flush toilets.
Fee per night: $8.
Agency: Los Padres National Forest, Santa Barbara Ranger District, 805-967-3481.
Activities: Hiking, swimming, fishing.
Finding the campground: From the intersection of U.S. Highway 101 and California 154 in Santa Barbara, drive northwest on CA 154 for 10 miles to Paradise Road. Turn right and drive east 3.3 miles.

About the campground: See Fremont Campground (No. 20 above) for a description of this scenic area only about a half hour north of Santa Barbara. Stay limit 14 days. Open all year.

22 Lower Santa Ynez Recreation Area: Los Prietos

Location: 14 miles north of Santa Barbara.
Sites: 37 sites for tents and RVs up to 23 feet long.
Facilities: Picnic tables, fire rings, drinking water, flush toilets.
Fee per night: $8.
Agency: Los Padres National Forest, Santa Barbara Ranger District, 805-967-3481.
Activities: Swimming, fishing.
Finding the campground: From the intersection of U.S. Highway 101 and California 154 in Santa Barbara, drive northwest on CA 154 for 10 miles to Paradise Road. Turn right (east) and drive 4.3 miles.

About the campground: See Fremont Campground (No. 20 above) for a description of this scenic area only about a half hour north of Santa Barbara. Stay limit 14 days. Open all year.

23 Lower Santa Ynez Recreation Area: Sage Hill

Location: 15.5 miles north of Santa Barbara.
Sites: 5 group sites that accommodate from 25 to 50 people each.
Facilities: Drinking water, flush toilets, centralized cooking and eating area, group barbecue, group fire pit. One site has hitching posts, corrals for horses, and parking space for horse trailers.
Fee per night: $35. Reservations required; call 800-280-CAMP. Reservation fee, $17.35.
Agency: Los Padres National Forest, Santa Barbara Ranger District, 805-967-3481.
Activities: Hiking, swimming, fishing, horseback riding.
Finding the campground: From the intersection of U.S. Highway 101 and California 154 in Santa Barbara, drive northwest on CA 154 for 10 miles to Paradise Road. Turn right (east) and drive 5 miles. Turn left onto a dirt road and proceed about half a mile.

About the campground: The Aliso National Recreational Trail, which provides a look at the native Chumash culture, is accessible near this campground. For more information about this scenic recreation area, see Fremont Campground (No. 20 above). Stay limit 14 days. Open all year.

24 | Lower Santa Ynez Recreation Area: Upper Oso

Location: 17 miles north of Santa Barbara.
Sites: 25 sites for tents and RVs up to 27 feet long; includes 5 equestrian sites.
Facilities: Picnic tables, fire rings, drinking water, flush toilets, horse corral.
Fee per night: $8. To reserve equestrian sites, call 800-280-CAMP. Reservation fee, $8.65.
Agency: Los Padres National Forest, Santa Barbara Ranger District, 805-967-3481.
Activities: Hiking, swimming, horseback riding.
Finding the campground: From the intersection of U.S. Highway 101 and California 154 in Santa Barbara, drive northwest on CA 154 for 10 miles to Paradise Road. Turn right (east) and drive 5.6 miles. Turn left toward Lower Oso Picnic Area and drive 1.8 miles, passing the picnic area.

About the campground: See Fremont Campground (No. 20 above) for more information about this scenic recreation area. Stay limit 14 days. Open all year.

25 | Upper Santa Ynez Recreation Area: Juncal

Location: 28 miles northeast of Santa Barbara.
Sites: 6 sites for tents.
Facilities: Picnic tables, fire rings, vault toilets. No drinking water.
Fee per night: None.
Agency: Los Padres National Forest, Santa Barbara Ranger District, 805-967-3481.
Activities: Hiking, fishing.
Finding the campground: From the intersection of U.S. Highway 101 and California 154 in Santa Barbara, drive northwest on CA 154 for 7.6 miles to East Camino Cielo (FR 5N12). Turn right and drive east for about 16 miles, to the end of the pavement. Continue on the dirt road (FR 5N15) for an additional 4 miles.

About the campground: A 1.5-hour drive on winding, sometimes unpaved mountain roads is required to reach the upper section of Santa Ynez Recreation Area, which follows the Santa Ynez River east of Gibraltar Reservoir. The four campgrounds in this upper section are for tent camping only, and there is no drinking water at either the campgrounds or the single picnic area. Two rustic hot springs and several trailheads are located in the area. There is no direct road connection between Upper and Lower Santa Ynez, and the dirt access road to the upper section is subject to seasonal flooding. Stay limit 14 days. Open all year.

26 | Upper Santa Ynez Recreation Area: Middle Santa Ynez

Location: 31 miles northeast of Santa Barbara.
Sites: 9 sites for tents.

Facilities: Picnic tables, fire rings, vault toilets. No drinking water.
Fee per night: None.
Agency: Los Padres National Forest, Santa Barbara Ranger District, 805-967-3481.
Activities: Hiking, fishing.
Finding the campground: From the intersection of U.S. Highway 101 and California 154 in Santa Barbara, drive northwest on CA 154 for 7.6 miles to East Camino Cielo (FR 5N12). Turn right and drive east for about 16 miles, to the end of the pavement. Continue on the dirt road (FR 5N15) for an additional 7 miles.

About the campground: See Juncal Campground (No. 25 above) for more information about this scenic area. Stay limit 14 days. Open all year.

27 Upper Santa Ynez Recreation Area: P-Bar Flat

Location: 31 miles northeast of Santa Barbara.
Sites: 4 sites for tents.
Facilities: Picnic tables, fire rings, vault toilets. No drinking water.
Fee per night: None.
Agency: Los Padres National Forest, Santa Barbara Ranger District, 805-967-3481.
Activities: Hiking, fishing.
Finding the campground: From the intersection of U.S. Highway 101 and California 154 in Santa Barbara, drive northwest on CA 154 for 7.6 miles to East Camino Cielo (FR 5N12). Turn right and drive east for about 16 miles to the end of the pavement. Continue east on the dirt road (FR 5N15) for another 7.5 miles.

About the campground: See Juncal Campground (above) for more information about this scenic area. Stay limit 14 days. Open all year.

28 Upper Santa Ynez Recreation Area: Mono

Location: 34 miles northeast of Santa Barbara.
Sites: 7 sites for tents.
Facilities: Picnic tables, fire rings, vault toilets. No drinking water.
Fee per night: None.
Agency: Los Padres National Forest, Santa Barbara Ranger District, 805-967-3481.
Activities: Hiking, fishing.
Finding the campground: From the intersection of U.S. Highway 101 and California 154 in Santa Barbara, drive northwest on CA 154 for 7.6 miles to East Camino Cielo (FR 5N12). Turn right and drive east for about 16 miles to the end of the pavement. Continue east on the dirt road (FR 5N15) for another 10.5 miles.

About the campground: See Juncal Campground (No. 25 above) for more information about this scenic area. Stay limit 14 days. Open all year.

Location: 10 miles east of Santa Barbara.
Sites: 262 sites for tents, RVs, and trailers up to 35 feet long, including 86 sites with full hookups and 33 with water and electricity.
Facilities: Picnic tables, barbecue grills, drinking water, flush toilets, showers, dump station, visitor center.
Fee per night: $14-$29, pets $1. For reservations, call Parknet, 800-444-7275. Reservation fee, $7.50.
Agency: California Department of Parks and Recreation, 805-684-2811.
Activities: Swimming, fishing, surfing.
Finding the campground: From Santa Barbara, drive 10 miles east on U.S. Highway 101. Exit at Carpinteria and follow the signs through town.

About the campground: Carpinteria is laid out in four separate beachfront loops in a grassy area dotted with trees on a wide, fine, sandy beach. The attractive town is within walking distance. A natural asphalt seep at the eastern end of this mile-long beach originally attracted the Chumash Indians to the site, where they found the tar to waterproof their boats. Trains pass by on a nearby track. Stay limit 7 days from June through September, 15 days from October through May. Open all year.

VENTURA COUNTY

Founded in 1782 as Mission San Buenaventura, the city of Ventura has evolved into a community of bookstores, coffee shops, and art and antique emporiums, with a more relaxed lifestyle than is typical of the rest of Southern California. The original mission and the Old Historic District surrounding it have been restored and are worth a visit. Although the coast here is not as dramatic as that to the north, there are fine, scenic beaches along the county's 42 miles of shoreline. Views of the Channel Islands are possible from almost any coastal location.

	Group sites	RV sites	Max. RV length	Hookups	Toilets	Showers	Drinking water	Dump station	Pets	Wheelchair	Recreation	Fee ($)	Season	Can reserve
1 Wheeler Gorge		•	23		V	•			•	•	HSF	16		•
2 Holiday	•	•	23		V				•		HO			•
3 Rose Valley		•	21		V				•		HFR			
4 Middle Lion		•	19		V				•		HSFR			
5 Piedra Blanca	•	•			V				•		HSFR			
6 Lion		•			V				•		HSFR			
7 Beaver		•			P				•		HF			
8 Potrero Seco		•			P				•		H		Apr–Oct	
9 Pine Mountain					V				•		H		Apr–Oct	

	Group sites	RV sites	Max. RV length	Hookups	Toilets	Showers	Drinking water	Dump station	Pets	Wheelchair	Recreation	Fee ($)	Season	Can reserve
10 Reyes Peak					V				•		H		Apr–Oct	
11 Ozena		•	23		V				•					
12 Reyes Creek	•	•	27		V				•		HSFR			
13 Dome Springs					P				•					
14 Rancho Nuevo					P				•		H		Apr–Oct	
15 Tinta					P				•		O		Apr–Oct	
16 Nettle Springs		•	23		V				•		HO			
17 Chuchupate		•			V				•		H		Apr–Oct	
18 Pine Springs		•	23		V				•		H		Apr–Oct	
19 Half Moon		•			V				•		HSO		Apr–Oct	
20 Thorn Meadows		•	19		P				•		HR		Apr–Oct	
21 Kings Camp		•	19		V				•		H			
22 Gold Hill		•			V				•		SFO			
23 Twin Pines					P				•		O			
24 Dutchman					V				•					
25 Lake Piru Rec Area		•		WES	F	•	•	•	•	•	SFB	14–22		
26 Blue Point		•			V				•		HSF	14–16		
27 Lake Casitas Rec Area		•		WES	F	•	•	•	•	•	FB	12–37		•
28 Camp Comfort County Park		•	34	E	F	•	•		•	•	H	14–17		•
29 Hobson County Park		•	34		F	•	•		•		SF	14–17		•
30 Faria County Park		•	34		F	•	•		•		SF	14–17		•
31 Rincon Parkway		•	34		C			•	•		SF	13–16		•
32 North End	•	•							•		HF	15		•
33 Ventura River	•	•			P	•	•		•		HSF	45		•
34 Steckel County Park		•		E	F		•		•	•	F	14–17		
35 Kenny Grove County Park		•		E	F		•		•			14–17		•
36 Oak County Park		•		E	F		•	•	•	•	H	14–17		•
37 Foster Regional Park		•			V	•		•			HSFB	14–17	Apr–Sep	
38 McGrath State Beach		•	34		F	•	•	•	•	•	SF	14–18		•
39 Big Sycamore Canyon		•	31		F	•		•	•	•	HSFR	14–18		•
40 Thornhill Broome		•	31		P	•	•		•	•	HSFR	7–11		•
41 La Jolla	•	•			P	•	•		•	•	HSFR	75		•

Hookups: W = Water E = Electric S = Sewer
Toilets: F = Flush V = Vault P = Pit C = Chemical
Recreation: H = Hiking S = Swimming F = Fishing B = Boating L = Boat Launch O = Off-highway Driving R = Horseback Riding
Maximum Trailer/RV Length given in feet. **Stay Limit** given in days. **Fee** given in dollars.
If no entry under **Season**, campground is open all year. If no entry under **Fee**, camping is free.

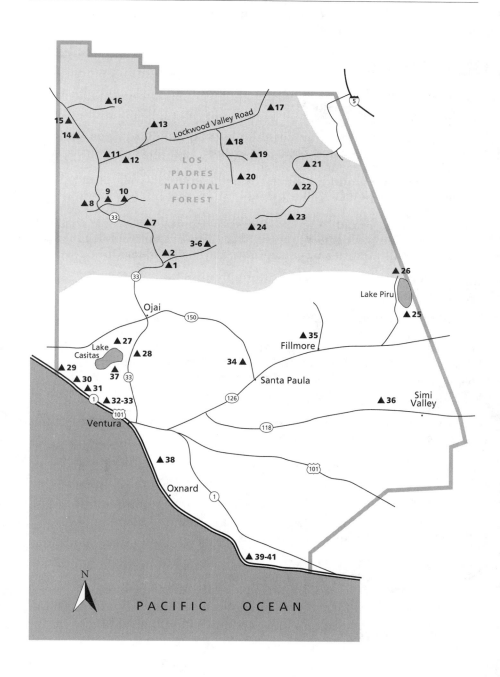

Inland, the Los Padres National Forest covers the county from its eastern to western borders and encompasses the Sespe and Chumash Wildernesses. Two large lakes, Casitas to the west and Piru to the east, provide visitors with a variety of water-sport opportunities.

1 Wheeler Gorge

Location: 20 miles north of Ventura.
Sites: 68 sites for tents and RVs up to 23 feet long.
Facilities: Picnic tables, fire rings, drinking water, vault toilets.
Fee per night: $16. For reservations, call 800-280-CAMP. Reservation fee, $8.65.
Agency: Los Padres National Forest, Ojai Ranger District, 805-646-3866.
Activities: Hiking, swimming, fishing.
Finding the campground: From the intersection of California 33 and CA 150 in Ojai, drive north on CA 33 for 7 miles.

About the campground: Wheeler Gorge lies beside Matilija Creek at an altitude of 2,000 feet. The Wheeler Gorge Nature Trail offers a varied walk along a stream and across fields with open mountain vistas. Stay limit 14 days. Open all year.

2 Holiday

Location: 9 miles north of Ojai.
Sites: 8 sites for tents and RVs up to 23 feet long, plus 1 group site.
Facilities: Picnic tables, fire rings, vault toilets. No drinking water.
Fee per night: None except for the group site, for which a fee is charged and a reservation is required. Contact the agency below for more information.
Agency: Los Padres National Forest, Ojai Ranger District, 805-646-3866.
Activities: Hiking, off-highway driving.
Finding the campground: From Wheeler Gorge Campground (see No.1 above), continue 2 miles north on California 33.

About the campground: The Ortega Trail leads northwest from the campground. It is open to both hikers and off-road vehicles, not usually a happy combination. Stay limit 14 days. Open all year.

3 Rose Valley Recreation Area: Rose Valley

Location: 18 miles north of Ojai.
Sites: 9 sites for tents and RVs up to 21 feet long.
Facilities: Picnic tables, fire rings, vault toilets. No drinking water.
Fee per night: None.
Agency: Los Padres National Forest, Ojai Ranger District, 805-646-3866.
Activities: Hiking, swimming, fishing, mountain biking, horseback riding, bird watching.
Finding the campground: From Ojai, drive north on California 33 for about 13 miles to Sespe River Road (FR 6N31). Turn right and continue another 5 miles.

Turn right again onto FR 5N42 and go half a mile.

About the campground: Rose Valley Recreation Area is one of the most popular locations in the Los Padres National Forest. It contains four separate campgrounds: Rose Valley, Middle Lion, Piedra Blanca, and Lion (see below). The Rose Valley Lakes are ideal places for fishing and bird watching. Beautiful Rose Valley Falls is just a short hike from Rose Valley Campground. Stay limit 14 days. Open all year.

4 Rose Valley Recreation Area: Middle Lion

Location: 20 miles north of Ojai.
Sites: 7 sites for tents and RVs up to 19 feet long.
Facilities: Picnic tables, fire rings, vault toilets. No drinking water.
Fee per night: None.
Agency: Los Padres National Forest, Ojai Ranger District, 805-646-3866.
Activities: Hiking, swimming, fishing, mountain biking, horseback riding, bird watching.
Finding the campground: From Ojai, drive north on California 33 for about 13 miles to Sespe River Road (FR 6N31). Turn right and continue for another 7.5 miles.

About the campground: See Rose Valley (No. 3 above) for a description of the attractions of this scenic recreation area. Stay limit 14 days. Open all year.

5 Rose Valley Recreation Area: Piedra Blanca

Location: 21 miles north of Ojai.
Sites: 4 sites for tents and RVs, plus 1 group site.
Facilities: Picnic tables, fire rings, vault toilets. No drinking water.
Fee per night: None.
Agency: Los Padres National Forest, Ojai Ranger District, 805-646-3866.
Activities: Hiking, swimming, fishing, mountain biking, horseback riding, bird watching.
Finding the campground: From Ojai, drive north on California 33 for about 13 miles to Sespe River Road (FR 6N31). Turn right and continue for another 8 miles.

About the campground: See Rose Valley (No. 3 above) for a description of the attractions of this scenic recreation area. Stay limit 14 days. Open all year.

6 Rose Valley Recreation Area: Lion

Location: 21.5 miles north of Ojai.
Sites: 30 sites for tents and RVs.
Facilities: Picnic tables, fire rings, vault toilets. No drinking water.
Fee per night: None.
Agency: Los Padres National Forest, Ojai Ranger District, 805-646-3866.

Activities: Hiking, swimming, fishing, mountain biking, horseback riding, bird watching.

Finding the campground: From Ojai, drive north on California 33 for about 13 miles to Sespe River Road (FR 6N31). Turn right and continue for 8.5 miles.

About the campground: A 7-mile trail leads from Lion Campground to Willet Hot Springs, with a primitive campsite nearby. Lion has been selected by *Sunset* as one of the best 100 campgrounds in the West. For more information about this scenic recreation area, see Rose Valley (No. 3 above). Stay limit 14 days. Open all year.

7 Beaver

Location: 15 miles north of Ojai.
Sites: 7 sites for tents and RVs.
Facilities: Picnic tables, fire rings, pit toilets. No drinking water.
Fee per night: None.
Agency: Los Padres National Forest, Ojai Ranger District, 805-646-3866.
Activities: Hiking, fishing.
Finding the campground: From Ojai, drive north on California 33 for about 15 miles.

About the campground: Situated along Sespe Creek at an elevation of 3,200 feet, this campground is the trailhead for the Middle Sespe Trail. Stay limit 14 days. Open all year.

8 Potrero Seco

Location: 29 miles north of Ojai.
Sites: 4 sites for tents and RVs.
Facilities: Picnic tables, fire rings, pit toilet. No drinking water.
Fee per night: None.
Agency: Los Padres National Forest, Ojai Ranger District, 805-646-3866.
Activities: Hiking.
Finding the campground: From Ojai, drive about 26 miles north on California 33 to FR 6N03. Turn left (west) onto this dirt road and continue 3 more miles.

About the campground: Campers need a special Forest Service permit to drive to Potrero Seco, but not to walk in. Stay limit 14 days. Open approximately April 1 to October 31, depending upon snow conditions.

9 Pine Mountain

Location: 30 miles north of Ojai.
Sites: 8 sites for tents.
Facilities: Picnic tables, fire rings, vault toilets. No drinking water.
Fee per night: None.

Agency: Los Padres National Forest, Ojai Ranger District, 805-646-3866.
Activities: Hiking.
Finding the campground: From Ojai, drive north on California 33 for 26.5 miles to Reyes Peak Road (FR 6N06). Turn right (east) onto this dirt road and go 3.5 miles.

About the campground: Sweeping vistas from the road and hiking trails are the main attractions at Pine Mountain, at an elevation of 6,650 feet. Views include the central coastline, the Channel Islands, and Sespe Gorge. Stay limit 14 days. Open approximately April 1 to October 31, depending upon snow conditions.

10 Reyes Peak

Location: 31 miles north of Ojai.
Sites: 7 sites for tents.
Facilities: Picnic tables, fire rings, vault toilets. No drinking water.
Fee per night: None.
Agency: Los Padres National Forest, Ojai Ranger District, 805-646-3866.
Activities: Hiking.
Finding the campground: From Ojai, drive north on California 33 for 26.5 miles to Reyes Peak Road (FR 6N06). Turn right (east) onto this dirt road and go 4.3 miles.

About the campground: At 7,000 feet, the campground and the surrounding area provide views of Sespe Gorge, the central coastline, and the Channel Islands. Stay limit 14 days. Open approximately April 1 to October 31, depending upon snow conditions.

11 Ozena

Location: 36 miles north of Ojai.
Sites: 10 sites for tents and RVs up to 23 feet long.
Facilities: Picnic tables, fire rings, vault toilets. No drinking water.
Fee per night: None.
Agency: Los Padres National Forest, Mount Pinos Ranger District, 805-245-3731.
Finding the campground: From Ojai, drive about 34 miles north on California 33 to Lockwood Valley Road. Turn right and drive 1.7 more miles.

About the campground: Situated close to the highway, Ozena is best used as an overnight stop. Reyes Creek Campground (below), which is only 3 miles farther east, is a better choice. Elevation 3,600 feet. Stay limit 14 days. Open all year.

12 Reyes Creek

Location: 39 miles north of Ojai.
Sites: 30 sites for tents and RVs up to 27 feet long, plus 1 group site.
Facilities: Picnic tables, fire rings, vault toilets, corral. No drinking water.

Fee per night: None.
Agency: Los Padres National Forest, Mount Pinos Ranger District, 805-245-3731.
Activities: Hiking, swimming, fishing, horseback riding.
Finding the campground: From Ojai, drive about 34 miles north on California 33 to Lockwood Valley Road. Turn right (east) onto Lockwood and drive 3.7 miles to FR 7N11. Turn right and drive 1.5 more miles.

About the campground: This attractive campground on the bank of Reyes Creek is shaded by oaks and cottonwoods. Elevation 4,000 feet. Stay limit 14 days. Open all year.

13 Dome Springs

Location: 43 miles north of Ojai.
Sites: 4 sites for tents.
Facilities: Picnic tables, fire rings, pit toilet. No drinking water.
Fee per night: None.
Agency: Los Padres National Forest, Mount Pinos Ranger District, 805-245-3731.
Activities: Hunting.
Finding the campground: From Ojai, drive about 34 miles north on California 33 to Lockwood Valley Road. Turn right and drive about 9 more miles. At the 6-mile mark, the pavement ends and the road surface becomes sandy dirt that is sometimes impassable except by four-wheel-drive vehicles.

About the campground: Hunters are the main users of this primitive, isolated spot situated in badlands terrain. Elevation 4,800 feet. Stay limit 14 days. Open all year.

14 Rancho Nuevo

Location: 37 miles north of Ojai.
Sites: 2 sites for tents.
Facilities: Picnic tables, fire rings, pit toilet. No drinking water.
Fee per night: None.
Agency: Los Padres National Forest, Mount Pinos Ranger District, 805-245-3731.
Activities: Hiking.
Finding the campground: From Ojai, drive about 34 miles north on California 33, watching for Lockwood Valley Road. Continue past Lockwood on CA 33 for almost 2 miles, and turn left onto a dirt road. Drive west 0.7 mile, bear left at a Y intersection, and drive another half mile. A sandy river crossing may require a four-wheel-drive vehicle.

About the campground: Rancho Nuevo lies in a grassy canyon bottom at an elevation of 3,600 feet. Trails lead west from the campground into the Dick Smith Wilderness. Stay limit 14 days. Open usually from April 1 to October 31.

15 Tinta

Location: 38 miles north of Ojai.
Sites: 3 sites for tents.
Facilities: Picnic tables, fire rings, pit toilet. No drinking water.
Fee per night: None.
Agency: Los Padres National Forest, Mount Pinos Ranger District, 805-245-3731.
Activities: Hunting, off-highway driving.
Finding the campground: From Ojai, drive about 34 miles north on California 33, watching for Lockwood Valley Road. Continue past Lockwood on CA 33 for almost 2 miles, and turn left onto a dirt road. Drive west 0.7 mile, bear right at a Y intersection, and drive an additional 1.6 miles. A sandy river crossing may require a four-wheel-drive vehicle.

About the campground: Hunters and off-road vehicle enthusiasts are the main users of this pinyon-shaded campground at an elevation of 3,600 feet. Stay limit 14 days. Open April through October.

16 Nettle Springs

Location: 48 miles north of Ojai.
Sites: 9 sites for tents and RVs up to 23 feet long.
Facilities: Picnic tables, fire rings, vault toilets. No drinking water.
Fee per night: None.
Agency: Los Padres National Forest, Mount Pinos Ranger District, 805-245-3731.
Activities: Hiking, off-highway driving, hunting.
Finding the campground: From Ojai, drive about 34 miles north on California 33, watching for Lockwood Valley Road. Continue past Lockwood on CA 33 for 5 miles, and turn right onto Apache Canyon Road, a graded dirt road. Drive east for about 9 miles.

About the campground: This is a pinyon-shaded camp at 4,400 feet. An OHV trail leads northeast from the campground to Toad Spring, and a hiking trail leads west into the Chumash Wilderness. Stay limit 14 days. Open all year.

17 Chuchupate

Location: 6 miles southwest of Frazier Park.
Sites: 24 sites for tents and RVs.
Facilities: Picnic tables, fire rings, vault toilets. No drinking water.
Fee per night: None.
Agency: Los Padres National Forest, Mount Pinos Ranger District, 805-245-3731.
Activities: Hiking.
Finding the campground: From the Frazier Park exit on Interstate 5, drive 5 miles west on Frazier Mountain Road to Frazier Park. From Frazier Park, continue west on Frazier Mountain Road for 6 miles, turning south after passing through Lake of the Woods. When Frazier Mountain Road splits off from Lockwood Valley Road it becomes Forest Road 8N01 which ends at the campground.

About the campground: This pinyon-shaded campground sits at an elevation of 6,200 feet. Stay limit 14 days. Open approximately April 1 to October 31, depending upon snowfall.

(AUTHOR'S NOTE: *Chuchupate was closed until further notice at the time of this writing. Check with the ranger district office for its current status.*)

18 Pine Springs

Location: 17 miles southwest of Frazier Park.
Sites: 12 sites for tents and RVs up to 23 feet long.
Facilities: Picnic tables, fire rings, vault toilets. No drinking water.
Fee per night: None.
Agency: Los Padres National Forest, Mount Pinos Ranger District, 805-245-3731.
Activities: Hiking, hunting.
Finding the campground: From the Frazier Park exit on Interstate 5, drive 5 miles west on Frazier Mountain Road to Frazier Park. From Frazier Park, continue west on Frazier Mountain Road for 4 miles, bear right onto Lockwood Valley Road, and drive about 10 miles to a junction with Forest Road 7N03. Turn left onto this road and drive another 2 miles. Turn right onto FR 7N03A and go 1 more mile.

About the campground: A pinyon-shaded site at 5,800 feet, Pine Springs is used mainly by hunters in the fall. Stay limit 14 days. Open approximately April 1 to October 31, depending upon snowfall.

19 Half Moon

Location: 23 miles southwest of Frazier Park.
Sites: 10 sites for tents and RVs.
Facilities: Picnic tables, fire rings, vault toilets. No drinking water.
Fee per night: None.
Agency: Los Padres National Forest, Mount Pinos Ranger District, 805-245-3731.
Activities: Hiking, swimming, off-highway driving.
Finding the campground: Follow directions for Pine Springs Campground (see No. 18 above). At the turnoff to Pine Springs (Forest Road 7N03A) continue south on FR 7N03 for 6 miles.

About the campground: Shaded by Jeffrey pines, Half Moon is situated along the bank of Piru Creek at an elevation of 4,700 feet. Stay limit 14 days. Open approximately April 1 to October 31, depending upon snowfall.

20 Thorn Meadows

Location: 22 miles southwest of Frazier Park.
Sites: 5 sites for tents and RVs up to 19 feet long.
Facilities: Picnic tables, fire rings, pit toilet, horse corral. No drinking water.
Fee per night: None.

Agency: Los Padres National Forest, Mount Pinos Ranger District, 805-245-3731.
Activities: Hiking, hunting, horseback riding.
Finding the campground: Follow directions for Pine Springs Campground (see No. 18 above). At the turnoff to Pine Springs (Forest Road 7N03A), continue south on FR 7N03 for 4 miles, turn right onto FR 7N03C and drive 1.5 miles.

About the campground: Located in a grassy meadow along Piru Creek, the campground lies at an elevation of 5,000 feet and is shaded by scattered Jeffrey pines. A trail leads 2 miles from the campground to Thorn Point Lookout Tower (elevation 6,935 feet). Stay limit 14 days. Open approximately April 1 to October 31, depending upon snowfall.

21 Kings Camp

Location: 12 miles southwest of Gorman.
Sites: 7 sites for tents and RVs up to 19 feet long.
Facilities: Picnic tables, fire rings, vault toilet. No drinking water.
Fee per night: None.
Agency: Los Padres National Forest, Mount Pinos Ranger District, 805-245-3731.
Activities: Hiking.
Finding the campground: Exit Interstate 5 at Gorman-Hungry Valley Road. Take Hungry Valley Road (FR 8N01) south for 5 miles, turn right onto FR 18N01 and drive about 7 miles.

About the campground: Kings Camp is situated in a pinyon and chaparral forest near Piru Creek, at an elevation of 4,200 feet. Stay limit 14 days. Open all year.

22 Gold Hill

Location: 13 miles southwest of Gorman.
Sites: 17 sites for tents and RVs.
Facilities: Picnic tables, fire rings, vault toilets. No drinking water.
Fee per night: None.
Agency: Los Padres National Forest, Mount Pinos Ranger District, 805-245-3731.
Activities: Swimming, fishing, off-highway driving.
Finding the campground: Exit Interstate 5 at Gorman-Hungry Valley Road. Take Hungry Valley Road (FR 8N01) south for 5 miles. Turn right onto FR 18N01 and drive about 8 miles.

About the campground: The campground lies at 3,800 feet and offers seasonal fishing and swimming in Piru Creek. An OHV trail leads west from the campground. Stay limit 14 days. Open all year.

23 Twin Pines

Location: 22 miles southwest of Gorman.
Sites: 5 sites for tents.

Facilities: Picnic tables, fire rings, vault toilets. No drinking water.
Fee per night: None.
Agency: Los Padres National Forest, Mount Pinos Ranger District, 805-245-3731.
Activities: Hunting, off-highway driving.
Finding the campground: From Interstate 5, exit at Gorman-Hungry Valley Road. Take Hungry Valley Road (FR 8N01) south for about 22 miles. Shortly after passing Gold Hill Campground (see No. 22 above), the road surface becomes graded dirt.

About the campground: Hunters and OHV enthusiasts are the main users of this campground shaded by Jeffrey pines at 6,600 feet. An OHV trail begins 1.5 miles southeast of the campground, on FR 7N01. Stay limit 14 days. Open all year.

24 Dutchman

Location: 24 miles southwest of Gorman.
Sites: 8 sites for tents.
Facilities: Fire rings, vault toilet. No drinking water.
Fee per night: None.
Agency: Los Padres National Forest, Mount Pinos Ranger District, 805-245-3731.
Activities: Hunting.
Finding the campground: From Interstate 5, exit at Gorman-Hungry Valley Road. Take Hungry Valley Road (FR 8N01) south for about 22 miles (the road surface becomes graded dirt after passing Gold Hill Campground) to Twin Pines Campground (see No. 23 above). Turn right onto FR 7N01 and drive about 2 miles. Occasionally, this road may be impassable except to four-wheel-drive vehicles.

About the campground: Jeffrey pines partially shade this campground, which lies at an elevation of 6,800 feet. Stay limit 14 days. Open all year.

25 Lake Piru Recreation Area

Location: 36 miles northeast of Ventura.
Sites: 238 sites for tents and RVs: 5 with full hookups, 101 with electricity, 132 dry.
Facilities: Picnic tables, barbecue grills, fire rings, drinking water, flush toilets, showers, dump station, snack bar, boat ramp, rentals, mooring.
Fee per night: $14-$22, pets $1.
Agency: United Water Conservation District, 805-521-1500.
Activities: Swimming, fishing, boating, waterskiing.
Finding the campground: From the intersection of U.S. Highway 101 and California 126 in Ventura, take CA 126 northeast for 30 miles to Piru Canyon Road. Turn north and follow this road for about 6 miles.

About the campground: Lake Piru has good fishing for bass and trout, especially in the spring. Boating on the main section of the lake is restricted to motorboats over 12 feet long. A separate area is designated for nonmotorized boats, such as kayaks and canoes. Stay limit 14 days from April through September, 30 days from October through March. Open all year.

26 Blue Point

Location: 40 miles northeast of Ventura.
Sites: 43 sites for tents and RVs.
Facilities: Picnic tables, fire rings, vault toilets. No drinking water.
Fee per night: $14-$16.
Agency: Los Padres National Forest, Mount Pinos Ranger District. Administered by Lake Piru Recreation Area, 805-521-1500.
Activities: Hiking, swimming, fishing.
Finding the campground: From the intersection of U.S. Highway 101 and California 126 in Ventura, take CA 126 northeast for 30 miles to Piru Canyon Road. Turn north and follow this road for about 10 miles.

About the campground: Blue Point is on the bank of Piru Creek, and trout fishing can be good in the spring. The Pothole Trailhead is located along the road a mile south of the campground, and another trail leads north from the campground itself. Stay limit 14 days. Open all year.

27 Lake Casitas Recreation Area

Location: 15 miles northwest of Ventura.
Sites: 450 sites for tents and RVs, including 21 with full hookups, 14 with TV, 120 with water and electricity.
Facilities: Picnic tables, fire rings, drinking water, flush and vault toilets, showers, two dump stations, snack bar, store, seven playgrounds, marina (boat ramps, rentals, slips, tackle and bait, etc.).
Fee per night: $12-$37, pets $1.50. Reservations accepted.
Agency: Casitas Municipal Water District, 805-649-1122.
Activities: Fishing, boating.
Finding the campground: From the intersection of U.S. Highway 101 and California 33 in Ventura, take CA 33 north for 11 miles to CA 150. Turn left (west) and drive 4 miles to Santa Ana Road, the campground entrance.

About the campground: Campsites are spread along the shore of Lake Casitas in a beautiful setting. Fishing is the major activity here, and the lake holds the state record for largemouth bass. Swimming and waterskiing are not permitted, nor, for some strange reason, are inflatable kayaks. Stay limit 14 days. Open all year.

28 Camp Comfort County Park

Location: 15 miles north of Ventura.
Sites: 43 sites for tents and RVs up to 34 feet long, some with electrical hookups.
Facilities: Picnic tables, barbecue grills, drinking water, flush toilets, showers, playground.

Fishing is the main attraction of Lake Casitas, which has yielded trophy-sized largemouth bass.

Fee per night: $14-$17, pets $1. Reservations accepted.
Agency: Ventura County Parks Department, 805-646-2314.
Activities: Hiking.
Finding the campground: From the intersection of U.S. Highway 101 and California 33 in Ventura, take CA 33 north for 11 miles to CA 150. Turn right (east) onto CA 150 and drive 3 miles to Creek Road. Turn right again and drive 1 mile. Stay limit 14 days. Open all year.

About the campground: The campground is situated on San Antonio Creek. The Old Creek Ranch Winery is south of the campground, near the intersection of Creek Road and CA 33. It offers tasting, tours, retail sales, and picnicking.

29 Hobson County Park

Location: 9 miles northwest of Ventura.
Sites: 31 sites for tents and RVs up to 34 feet long.
Facilities: Picnic tables, barbecue grills, drinking water, flush toilets, showers, snack bar.
Fee per night: $14-$17, pets $1. Reservations accepted.
Agency: Ventura County Parks Department, 805-654-3951.
Activities: Swimming, fishing.
Finding the campground: From Ventura, drive 9 miles northwest on U.S. Highway 101 and follow the State Beaches sign. The campground is just off the beach-front road, which parallels US 101.

About the campground: Hobson is a small oceanside location, with a rock wall dividing the campground from the water. There was no beach at the time of this writing. The campground is congested when full, but it offers a good view of the Channel Islands. Stay limit 14 days. Open all year.

30 Faria County Park

Location: 7 miles northwest of Ventura.
Sites: 42 sites for tents and RVs up to 34 feet long.
Facilities: Picnic tables, fire rings, drinking water, flush toilets, showers, playground, snack bar.
Fee per night: $14-$17, pets $1. Reservations accepted.
Agency: Ventura County Parks Department, 805-654-3951.
Activities: Swimming, fishing.
Finding the campground: From Ventura, drive 7 miles northwest on U.S. Highway 101 and follow the State Beaches sign. The campground is just off the beachfront road, which parallels US 101.

About the campground: Faria is a small oceanside campground on a waterfront composed of sand and large boulders. A rock wall stands between the campground and the waves. The park is attractive when lightly occupied but congested when full. There is a good view of the Channel Islands. Stay limit 14 days. Open all year.

31 Rincon Parkway

Location: 6 miles northwest of Ventura.
Sites: 100 sites for self-contained RVs up to 34 feet long.
Facilities: Portable toilets, dump station.
Fee per night: $13-$16, pets $1.
Agency: Ventura County Parks Department, 805-654-3951.
Activities: Swimming, fishing.
Finding the campground: From Ventura, drive 6 miles northwest on U.S. Highway 101 and follow the State Beaches sign. The campground is along a beachfront road that parallels US 101.

About the campground: Rincon Parkway is more like a large parking lot for RVs than a conventional campground, but it is on the ocean, and each site is directly off the road. RVs can park broadside to the water. Large boulders make a wall between the road and the sea. Railroad tracks run between the beach road and US 101, but the closest sound is the breaking of the waves. There is a good view of the Channel Islands. Stay limit 5 days from April 1 to October 31, 10 days from November 1 to March 31. Open all year.

32 Emma Wood State Beach: North End

Location: 2 miles northwest of Ventura.
Sites: 93 primitive sites for tents and RVs, plus 2 group sites.

Facilities: Chemical toilets.
Fee per night: $15, group site $75, pets $1. For group reservations, call Parknet, 800-444-7275. Reservation fee, $13.50.
Agency: California Department of Parks and Recreation, 805-654-4610.
Activities: Hiking, fishing, bicycling, beachcombing.
Finding the campground: From Ventura, drive 2 miles northwest on U.S. Highway 101.

About the campground: There are two campgrounds in this 116-acre park, North End and Ventura River (see No. 33 below); they are about a mile apart. Emma Wood Beach is a narrow, cobblestone-strewn beach that is sometimes completely underwater in winter. The campsites at North End are side by side, making them most suitable for RVs. The Ventura Oceanfront Bike Route connects Emma Wood and San Buenaventura Beaches. Stay limit 14 days. Open all year.

33 Emma Wood State Beach: Ventura River

Location: In Ventura.
Sites: 4 group tent sites, 1 group RV site, 1 hike/bike site.
Facilities: Picnic tables, barbecue grills, drinking water, cold showers, pit toilets.
Fee per night: $45 for tent sites, $75 for RV site, $6 per day for hike/bike site. For reservations, call Parknet, 800-444-7275. Reservation fee, $13.50.
Agency: California Department of Parks and Recreation, 805-654-4610.
Activities: Hiking, fishing, cycling, beachcombing, swimming.
Finding the campground: The campground is located at 900 West Main Street in northwestern Ventura, off U.S. Highway 101.

About the campground: See North End (No. 32 above) for information about Emma Wood State Beach. Stay limit 14 days. Open all year.

34 Steckel County Park

Location: 16 miles northeast of Ventura.
Sites: 75 sites for tents and RVs, most with electrical hookups.
Facilities: Picnic tables, barbecue grills, drinking water, flush toilets, playground.
Fee per night: $14-$17, pets $1.
Agency: Ventura County Parks Department, 805-654-3951.
Activities: Fishing.
Finding the campground: From the intersection of U.S. Highway 101 and California 126 in Ventura, drive northeast on CA 126 for 12 miles to CA 150 in Santa Paula. Turn left (north) and drive 4 miles.

About the campground: The campground is located along the bank of Santa Paula Creek. Stay limit 14 days. Open all year.

35 Kenny Grove County Park

Location: 22 miles northeast of Ventura.
Sites: 40 sites for tents and RVs, some with electrical hookups.
Facilities: Picnic tables, grills, drinking water, flush toilets, playground.
Fee per night: $14-$17, pets $1. Reservations accepted.
Agency: Ventura County Parks Department, 805-654-3951.
Finding the campground: From the intersection of U.S. Highway 101 and California 126 in Ventura, drive northeast on CA 126 for about 20 miles to Old Telegraph Road, on the left. Take Old Telegraph Road to Seventh Street in the town of Fillmore, turn right, and drive 2 miles.

About the campground: Kenny Grove is best used as an overnight stop. Stay limit 14 days. Open all year.

36 Oak County Park

Location: 24 miles east of Ventura.
Sites: 20 sites for tents; 35 sites for RVs, some with electrical hookups.
Facilities: Picnic tables, barbecue grills, drinking water, flush toilets, dump station, playground.
Fee per night: $14-$17, pets $1. Reservations accepted.
Agency: Ventura County Parks Department, 805-654-3951.
Activities: Hiking.
Finding the campground: From the intersection of California 126 and U.S. Highway 101 in Ventura, take US 101 southeast for 12 miles to CA 34. Turn left (north) on CA 34 for 5 miles to CA 118. Drive east on CA 118 for about 7 miles.

About the campground: Relatively secluded for the area, this campground has access to nearby hiking trails. Stay limit 14 days. Open all year.

37 Foster Regional Park

Location: 7 miles north of Ventura.
Sites: 30 sites for tents and RVs.
Facilities: Picnic tables, fire rings, grills, drinking water, vault toilets, playground, ball field.
Fee per night: $14-$17, pets $1.
Agency: Ventura County Parks Department, 805-654-3951.
Activities: Hiking, swimming, fishing, boating.
Finding the campground: From the intersection of U.S. Highway 101 and California 33 in Ventura, drive north on CA 33 for 6 miles. Turn left onto Casitas Vista Road and drive about 1 mile.

About the campground: Foster Park is on the bank of the Ventura River. Stay limit 14 days. Open April 1 through September 30.

38 McGrath State Beach

Location: 3 miles south of Ventura.
Sites: 174 sites for tents and RVs up to 34 feet long.
Facilities: Picnic tables, grills, drinking water, flush toilets, showers, dump station.
Fee per night: $14-$18, pets $1. For reservations, call Parknet, 800-444-7275. Reservation fee, $7.50.
Agency: California Department of Parks and Recreation, 805-654-4744.
Activities: Swimming, fishing, surfing.
Finding the campground: From U.S. Highway 101 in Ventura, take Seaward Avenue to Harbor Boulevard and drive 3 miles south.

About the campground: This 2-mile-long sandy beach attracts water-sports lovers, but swimmers should beware of occasional strong currents and rip tides. Grunion runs occur between March and August. Stay limit 7 days from June through September, 15 days from October through May. Open all year.

39 Point Mugu State Park: Big Sycamore Canyon

Location: 16 miles southeast of Oxnard.
Sites: 50 sites for tents and RVs up to 31 feet long.
Facilities: Picnic tables, barbecue grills, flush toilets, showers, dump station.
Fee per night: $14-$18, pets $1. For reservations, call Parknet, 800-444-7275. Reservation fee, $7.50.
Agency: California Department of Parks and Recreation, 818-880-0350.
Activities: Hiking, swimming, fishing, horseback riding, mountain biking.
Finding the campground: From Oxnard, drive southeast on California 1 for about 16 miles.

About the campground: This 14,980-acre state park features three campgrounds: Big Sycamore Canyon, Thornhill Broome, and La Jolla (see Nos. 40, 41 below). They are all within about a mile of each other. Big Sycamore lies in an attractive wooded area across the highway from Sycamore Cove Beach. Many trails wind through the park's backcountry, including 10-mile Sycamore Canyon Loop and 8-mile La Jolla Valley Loop. Interpretive displays are provided throughout the park. Stay limit 7 days from June through September, 15 days from October through May. Open all year.

40 Point Mugu State Park: Thornhill Broome

Location: 15 miles southeast of Oxnard.
Sites: 80 sites for tents and RVs up to 31 feet long.
Facilities: Picnic tables, drinking water, showers, pit toilets.
Fee per night: $7-$11, pets $1. For reservations, call Parknet, 800-444-7275. Reservation fee, $7.50.
Agency: California Department of Parks and Recreation, 818-880-0350.

Activities: Hiking, swimming, fishing, horseback riding, mountain biking.
Finding the campground: From Oxnard, drive 15 miles southeast on California 1.

About the campground: Thornhill Broome spreads for almost a mile along Thornhill Broome Beach. See Big Sycamore Canyon (see No. 39 above) for more about the attractions of Point Mugu State Park. Stay limit 7 days from June through September, 15 days from October through May. Open all year.

41 Point Mugu State Park: La Jolla

Location: 15 miles southeast of Oxnard.
Sites: 1 group site for tents or RVs that accommodates up to 50 people and 16 vehicles.
Facilities: Picnic tables, drinking water, showers, pit toilets.
Fee per night: $75. For reservations, call Parknet, 800-444-7275. Reservation fee, $13.50.
Agency: California Department of Parks and Recreation, 818-880-0350.
Activities: Hiking, swimming, fishing, horseback riding, mountain biking.
Finding the campground: From Oxnard, drive 15 miles southeast on California 1.

About the campground: See Big Sycamore Canyon (above) for more about the attractions of Point Mugu State Park. Stay limit 7 days from June through September, 15 days from October through May. Open all year.

CENTRAL VALLEY

The Central Valley of California is one of the most productive farming areas in the world. A drive along Interstate 5 or California 99 reveals a surprisingly diverse agricultural bounty. Miles and miles of orchards, vineyards, rice paddies, and vegetable crops seem to stretch to an endless horizon. The Fresno area bursts into color in late winter as peach, apricot, nectarine, plum, and almond orchards come into bloom. To a traveler accustomed to the smaller farms of the East, agriculture on a California scale boggles the mind. Even in the oil fields surrounding Bakersfield, pumping wells share the same fields with grazing sheep and growing crops.

But not all of the Central Valley is farmland. The eastern foothills of the Sierra Nevada offer a variety of outdoor adventures. Large lakes host a full range of water sports, and the foothills provide miles of hiking, equestrian, and mountain biking trails, as well as picnicking and wildlife-watching opportunities.

Cool winters and warm summers mean a long growing season, which contributes significantly to the agricultural success of the region. Average summer temperatures range from a high of 96 degrees F to a low of 65 degrees, while winter brings highs of 56 and lows of 39 degrees. Spring temperatures range from 73 to 49 degrees F, and in the fall temperatures are somewhat warmer, averaging highs of 78 and lows of 52 degrees F. In the summer, an average of 91 percent of the days are sunny. The sun shines an average of 71 percent of the time in the fall, 44 percent in the winter, and 61 percent in the spring.

Although the Central Valley (as defined by the California Division of Tourism) extends into Northern California, this book features only the campgrounds in its southern half. For the northern campgrounds, please see the upcoming FalconGuide *Camping Northern California*, by the same author.

This book divides the Central Valley into two areas: Fresno/Kings/Tulare Counties, and Kern County.

FRESNO, KINGS & TULARE COUNTIES

Although the Central Valley is one of the most productive agricultural regions in the nation, visitors will find much to see besides rich farmland and bountiful vineyards. Tucked among the immense fruit orchards south of Fresno, the Swedish theme town of Kingsburg offers a small slice of Old World culture. In this unlikely rural setting, costumes, architecture, and restaurants reflect the heritage of the community's early settlers.

FRESNO, KINGS & TULARE COUNTIES AREA MAP

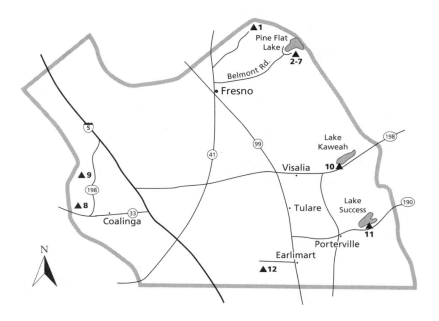

	Group sites	RV sites	Max. RV length	Hookups	Toilets	Showers	Drinking water	Dump station	Pets	Wheelchair	Recreation	Fee ($)	Season	Can reserve
1 Lost Lake Rec Area		•			V				•		HF	11		
2 Choinumni Park	•	•			F			•	•	•	HF	11		
3 Upper Pine Flat Rec Area	•	•			F		•	•	•	•	HF	11		
4 Deer Creek Point	•	•			V	•		•			HSB	50–75		•
5 Island Park		•			F	•	•	•	•	•	SFB	10–14		
6 Trimmer		•			F	•	•		•		SFB	10		
7 Sycamore		•	23		V			•			SFB	6		
8 Coalinga Mineral Springs		•			F			•			H	11		
9 Los Gatos Creek Park		•			F	•		•	•		H	11		
10 Lake Kaweah/Horse Creek		•			F	•	•	•	•	•	SFBL	8–12		
11 Lake Success		•	31		F	•	•	•	•	•	SFBL	8–12		
12 Col. Allensworth Historic Park		•	30		F	•	•		•			8		

Hookups: W = Water E = Electric S = Sewer
Toilets: F = Flush V = Vault P = Pit C = Chemical
Recreation: H = Hiking S = Swimming F = Fishing B = Boating L = Boat Launch O = Off-highway Driving R = Horseback Riding
Maximum Trailer/RV Length given in feet. **Stay Limit** given in days. **Fee** given in dollars.
If no entry under **Season,** campground is open all year. If no entry under **Fee,** camping is free.

Farther south, Colonel Allensworth State Historic Park preserves the first community in the nation founded, financed, and governed entirely by African-Americans. Eastward, in the Sierra Nevada foothills, Pine Flat, Kaweah, and Success Lakes provide complete water-sports activities in a scenic environment. At Fort Tejon, home of the former U.S. Army Camel Corps, a state historic park features a restored dragoon barracks and a small museum.

1 Lost Lake Recreation Area

Location: 14 miles north of Fresno.
Sites: 42 sites for tents and RVs.
Facilities: Vault toilets, playground, ball field.
Fee per night: $11.
Agency: Fresno County Parks Division, 209-488-3004.
Activities: Hiking, fishing, bird watching.
Finding the campground: From the intersection of California 168 and CA 41 in Fresno, drive north on CA 41 for 2.5 miles, turn right on Friant Road, and drive 11 miles northeast.

About the campground: The recreation area includes a 38-acre lake and a 70-acre primitive nature study area. Stay limit 14 days. Open all year.

(AUTHOR'S NOTE: *As of this writing, Lost Lake was closed to camping due to flooding. Whether the campground reopens depends upon future funding. Check with the Fresno County Parks Division for its current status.*)

2 Choinumni Park

Location: 31 miles east of Fresno.

Sites: 75 spaces for tents and RVs, plus 20 overflow sites and 1 group site.

Facilities: Picnic tables, fire rings, flush toilets, dump station. Check at entry booth for information on potability of water.

Fee per night: $11, pets $1.

Agency: Fresno County Parks Division, 209-488-3004.

Activities: Hiking, fishing.

Finding the campground: From the intersection of California 99 and Belmont Road in Fresno, drive east on Belmont for about 30 miles. (Belmont will become Trimmer Springs Road.) Turn right at Piedra onto Pine Flat Road and drive about 1 mile to the campground entrance on the right.

About the campground: Located in an attractive, grassy field interspersed with trees, Choinumni is near the north bank of the Kings River and close to Pine Flat Reservoir, where swimming, boating, and additional fishing are available. Stay limit 14 days. Open all year.

3 Upper Pine Flat Recreation Area

Location: 34 miles east of Fresno.

Sites: 52 spaces for tents and RVs, with many small pull-thrus, plus 60 overflow spaces and some group spaces.

Facilities: Picnic tables, grills, drinking water, flush toilets, dump station, playground.

Fee per night: $11, pets $1.

Agency: Fresno County Parks Division, 209-488-3004.

Activities: Hiking, fishing.

Finding the campground: From the intersection of California 99 and Belmont Road in Fresno, drive east on Belmont for about 30 miles. (Belmont will become Trimmer Springs Road.) Turn right at Piedra onto Pine Flat Road and drive 4 miles.

About the campground: Located at the base of Pine Flat Dam along the Kings River, this attractive campground occupies a flat, grassy field dotted with trees. About a mile past the campground on Pine Flat Road is the park headquarters, where information and brochures are available. A mile past the headquarters is the top of the dam, with a picnic area and an observation point that looks out over the reservoir. The campground is also close to other locations on Pine Flat Reservoir where swimming, boating, and additional fishing are available. Stay limit 14 days. Open all year.

4 Pine Flat Lake: Deer Creek Point

Location: 33 miles north of Fresno.

Sites: 2 group sites for tents and RVs, each accommodating up to 50 people.

Facilities: Picnic tables, fire rings, drinking water, vault toilets.

Nestled in the western foothills of the Sierra Nevada, Pine Flat Reservoir offers a choice of four campgrounds on its north shore.

Fee per night: $50-$75. Reservations required. Call 209-787-2589.

Agency: U.S. Army Corps of Engineers, 209-787-2589.

Activities: Swimming, fishing, boating, waterskiing.

Finding the campground: From the intersection of California 180 and CA 41 in Fresno, drive north on CA 41 for 1.1 miles to Belmont Road. Turn right onto Belmont and drive about 17 miles, to where Belmont becomes Trimmer Springs Road. Continue for another 15 miles and turn right onto the campground entrance road.

About the campground: Pine Flat, a large and scenic lake in the western foothills of the Sierra Nevada, offers a full range of water activities. Rainbow and brown trout, large and smallmouth bass, kokanee salmon, bluegill, crappie, and catfish are the most common catches. The reservoir has four campgrounds on its north shore: Deer Creek Point, Island Park, Trimmer, and Sycamore (see Nos. 5, 6, and 7 below). In addition, two county campgrounds are located just below Pine Flat Dam on Kings River (see Nos. 2 and 3 above).

Because the lake is subject to irrigation drawdowns, water levels can fluctuate daily, making established beaches impractical. The water level is usually highest in spring. A commercial marina is located at Deer Creek Point. It offers boat and slip rentals and camping and fishing supplies. Stay limit 14 days. Open all year.

5 ☐ Pine Flat Lake: Island Park

Location: 34 miles north of Fresno.
Sites: 52 sites for tents and RVs, plus 60 overflow sites.
Facilities: Picnic tables, fire rings, drinking water, flush toilets, showers, dump station, boat launch, fish-cleaning stations.
Fee per night: $14 in summer ($10 overflow), $10 in winter.
Agency: U.S. Army Corps of Engineers, 209-787-2589.
Activities: Swimming, fishing, boating, waterskiing.
Finding the campground: From the intersection of California 180 and CA 41 in Fresno, drive north on CA 41 for 1.1 miles to Belmont Road. Turn right onto Belmont and drive about 17 miles, to where Belmont becomes Trimmer Springs Road. Continue for another 16 miles.

About the campground: Island Park is beautifully situated on a small neck of land that juts out into the lake. It offers great lake and mountain views. For more information about the attractions of Pine Flat Reservoir, see Deer Creek Point (No. 4 above). Stay limit 14 days. Open all year.

6 ☐ Pine Flat Lake: Trimmer

Location: 41 miles north of Fresno.
Sites: 27 sites for tents and RVs.
Facilities: Picnic tables, fire rings, flush toilets, showers, boat ramp, marina, fish-cleaning stations, public phone, drinking water.
Fee per night: $10.
Agency: U.S. Army Corps of Engineers, 209-787-2589.
Activities: Swimming, fishing, boating, waterskiing.
Finding the campground: From the intersection of California 180 and CA 41 in Fresno, drive north on CA 41 for 1.1 miles to Belmont Road. Turn right and drive about 17 miles to where Belmont becomes Trimmer Springs Road. Continue on for another 23 miles.

About the campground: A commercial marina is located on the lake at Trimmer. For more information about the attractions of the area, see Deer Creek Point (above). Stay limit 14 days. Open all year.

7 ☐ Pine Flat Lake: Sycamore

Location: 48 miles north of Fresno.
Sites: 20 sites for tents and RVs up to 23 feet long.
Facilities: Picnic tables, fire rings, vault toilets. No drinking water.
Fee per night: $6.
Agency: U.S. Army Corps of Engineers, 209-787-2589.
Activities: Swimming, fishing, boating, waterskiing.
Finding the campground: From the intersection of California 180 and CA 41 in Fresno, drive north on CA 41 for 1.1 miles to Belmont Road. Turn right and

drive about 17 miles to where Belmont becomes Trimmer Springs Road. Continue on for another 30 miles.

About the campground: As of this writing, Sycamore Campground was closed until further notice. Call the Corps of Engineers for current information.

8 Coalinga Mineral Springs Recreation Area

Location: 18 miles west of Coalinga.
Sites: Undesignated sites for tents and RVs.
Facilities: Picnic tables, barbecue grills, flush toilets. No drinking water.
Fee per night: $11.
Agency: Fresno County Parks Division, 209-488-3004.
Activities: Hunting, hiking.
Finding the campground: From Coalinga, drive west on California 198 for 13 miles. Turn right onto Coalinga Mineral Springs Road and drive 5 miles.

About the campground: Hot, dry, and isolated, this campground is located in a former hot-springs resort area, now closed and abandoned. It is used mainly by hunters. Written permission is required to camp here; call the Fresno County Parks Division for information. Stay limit 14 days. Open all year.

9 Los Gatos Creek Park

Location: 19 miles west of Coalinga.
Sites: 44 sites for tents and RVs, plus 17 overflow sites.
Facilities: Picnic tables, barbecue grills, drinking water, flush toilets, ball field.
Fee per night: $11.
Agency: Fresno County Parks Division, 209-488-3004.
Activities: Hiking.
Finding the campground: From Coalinga, drive north on California 198/33 for 3.5 miles, turn left (west) onto Los Gatos Creek Road, and drive about 15 miles.

About the campground: Stay limit 14 days. Open all year.

10 Lake Kaweah/Horse Creek Recreation Area

Location: 24 miles east of Visalia.
Sites: 80 sites for tents and RVs.
Facilities: Picnic tables, fire rings, drinking water, flush toilets, showers, dump station, playground, boat ramp, fish-cleaning station.
Fee per night: $8-$12.
Agency: U.S. Army Corps of Engineers, 209-597-2301.
Activities: Swimming, fishing, boating, waterskiing.
Finding the campground: From the intersection of California 63 and CA 198 in Visalia, drive east and then northeast on CA 198 for about 24 miles.

About the campground: A large, scenic lake in the foothills of the southern Sierra Nevada, Kaweah offers a full range of water activities. The campground is directly on the lakefront. Rainbow trout, largemouth bass, bluegill, crappie, and catfish are the most common catches. Spring is the best time to visit; during the hot summers, the level of the lake drops significantly, because surrounding farms draw on it for irrigation. Stay limit 14 days. Open all year.

11 Lake Success/Tule Recreation Area

Location: 8 miles east of Porterville.
Sites: 104 sites for tents and RVs up to 31 feet long.
Facilities: Picnic tables, barbecue grills, drinking water, flush toilets, showers, dump station, playground, 2 boat ramps.
Fee per night: $8-$12, $2 boat-launching fee.
Agency: U.S. Army Corps of Engineers, 209-784-0215.
Activities: Swimming, fishing, boating, waterskiing, hiking.
Finding the campground: From Porterville, drive 8 miles east on California 190 and turn left onto Success Drive.

About the campground: Tule is located on the shore of Lake Success, in the scenic foothills of the Sierra Nevada. Gentle winds make it an ideal environment for small sailboats, which are popular on the lake. Black bass, bluegill, crappie, and catfish are the most common catches. Big Sycamore Nature Trail begins at the dam at the south end of the lake, below park headquarters. Stay limit 14 days. Open all year.

12 Colonel Allensworth State Historic Park

Location: 70 miles southwest of Fresno.
Sites: 15 sites for tents and RVs up to 30 feet long.
Facilities: Picnic tables, barbecue grills, drinking water, flush toilets, showers.
Fee per night: $8, pets $1.
Agency: California Department of Parks and Recreation, 805-849-3433.
Activities: Sightseeing, museum.
Finding the campground: Take California 99 south from Fresno and drive about 60 miles to Earlimart. Turn right (west) onto Sierra Avenue (Route J22) and drive 7.3 miles. Then turn left (south) onto CA 43 and go 2.3 miles.

About the campground: The park preserves the site of the only town in California founded, financed, and governed by African-Americans. The town, named for a U.S. Army chaplain, has been partially restored, and visitors can tour former homes and other buildings, many with original or period furnishings. Guided tours may also be arranged by calling the Department of Parks and Recreation. Stay limit 15 days from June through September, 30 days from October through May. Open all year.

KERN COUNTY

KERN COUNTY AREA MAP

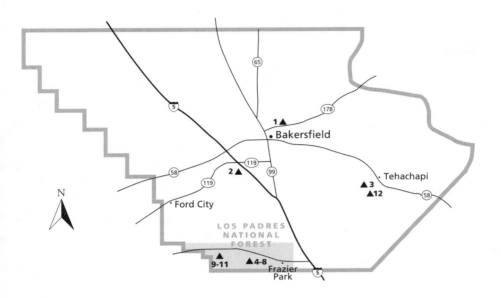

		Group sites	RV sites	Max. RV length	Hookups	Toilets	Showers	Drinking water	Dump station	Pets	Wheelchair	Recreation	Fee ($)	Season	Can reserve
1	Kern River County Park		•			F	•	•	•	•		SFBL	12		
2	Buena Vista Aquatic Rec Area		•		WES	F	•	•	•	•		SFBL	18–26		•
3	Brite Valley Aquatic Rec Area		•		WE	F	•	•	•	•	•	HSFB	9–12	May–Oct	
4	McGill	•	•			V			•		•	H	8	June–Sep	•
5	Mount Pinos		•	21		V			•			H	8	June–Sep	
6	Chula Vista					V			•			H		June–Sep	
7	Campo Alto	•	•	23		V			•		•	H		June–Sep	
8	Toad Springs		•	15		V			•			H			
9	Caballo		•	15		V			•			H		May–Oct	
10	Marian		•	15		V			•			H		May–Oct	
11	Valle Vista		•			V			•			H			
12	Tehachapi Mountain Park		•			V			•		•	HR	8–12		

Hookups: W = Water   E = Electric   S = Sewer
Toilets: F = Flush   V = Vault   P = Pit   C = Chemical
Recreation: H = Hiking   S = Swimming   F = Fishing   B = Boating   L = Boat Launch   O = Off-highway Driving   R = Horseback Riding
Maximum Trailer/RV Length given in feet.   **Stay Limit** given in days.   **Fee** given in dollars.
If no entry under **Season,** campground is open all year. If no entry under **Fee,** camping is free.

At Bakersfield, steadily pumping oil wells begin to share the landscape—and often the same fields—with agricultural crops and livestock. The city is home to the Kern County Museum, which includes 50 historic buildings, and to the California Living Museum, the Lori Breck Children's Discovery Center, and the Cunningham Memorial Art Gallery. Farther south, near Lebec, Fort Tejon features a restored dragoon barracks and museum. Eastward, a few small but picturesque lakes dot the Sierra Nevada foothills, offering fishing and water sports.

1 Kern River County Park

Location: 15 miles northeast of Bakersfield.
Sites: 50 sites for tents and RVs, all with pull-thrus.
Facilities: Picnic tables, barbecue grills, fire rings, drinking water, flush toilets, showers, dump station, boat launch, playground.
Fee per night: $12, pets $2.
Agency: Kern County Parks Department, 805-861-2345.
Activities: Swimming, fishing, boating, waterskiing.
Finding the campground: From the intersection of California 99 and CA 178 in Bakersfield, drive east on CA 178 for 8.5 miles to Alfred Harrell Highway. Turn left (north) and drive about 6 miles, watching for signs to the park.

About the campground: This attractive campground is situated along the bank of the Kern River, adjacent to relatively small Lake Ming. Lots of grass and scattered trees give a feeling of spaciousness to the sites, which are all semicircular pull-thrus off the camp road. Large rigs may have trouble fitting. Stay limit 14 days. Open all year.

2 Buena Vista Aquatic Recreation Area

Location: 22 miles southwest of Bakersfield.
Sites: 130 sites for tents and RVs, including 82 sites with full hookups.
Facilities: Picnic tables, barbecue grills, drinking water, flush toilets, showers, boat ramps, dump station, playground, store.
Fee per night: $18-$26, pets $3. For reservations, call 800-950-7275.
Agency: Kern County Parks Department, 805-763-1526.
Activities: Swimming, fishing, boating, waterskiing, golfing.
Finding the campground: From the intersection of California 58 and CA 119 in Bakersfield, take CA 99 south for 6 miles, turn right (west) onto CA 119 and drive 13 miles, turn left (south) onto Enos Lane, and drive about 2.5 more miles.

About the campground: The camping area is located on Lake Webb, the larger of two lakes that comprise the recreation area. A public golf course is located a short distance west of the park. Stay limit 14 days. Open all year.

3 Brite Valley Aquatic Recreation Area

Location: 7 miles southwest of Tehachapi.
Sites: Unlimited sites for tents, 12 sites with water and electrical hookups for RVs.
Facilities: Picnic tables, barbecue grills, drinking water, flush toilets, showers, playground, dump station, fish-cleaning station, and 3 pavilions with electricity.
Fee per night: $9-$12.
Agency: Kern County Parks Department, 805-822-3228.
Activities: Hiking, swimming, fishing, boating.
Finding the campground: From California 58 in Tehachapi, take the exit for CA 202, and drive west on CA 202 for about 5 miles to Banducci Road. Turn left and drive 1 mile.

About the campground: Fishing for trout in the spring and catfish in the summer is the major activity at Brite Lake. No gasoline motors are allowed on the lake. Stay limit 14 days. Open May through October.

4 Mount Pinos Recreation Area: McGill

Location: 18 miles west of Frazier Park.
Sites: 73 sites for tents and RVs, plus 2 group sites, 1 accommodating up to 60 people, the other up to 80 people.
Facilities: Picnic tables, fire rings, vault toilets. No drinking water.
Fee per night: $8. For group reservations, call 800-280-CAMP. Reservation fee, $15.
Agency: Los Padres National Forest, Mount Pinos Ranger District, 805-245-3731.
Activities: Hiking.
Finding the campground: From Frazier Park, drive west on Cuddy Valley Road about 12 miles. Turn left onto Mount Pinos Road (FR 9N24) and drive 6 miles.

About the campground: Mount Pinos Recreation Area is located on the slopes of Mount Pinos, which, at 8,831 feet, is the highest point in the Los Padres National Forest. There are five campgrounds in the area: McGill, Mount Pinos, Chula Vista, Campo Alto, and Toad Springs (see below). McGill sits at an elevation of 7,400 feet. The forest cover consists mainly of Jeffrey pine and white fir. Hiking trails with sweeping vistas are the main attraction here. A 5-mile trail leads from Mount Pinos to Mount Abel. Stay limit 14 days. Open June through September.

5 Mount Pinos Recreation Area: Mount Pinos

Location: 19 miles west of Frazier Park.
Sites: 19 sites for tents and RVs up to 21 feet long.
Facilities: Picnic tables, fire rings, vault toilets. No drinking water.
Fee per night: $8.
Agency: Los Padres National Forest, Mount Pinos Ranger District, 805-245-3731.
Activities: Hiking.
Finding the campground: From Frazier Park, drive west on Cuddy Valley Road about 12 miles. Turn left onto Mount Pinos Road (FR 9N24) and drive

another 7 miles.

About the campground: Mount Pinos Campground sits at an elevation of 8,000 feet. For more information about the attractions of the recreation area, see McGill Campground (above). Stay limit 14 days. Open June through September.

6 Mount Pinos Recreation Area: Chula Vista

Location: 21 miles west of Frazier Park.
Sites: 12 sites for tents.
Facilities: Picnic tables, fire rings, vault toilets. No drinking water.
Fee per night: None.
Agency: Los Padres National Forest, Mount Pinos Ranger District, 805-245-3731.
Activities: Hiking.
Finding the campground: From Frazier Park, drive west on Cuddy Valley Road about 12 miles. Turn left onto Mount Pinos Road (FR 9N24) and drive another 8.5 miles.

About the campground: There is a 500-foot walk between the parking lot for Chula Vista and the tent sites. This campground sits at an elevation of 8,300 feet, at one end of a 5-mile trail leading from Mount Pinos to Mount Abel. For more information about the attractions of this recreation area, see McGill Campground (No. 4 above). Stay limit 14 days. Open June through September.

7 Mount Pinos Recreation Area: Campo Alto

Location: 26 miles west of Frazier Park.
Sites: 17 sites for tents and RVs up to 23 feet long, plus 2 group sites.
Facilities: Picnic tables, fire rings, vault toilets. No drinking water.
Fee per night: None.
Agency: Los Padres National Forest, Mount Pinos Ranger District, 805-245-3731.
Activities: Hiking.
Finding the campground: From Frazier Park, drive west about 20 miles on Cuddy Valley Road (which turns into Mil Potrero Highway). Turn left onto FR 9N07 and drive about 6 more miles.

About the campground: Campo Alto sits at an elevation of 8,300 feet and anchors one end of a 5-mile trail from Mount Pinos to Mount Abel. For more information about the recreation area, see McGill Campground (No. 4 above). Stay limit 14 days. Open June through September.

8 Mount Pinos Recreation Area: Toad Springs

Location: 22 miles west of Frazier Park.
Sites: 5 sites for tents and RVs up to 15 feet long.
Facilities: Picnic tables, fire rings, vault toilets. No drinking water.
Fee per night: None.

Agency: Los Padres National Forest, Mount Pinos Ranger District, 805-245-3731.
Activities: Hiking.
Finding the campground: From Frazier Park, drive west about 21 miles on Cuddy Valley Road (which becomes Mil Potrero Highway), and go about 1.2 miles past Apache Saddle.

About the campground: Toad Springs, at an elevation of 5,700 feet, is the only campground in Mount Pinos Recreation Area that is open year-round. For more information about the recreation area, see McGill Campground (No. 4 above). Stay limit 14 days.

9 Caballo

Location: 23 miles west of Frazier Park.
Sites: 5 sites for tents and RVs up to 15 feet long.
Facilities: Picnic tables, fire rings, vault toilets. No drinking water.
Fee per night: None.
Agency: Los Padres National Forest, Mount Pinos Ranger District, 805-245-3731.
Activities: Hiking, hunting.
Finding the campground: From Frazier Park, drive west about 21 miles on Cuddy Valley Road (which becomes Mil Potrero Highway). Go about 1.3 miles beyond Apache Saddle, turn right (north) onto FR 9N27, a dirt road, and drive half a mile.

About the campground: Caballo is a pinyon-shaded campground at an elevation of 5,800 feet. Stay limit 14 days. Open May through October.

10 Marian

Location: 23 miles west of Frazier Park.
Sites: 5 sites for tents and RVs up to 15 feet long.
Facilities: Picnic tables, fire rings, vault toilets. No drinking water.
Fee per night: None.
Agency: Los Padres National Forest, Mount Pinos Ranger District, 805-245-3731.
Activities: Hiking, hunting.
Finding the campground: From Frazier Park, drive west about 21 miles on Cuddy Valley Road (which becomes Mil Potrero Highway). Go about 1.3 miles beyond Apache Saddle, turn right (north) onto FR 9N27, a dirt road, and drive 1.5 miles.

About the campground: This campground sits at an elevation of 6,600 feet. Stay limit 14 days. Open May through October.

11 Valle Vista

Location: 19 miles southeast of Maricopa.
Sites: 7 sites for tents and RVs.

Facilities: Picnic tables, fire rings, vault toilets. No drinking water.
Fee per night: None.
Agency: Los Padres National Forest, Mount Pinos Ranger District, 805-245-3731.
Activities: Hiking.
Finding the campground: From the intersection of California 166 and CA 33 in Maricopa, drive south on CA 33/166 about 8 miles to Cerro Noroeste Road. Turn left (east) and drive about 11 miles.

About the campground: Valle Vista sits at an elevation of 4,800 feet. Stay limit 14 days. Open all year.

12 Tehachapi Mountain Park

Location: 7 miles south of Tehachapi.
Sites: 61 sites for tents and RVs.
Facilities: Picnic tables, barbecue grills, drinking water, showers, vault toilets, corral.
Fee per night: $8-$12, pets $2.
Agency: Kern County Parks Department, 805-822-4632.
Activities: Hiking, horseback riding.
Finding the campground: From the intersection of California 202 and Summit Road in Tehachapi, take Summit Road south about 1 mile and turn right (west) onto Highline Road. Drive 2.5 miles to Water Canyon Road and turn left (south). Drive about 3 miles to the campground at the end of the road.

About the campground: Stay limit 14 days. Open all year.

HIGH SIERRA

Some of the most majestic scenery in all of California is found in the high country that separates Owens Valley to the east and the fertile San Joaquin Valley to the west. The Sierra Nevada, the highest mountain range in North America, is the centerpiece of this tour region. Extending like a giant spine from north to south, its rugged peaks and granite-walled valleys prevent all vehicles from crossing from east to west. The region is a paradise for outdoor enthusiasts year-round, and virtually every type of outdoor activity takes place within its borders.

Sequoia and Kings Canyon National Parks provide miles of roads and trails through a magnificent wilderness, affording access to the largest trees on earth and the deepest canyon in the United States. Three national forests encompass more than 2 million acres and eight wilderness areas and contain hundreds of miles of roads and trails through equally breathtaking scenery.

The most prominent peak of the Sierra Nevada, Mount Whitney, is also the highest in the contiguous 48 states. Dozens of lakes, large and small, dot the landscape. Many are in wild, remote places—havens of solitude where little more than an angler's line disturbs their placid surfaces. Others, more easily accessible by car and RV, welcome power boats and water skiers. Wild and Scenic Rivers beckon kayakers and whitewater rafters, while special trails attract equestrians, mountain bikers, and off-highway drivers. Ski areas cater to both downhill and cross-country skiers. Although most campgrounds are closed in winter, the national forests permit camping anywhere within their borders as long as certain rules are followed (see How To Use This Guide, on page 7). This allows the self-contained RVer and the hardy, all-season camper the opportunity to enjoy these special places in their wonderful winter settings.

The climate here is typical of mountainous areas: warm summers, cool springs and falls, and cold winters (although the latter are more moderate than in many mountainous regions). The average maximum and minimum temperatures range in summer from 79 to 45 degrees F and in winter from 44 to 16 degrees F. Spring brings temperatures from 60 to 32 F, and fall from 51 to 35 F. Altitude affects these temperatures; the higher elevations tend to have colder averages, while the lowest elevations are generally warmer. The percentage of average days of sunshine is fairly consistent year-round: 80 percent in summer, 79 in fall, 74 in winter, and 77 percent in spring.

Although the High Sierra region, as defined by the California Division of Tourism, extends into Northern California, this book features campgrounds only in its southern half. For the northern Sierra, see the upcoming Falcon-Guide, *Camping Northern California*.

This book divides the High Sierra into five areas: Sierra & Inyo National Forests, Sequoia National Park, Kings Canyon National Park, Sequoia National Forest (North), and Sequoia National Forest (South). Each contains a variety of campgrounds that will satisfy virtually all outdoor enthusiasts, whatever their recreational preferences may be.

HIGH SIERRA MAP

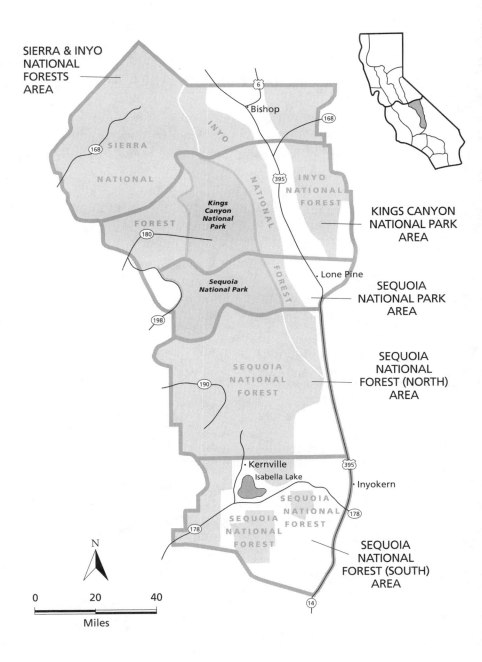

SIERRA & INYO NATIONAL FORESTS AREA

6

Bishop

168

SIERRA

168

NATIONAL

INYO

NATIONAL

395

INYO NATIONAL FOREST

Kings Canyon National Park

FOREST

180

KINGS CANYON NATIONAL PARK AREA

Sequoia National Park

FOREST

Lone Pine

SEQUOIA NATIONAL PARK AREA

198

SEQUOIA NATIONAL FOREST

190

SEQUOIA NATIONAL FOREST (NORTH) AREA

Kernville

395

Isabella Lake

Inyokern

SEQUOIA NATIONAL FOREST

178

178

SEQUOIA NATIONAL FOREST

SEQUOIA NATIONAL FOREST (SOUTH) AREA

N

0   20   40

Miles

14

SIERRA & INYO NATIONAL FORESTS & VICINITY

Virtually all of this area consists of portions of the Sierra and Inyo National Forests, which are possibly the most scenic national forests in the nation. Rugged mountain peaks, crystal-clear streams, and pristine alpine lakes combine

SIERRA & INYO NATIONAL FORESTS AREA MAP

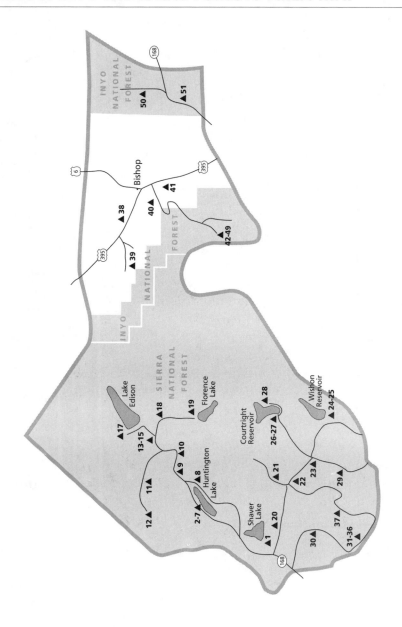

#	Name	Group sites	RV sites	Max. RV length	Hookups	Toilets	Showers	Drinking water	Dump station	Pets	Wheelchair	Recreation	Fee ($)	Season	Can reserve
1	Dorabelle		•			V		•		•		SFB	12	May–Oct	•
2	Lower Billy Creek		•			V		•		•		HSRFB	14	June–Oct	•
3	Billy Creek		•			F		•		•		HSRFB	14	June–Oct	•
4	Catavee		•			V		•		•	•	HSRFB	14	June–Oct	•
5	Kinnikinnick		•			F		•		•		HSRFB	14	June–Oct	•
6	Deer Creek		•			F		•		•	•	HSRFB	14	June–Oct	•
7	College		•			V		•		•		HSRFB	14	June–Oct	•
8	Rancheria		•			F		•		•		HSRFB	14	June–Oct	•
9	Midge Creek	•	•			C				•		H	75	June–Oct	•
10	Badger Flat	•	•			V				•		HRO	8	June–Oct	
11	Sample Meadow		•			V				•		H		June–Oct	
12	West Kaiser		•			P				•		H		June–Oct	
13	Portal Forebay		•			V				•		HSFB	8	June–Oct	
14	Bolsillo		•			V		•		•		HF		June–Oct	
15	Mono Hot Springs		•			V		•		•		HSFR	10	May–Nov	
16	Mono Creek		•			V		•		•		HSF	10	June–Sep	
17	Vermillion		•			V		•		•		HSFBR	10	June–Oct	•
18	Ward Lake		•			V				•		HSF	8	June–Oct	
19	Jackass Meadow		•			V		•		•	•	HSFB	10	June–Oct	•
20	Swanson Meadow		•			V				•			8	May–Nov	
21	Dinkey Creek	•	•			F		•		•		HSFO	12	May–Oct	•
22	Gigantea		•			V				•		H		June–Oct	
23	Buck Meadow		•			V				•		H		June–Oct	
24	Lily Pad		•			V		•		•	•	HSFB	10	June–Oct	
25	Upper Kings River	•	•			V		•		•	•	HSFB	Call	June–Oct	•
26	Marmot Rock					V		•		•		HSFB	8	June–Oct	
27	Trapper Springs		•	23		V		•		•		HSFB	10	June–Oct	
28	Voyager Rock					V				•		HSFB		June–Oct	
29	Sawmill Flat		•			V				•		H		June–Oct	
30	Bretz		•			V				•		H		May–Oct	
31	Kirch Flat	•	•			V				•		HSFB			•
32	Camp 4½					V				•		HF			
33	Gravel Flat	•	•			V				•		HF			•
34	Camp 4					V				•		HF			
35	Bear Wallow	•	•			V				•		HF			•
36	Mill Flat					V				•		HF			
37	Black Rock		•			V		•		•	•	F	8	May–Oct	
38	Pleasant Valley		•			P		•		•		F	6		
39	Horton Creek		•			P				•		HF		May–Oct	
40	Millpond Rec Area		•		WE	F		•		•	•	HSB	12–15	Mar–Nov	•

	Group sites	RV sites	Max. RV length	Hookups	Toilets	Showers	Drinking water	Dump station	Pets	Wheelchair	Recreation	Fee ($)	Season	Can reserve
41 Shober Lane		•		WE	F	•	•		•	•		17	Mar–Nov	•
42 Big Trees		•			F		•		•		HF	11	Mem. Day–Labor Day	
43 Forks		•			F		•		•		H	8	May–Oct	
44 Four Jeffrey		•			F	•	•	•	•		HF	11	Apr–Oct	
45 Intake 2		•			F		•		•		HFBL	8	Apr–Oct	
46 Bishop Park	•	•			F		•		•	•	H	8	Apr–Oct	
47 Sabrina		•			V		•		•		H	8	June–Sep	
48 North Lake					V		•		•		HFR	11	July–Sep	
49 Willow		•			P				•		HFB	8	July–Sep	
50 Grandview		•			P				•		H		Apr–Nov	
51 Pinon, Fossil, Poleta, Juniper	•				P				•		H		Apr–Nov	

Hookups: W = Water E = Electric S = Sewer
Toilets: F = Flush V = Vault P = Pit C = Chemical
Recreation: H = Hiking S = Swimming F = Fishing B = Boating L = Boat Launch O = Off-highway Driving R = Horseback Riding
Maximum Trailer/RV Length given in feet. **Stay Limit** given in days. **Fee** given in dollars.
If no entry under **Season,** campground is open all year. If no entry under **Fee,** camping is free.

with a diverse forest to provide spectacular open vistas and wooded groves and glens. The forests are home to more than 315 animal species, including black bears, coyotes, bobcats, gray foxes, porcupines, mule deer, beavers, marmots, and pikas. Thirty-one species of fish include bass, crappie, bluegill, and four types of trout.

At lower altitudes, the forests consist primarily of oak and chaparral. Between 4,000 and 8,000 feet, mixed conifers are predominantly ponderosa pine. Red fir forests begin at 6,000 feet and range up to 8,000 feet. Just below timberline, mixed pines (lodgepole and Western white) and hemlock take over the scene. In addition, fine groves of giant sequoia can be found at various locations in the Sierra National Forest, and ancient bristlecone pines can be seen in the Inyo.

The forests contain hundreds of miles of trails, including the Kings River National Recreation Trail, the Mount Whitney Trail, and a 30-mile segment of the Pacific Crest Trail. Large, secluded alpine lakes, such as Florence, Cartwright, and Wishon, and numerous smaller ones, such as the Dinkey Lakes, glisten like jewels in their High Sierra setting. The Kings Wild and Scenic River challenges kayakers and rafters. The Sierra Heritage Scenic Byway (California 168) passes through a landscape of granite walls and domes, untrammeled wilderness areas, and majestic mountain vistas. These and other attractions can be enjoyed from the 51 public campgrounds described below.

1 | Dorabelle

Location: Half a mile east of the center of the town of Shaver Lake.
Sites: 34 sites for tents only, 34 sites for tents and RVs.
Facilities: Picnic tables, fire rings, drinking water, vault toilets.
Fee per night: $12. For reservations, call 800-280-CAMP. Reservation fee, $8.65.
Agency: Sierra National Forest, Pineridge Ranger District, 209-855-5360.
Activities: Swimming, fishing, boating, waterskiing.
Finding the campground: From the intersection of California 168 and County Road N257 (Dorabelle Road) near the center of the town of Shaver Lake, drive east on Dorabelle Road for half a mile.

About the campground: Located on the south shore of Shaver Lake, Dorabelle offers a complete range of water sports. A nearby marina offers boat rentals. Elevation 5,400 feet. Stay limit 14 days. Open May through October.

2 | Huntington Lake: Lower Billy Creek

Location: 15 miles north of the town of Shaver Lake.
Sites: 8 sites for tents only, 5 sites for tents and RVs.
Facilities: Picnic tables, fire rings, drinking water, vault toilets.
Fee per night: $14. For reservations, call 800-280-CAMP. Reservation fee, $8.65.
Agency: Sierra National Forest, Pineridge Ranger District, 209-855-5360.
Activities: Hiking, swimming, fishing, boating, waterskiing, horseback riding.
Finding the campground: From the town of Shaver Lake, drive north on California 168 for 4 miles, turn left onto Huntington Lake Road, and drive 10 miles to Huntington Lake. The campground is half a mile east of Huntington Lake Resort, at the northwestern end of the lake, on County Road M2710.

About the campground: A scenic, high-country lake at an elevation of 7,000 feet, Huntington Lake offers a full range of water sports but is best known for its excellent sailing conditions. Sailing regattas are held here every summer. The area also contains many fine hiking trails, including the 10-mile Kaiser Loop Trail, which leads to the top of Kaiser Peak; a short trail to a fine view atop Black Point; and a mile-long hike to Rancheria Falls (150 feet). There are seven campgrounds on the north shore of the lake, five of which are on the water. This is one of them. Stay limit 14 days. Open June through October.

3 | Huntington Lake: Billy Creek

Location: 15 miles north of the town of Shaver Lake.
Sites: 29 sites for tents only, 15 sites for tents and RVs.
Facilities: Picnic tables, fire rings, drinking water, flush toilets.
Fee per night: $14. For reservations, call 800-280-CAMP. Reservation fee, $8.65.
Agency: Sierra National Forest, Pineridge Ranger District, 209-855-5360.
Activities: Hiking, swimming, fishing, boating, waterskiing, horseback riding.
Finding the campground: From Lower Billy Creek Campground (see No. 2 above), continue 0.1 mile east on County Road M2710.

About the campground: See Lower Billy Creek Campground (above) for more information about the attractions of this area. Billy Creek is on the opposite side of the road from the lakeshore. Stay limit 14 days. Open June through October.

4 ∎ Huntington Lake: Catavee

Location: 18 miles north of the town of Shaver Lake.
Sites: 18 sites for tents only, 9 sites for tents and RVs.
Facilities: Picnic tables, fire rings, drinking water, vault toilets.
Fee per night: $14. For reservations, call 800-280-CAMP. Reservation fee, $8.65.
Agency: Sierra National Forest, Pineridge Ranger District, 209-855-5360.
Activities: Hiking, swimming, fishing, boating, waterskiing, horseback riding.
Finding the campground: From lower Billy Creek Campground (see No. 2 above), continue east 3 miles on County Road M2710.

About the campground: See Lower Billy Creek Campground (No. 2 above) for more information about the attractions of this area. Stay limit 14 days. Open June through October.

5 ∎ Huntington Lake: Kinnikinnick

Location: 18 miles north of the town of Shaver Lake.
Sites: 19 sites for tents only, 13 for tents and RVs.
Facilities: Picnic tables, fire rings, drinking water, flush toilets.
Fee per night: $14. For reservations, call 800-280-CAMP. Reservation fee, $8.65.
Agency: Sierra National Forest, Pineridge Ranger District, 209-855-5360.
Activities: Hiking, swimming, fishing, boating, waterskiing, horseback riding.
Finding the campground: From Lower Billy Creek Campground (see No. 2 above), continue east 3.2 miles on County Road M2710.

About the campground: See Lower Billy Creek Campground (above) for more information about the attractions of this area. Stay limit 14 days. Open June through October.

6 ∎ Huntington Lake: Deer Creek

Location: 18 miles north of the town of Shaver Lake.
Sites: 13 sites for tents only, 16 sites for tents and RVs.
Facilities: Picnic tables, fire rings, drinking water, flush toilets.
Fee per night: $14. For reservations, call 800-280-CAMP. Reservation fee, $8.65.
Agency: Sierra National Forest, Pineridge Ranger District, 209-855-5360.
Activities: Hiking, swimming, fishing, boating, waterskiing, horseback riding.
Finding the campground: Deer Creek is across the road from Kinnikinnick Campground (see No. 5 above).

About the campground: See Lower Billy Creek Campground (No. 2 above) for

more information about the attractions of this area. Stay limit 14 days. Open
June through October.

7 Huntington Lake: College

Location: 19 miles north of the town of Shaver Lake.
Sites: 9 sites for tents only, 2 sites for tents and RVs.
Facilities: Picnic tables, fire rings, drinking water, vault toilets.
Fee per night: $14. For reservations, call 800-280-CAMP. Reservation fee, $8.65.
Agency: Sierra National Forest, Pineridge Ranger District, 209-855-5360.
Activities: Hiking, swimming, fishing, boating, waterskiing, horseback riding.
Finding the campground: From Lower Billy Creek Campground (see No. 2
above), continue east 3.7 miles on County Road M2710.

About the campground: See Lower Billy Creek Campground (No. 2 above) for
more information about the attractions of this area. Stay limit 14 days. Open
June through October.

8 Huntington Lake: Rancheria

Location: 18 miles northeast of the town of Shaver Lake.
Sites: 82 sites for tents, 67 sites for RVs.
Facilities: Picnic tables, fire rings, drinking water, flush toilets.
Fee per night: $14. For reservations, call 800-280-CAMP. Reservation fee, $8.65.
Agency: Sierra National Forest, Pineridge Ranger District, 209-855-5360.
Activities: Hiking, swimming, fishing, boating, waterskiing, horseback riding.
Finding the campground: From the town of Shaver Lake, drive northeast 18
miles on California 168.

About the campground: See Lower Billy Creek Campground (No. 2 above) for
more information about the attractions of this area. Stay limit 14 days. Open
June through October.

9 Midge Creek

Location: 20 miles northeast of Shaver Lake.
Sites: 2 group sites for tents and RVs, each accommodating up to 50 people.
Facilities: Picnic tables, fire rings, portable toilets. No drinking water.
Fee per night: $75. For reservations, call 800-280-CAMP. Reservation fee, $15.
Agency: Sierra National Forest, Pineridge Ranger District, 209-855-5360.
Activities: Hiking.
Finding the campground: From the town of Shaver Lake, drive north 18 miles
on California 168 to the town of Lakeshore, where the road becomes Kaiser Pass
Road (FR 80). Continue northeast on Kaiser Pass Road for 1.5 miles.

About the campground: Elevation 7,400 feet. Stay limit 14 days. Open June
through October.

10 Badger Flat

Location: 24 miles northeast of Shaver Lake.
Sites: 10 sites for tents only, 5 sites for tents and RVs, 1 group site for tents or RVs that accommodates up to 100 people.
Facilities: Picnic tables, fire rings, vault toilets. No drinking water.
Fee per night: $8 for individual sites, $150 for group site.
Agency: Sierra National Forest, Pineridge Ranger District, 209-855-5360.
Activities: Hiking, horseback riding, off-highway driving.
Finding the campground: From the town of Shaver Lake, drive north 18 miles on California 168 to the town of Lakeshore, where the road becomes Kaiser Pass Road (FR 80). Continue northeast on Kaiser Pass Road for 6 miles.

About the campground: A trail leads southeast from the camp to the Dinkey Lakes Wilderness, and another goes northwest to several lakes in the Kaiser Wilderness via Potter's Pass. White Bark Vista (2 miles northeast of the campground on Kaiser Pass Road, then a 2-mile round-trip hike on a four-wheel-drive road) provides spectacular views of the Sierra crest and Edison and Florence Lakes. This same road affords access to the 20-mile Dusy Ershim OHV Route. Elevation 8,200 feet. Stay limit 14 days. Open June through October.

11 Sample Meadow

Location: 32 miles north of Shaver Lake.
Sites: 16 sites for tents and RVs.
Facilities: Picnic tables, fire rings, vault toilets. No drinking water.
Fee per night: None.
Agency: Sierra National Forest, Pineridge Ranger District, 209-855-5360.
Activities: Hiking.
Finding the campground: From the town of Shaver Lake, drive north 18 miles on California 168 to the town of Lakeshore, where the road becomes Kaiser Pass Road (FR 80). Continue northeast on Kaiser Pass Road for about 10 miles, turn left onto unpaved FR 5, and drive about 4 miles.

About the campground: A trail leads 3 miles south from the campground to three attractive, small lakes in the Kaiser Wilderness. Elevation 7,800 feet. Stay limit 14 days. Open June through October.

12 West Kaiser

Location: 39 miles north of Shaver Lake.
Sites: 10 sites for tents and RVs.
Facilities: Picnic tables, fire rings, pit toilets. No drinking water.
Fee per night: None.
Agency: Sierra National Forest, Pineridge Ranger District, 209-855-5360.
Activities: Hiking.
Finding the campground: From the town of Shaver Lake, drive north 18 miles

on California 168 to the town of Lakeshore, where the road becomes Kaiser Pass Road (FR 80). Continue northeast on Kaiser Pass Road for about 10 miles, turn left onto unpaved FR 5, and drive about 11 miles.

About the campground: A 4-mile trail to Mammoth Pool Reservoir begins a mile north of the campground. Elevation 7,800 feet. Stay limit 14 days. Open June through October.

13 Portal Forebay

Location: 32 miles northeast of Shaver Lake.
Sites: 6 sites for tents only, 3 sites for tents and RVs.
Facilities: Picnic tables, fire rings, vault toilets. No drinking water.
Fee per night: $8.
Agency: Sierra National Forest, Pineridge Ranger District, 209-855-5360.
Activities: Hiking, swimming, fishing, boating.
Finding the campground: From the town of Shaver Lake, drive north 18 miles on California 168 to the town of Lakeshore, where the road becomes Kaiser Pass Road (FR 80). Continue northeast on Kaiser Pass Road for about 14 miles.

About the campground: Portal Forebay is located on the shore of Forebay Lake at an elevation of 7,200 feet. Trails lead south from the campground to Kaiser Pass Meadow and north into the John Adams Wilderness and to Lake Edison. Stay limit 14 days. Open June through October.

14 Bolsillo

Location: 33 miles northeast of Shaver Lake.
Sites: 4 sites for tents and RVs.
Facilities: Picnic tables, fire rings, drinking water, vault toilets.
Fee per night: None.
Agency: Sierra National Forest, Pineridge Ranger District, 209-855-5360.
Activities: Hiking, fishing.
Finding the campground: From the town of Shaver Lake, drive north 18 miles on California 168 to the town of Lakeshore, where the road becomes Kaiser Pass Road (FR 80). Continue northeast on Kaiser Pass Road for about 15 miles.

About the campground: This campground is located on the bank of Bolsillo Creek at an elevation of 7,400 feet. A trail leads 2 miles south from the campground to tiny Corbett Lake and 1.5 miles northeast to Mono Hot Springs. Stay limit 14 days. Open June through October.

15 Mono Hot Springs

Location: 35 miles northeast of Shaver Lake.
Sites: 4 sites for tents only, 26 sites for tents and RVs.
Facilities: Picnic tables, fire rings, drinking water, vault toilets.

Fee per night: $10. For reservations, call 800-280-CAMP. Reservation fee, $8.65.
Agency: Sierra National Forest, Pineridge Ranger District, 209-855-5360.
Activities: Hiking, swimming, fishing, horseback riding.
Finding the campground: From the town of Shaver Lake, drive north 18 miles on California 168 to the town of Lakeshore, where the road becomes Kaiser Pass Road (FR 80). Continue northeast on Kaiser Pass Road for about 17 miles.

About the campground: On the bank of the San Joaquin River, adjacent to Mono Hot Springs Resort, the campground is directly across a small creek from several natural hot springs. Elevation 6,500 feet. Stay limit 14 days. Open May through November.

16 Mono Creek

Location: 38 miles northeast of Shaver Lake.
Sites: 16 sites for tents and RVs.
Facilities: Picnic tables, fire rings, drinking water, vault toilets.
Fee per night: $10. For reservations, call 800-280-CAMP. Reservation fee, $8.65.
Agency: Sierra National Forest, Pineridge Ranger District, 209-855-5360.
Activities: Hiking, swimming, fishing.
Finding the campground: From the town of Shaver Lake, drive north 18 miles on California 168 to the town of Lakeshore, where the road becomes Kaiser Pass Road (FR 80). Continue northeast on Kaiser Pass Road for about 19.5 miles. (The road becomes Edison Lake Road after Mono Hot Springs.)

About the campground: On the bank of Mono Creek at an elevation of 7,400 feet, this campground is reachable by a narrow, winding road that prohibits access by large RVs and trailers. Stay limit 14 days. Open June through September.

17 Vermillion

Location: 43 miles northeast of Shaver Lake.
Sites: 10 sites for tents only, 20 sites for tents and RVs.
Facilities: Picnic tables, fire rings, drinking water, vault toilets.
Fee per night: $10. For reservations, call 800-280-CAMP. Reservation fee, $8.65.
Agency: Sierra National Forest, Pineridge Ranger District, 209-855-5360.
Activities: Hiking, swimming, fishing, boating, horseback riding.
Finding the campground: From the town of Shaver Lake, drive north 20 miles on California 168 to the town of Lakeshore, where the road becomes Kaiser Pass Road (FR 80). Continue northeast on Kaiser Pass Road for about 23 miles.

About the campground: On the western shore of beautiful, 5-mile-long Lake Edison, Vermillion offers a full range of water sports, except for waterskiing. Boat speed is limited to 15 miles an hour. A boat ramp and riding stable are located near the campground. A ferry operates in summer, taking hikers and backpackers into the John Muir Wilderness and to the Pacific Crest Trail. The 5-mile Onion Spring OHV Route begins less than a mile north of the campground. The road to Vermillion is narrow and winding, prohibiting access by large RVs and trailers. Elevation 7,700 feet. Stay limit 14 days. Open June through October.

18 Ward Lake

Location: 39 miles northeast of Shaver Lake.
Sites: 6 sites for tents and RVs.
Facilities: Picnic tables, fire rings, vault toilets. No drinking water.
Fee per night: $8.
Agency: Sierra National Forest, Pineridge Ranger District, 209-855-5360.
Activities: Hiking, swimming, fishing.
Finding the campground: From the town of Shaver Lake, drive north 20 miles on California 168 to the town of Lakeshore, where the road becomes Kaiser Pass Road (FR 80). Continue northeast on Kaiser Pass Road for about 16 miles, turn right onto Florence Lake Road, and drive 3 miles.

About the campground: Located on the shore of a small lake at an elevation of 7,300 feet, this campground is reached by a narrow, winding road that prohibits access by large RVs and trailers. Stay limit 14 days. Open June through October.

19 Jackass Meadow

Location: 42 miles northeast of Shaver Lake.
Sites: 50 sites for tents and RVs.
Facilities: Picnic tables, fire rings, drinking water, vault toilets.
Fee per night: $10. For reservations, call 800-280-CAMP. Reservation fee, $8.65.
Agency: Sierra National Forest, Pineridge Ranger District, 209-855-5360.
Activities: Hiking, swimming, fishing, boating.
Finding the campground: From the town of Shaver Lake, drive north 20 miles on California 168 to the town of Lakeshore, where the road becomes Kaiser Pass Road (FR 80). Continue northeast on Kaiser Pass Road for about 16 miles, turn right onto Florence Lake Road, and drive 6 miles.

About the campground: Located on beautiful Florence Lake, Jackass Meadow offers most water sports except waterskiing. Boat speed is limited to 15 miles an hour. A ferry operates in summer, taking hikers and backpackers to several trails, including the Pacific Crest Trail. The ferry ride may also be combined with a 5-mile return hike along the western shore of the lake. A narrow, winding road prohibits access by large RVs and trailers. Stay limit 14 days. Open June through October.

20 Swanson Meadow

Location: 2 miles east of Shaver Lake.
Sites: 9 sites for tents and RVs.
Facilities: Picnic tables, fire rings, vault toilets. No drinking water.

Fee per night: $8.
Agency: Sierra National Forest, Pineridge Ranger District, 209-855-5360.
Finding the campground: From the town of Shaver Lake, drive 2 miles east on Dinkey Creek Road.

About the campground: Swanson Meadow is primarily an overflow campground, useful when lakeside locations are full. Elevation 5,600 feet. Stay limit 14 days. Open May through November.

21 Dinkey Creek

Location: 12 miles east of Shaver Lake.
Sites: 128 sites for tents and RVs, plus 1 group site for tents or RVs that accommodates up to 50 people.
Facilities: Picnic tables, fire rings, drinking water, flush and vault toilets.
Fee per night: $12 for individual sites, $75 for group site. For reservations, call 800-280-CAMP. Reservation fee, $8.65 for individual sites, $15 for group site.
Agency: Sierra National Forest, Kings River Ranger District, 209-855-8321.
Activities: Hiking, swimming, fishing, off-highway driving.
Finding the campground: From the town of Shaver Lake, drive 12 miles east on Dinkey Creek Road.

About the campground: Located on the bank of Dinkey Creek, the campground is an excellent base for day hikes or backpacking trips into the Dinkey Lakes Wilderness. More than a dozen small, pretty lakes are easily accessible; several can be reached in the course of a day trip. The Dinkey Lakes trailhead is 11 miles north of the campground via Rock Creek Road (FR 9S09) and FR 9S62. For those who like scenic vistas, the Bald Mountain Summit Trail (3.5 miles round trip) begins about 3 miles from the campground, back toward Shaver Lake on Dinkey Creek Road. The trail joins the Bald Mountain OHV Route before reaching the summit. Elevation 5,700 feet. Stay limit 14 days. Open May through October.

22 Gigantea

Location: 18 miles southeast of Shaver Lake.
Sites: 4 sites for tents only, 6 sites for tents and RVs.
Facilities: Picnic tables, fire rings, vault toilets. No drinking water.
Fee per night: None.
Agency: Sierra National Forest, Kings River Ranger District, 209-855-8321.
Activities: Hiking.
Finding the campground: From the town of Shaver Lake, drive east on Dinkey Creek Road for 12 miles, turn right onto McKinley Grove Road (FR 40) and drive about 6 miles.

About the campground: Gigantea is located on the edge of McKinley Grove, a relatively isolated stand of more than 170 giant sequoia trees spread out over 100 acres. A paved, wheelchair-accessible interpretive trail leads through these towering trees. Elevation 6,500 feet. Stay limit 14 days. Open June through October.

23 Buck Meadow

Location: 21 miles southeast of Shaver Lake.
Sites: 5 sites for tents only, 5 sites for tents and RVs.
Facilities: Picnic tables, fire rings, vault toilets. No drinking water.
Fee per night: None.
Agency: Sierra National Forest, Kings River Ranger District, 209-855-8321.
Activities: Hiking.
Finding the campground: From the town of Shaver Lake, drive east on Dinkey Creek Road for 12 miles, turn right onto McKinley Grove Road (FR 40) and drive about 9 miles.

About the campground: Elevation 6,800 feet. Stay limit 14 days. Open June through October.

24 Wishon Reservoir: Lily Pad

Location: 27 miles southeast of Shaver Lake.
Sites: 5 sites for tents only, 10 sites for tents and RVs.
Facilities: Picnic tables, fire rings, drinking water, vault toilets.
Fee per night: $10.
Agency: Sierra National Forest, Kings River Ranger District, 209-855-8321.
Activities: Hiking, swimming, fishing, boating.
Finding the campground: From the town of Shaver Lake, drive east on Dinkey Creek Road for 12 miles, turn right onto McKinley Grove Road (FR 40), and drive 15 miles.

About the campground: Wishon is a beautiful high-country lake with spectacular alpine scenery. Water sports other than waterskiing are permitted on the lake, and boat speed is limited to 15 miles an hour. Because Wishon is a reservoir, it is subject to periodic drawdowns that affect the shoreline. Two campgrounds are located in close proximity on the southwest shore of the lake. Lily Pad, for individuals and families, is located directly on the water. A group camp, Upper Kings River (see No. 25 below), is located near the shoreline. A trail leads east from the campground area to a series of lakes in the John Muir Wilderness. Elevation 6,500 feet. Stay limit 14 days. Open June through October.

25 Wishon Reservoir: Upper Kings River

Location: 27 miles southeast of Shaver Lake.
Sites: 1 group site for tents or RVs that accommodates up to 100 people.
Facilities: Picnic tables, fire rings, drinking water, vault toilets.
Fee per night: Call for fees. Reservations required; call 209-263-5230.
Agency: Pacific Gas & Electric Company, 916-386-5164.

Activities: Hiking, swimming, fishing, boating.
Finding the campground: From the town of Shaver Lake, drive east on Dinkey Creek Road for 12 miles, turn right onto McKinley Grove Road (FR 40), and drive 15 miles.

About the campground: See Lily Pad Campground (No. 24 above) for information about the attractions of the Wishon Reservoir area. Elevation 6,400 feet. Stay limit 14 days. Open June through October.

26 Courtright Reservoir: Marmot Rock

Location: 33 miles east of Shaver Lake.
Sites: 15 sites for tents.
Facilities: Picnic tables, fire rings, vault toilets, drinking water.
Fee per night: $8, pets $1.
Agency: Sierra National Forest, Kings River Ranger District, 209-855-8321.
Activities: Hiking, swimming, fishing, boating.
Finding the campground: From the town of Shaver Lake, drive east on Dinkey Creek Road for 12 miles, turn right onto McKinley Grove Road (FR 40), and drive 13 miles. Turn left onto Courtright Reservoir Road (FR 10S16) and drive north 8 miles to the south shore of the reservoir.

About the campground: Courtright is another beautiful high-country lake with spectacular scenery. Water sports other than waterskiing are permitted, and boat speed is limited to 15 miles an hour. One small disadvantage to an otherwise idyllic location is that periodic drawdowns affect the shoreline and level of the lake. There are three campgrounds on the shoreline: Marmot Rock, Trapper Springs, and Voyager Rock (see Nos. 27 and 28 below). Elevation 8,200 feet. Stay limit 14 days. Open June through October.

27 Courtright Reservoir: Trapper Springs

Location: 35 miles east of Shaver Lake.
Sites: 75 sites for tents and RVs up to 23 feet long.
Facilities: Picnic tables, fire rings, vault toilets, drinking water.
Fee per night: $10.
Agency: Sierra National Forest, Kings River Ranger District, 209-855-8321.
Activities: Hiking, swimming, fishing, boating.
Finding the campground: From the town of Shaver Lake, drive east on Dinkey Creek Road for 12 miles, turn right onto McKinley Grove Road (FR 40), and drive 13 miles. Turn left onto Courtright Reservoir Road (FR 10S16) and drive north 8 miles to Marmot Rock Campground on the south shore of the reservoir. Drive north for another 2 miles on FR 8S07 on the west side of the lake.

About the campground: See Marmot Rock Campground (No. 26 above) for information about the attractions of the reservoir and surrounding area. A trail leads northwest from Trapper Springs to a dozen small lakes in the Dinkey Lakes Wilderness. Elevation 8,200 feet. Stay limit 14 days. Open June through October.

28 Courtright Reservoir: Voyager Rock

Location: 36 miles east of Shaver Lake.
Sites: 14 sites for tents.
Facilities: Picnic tables, fire rings, vault toilets. No drinking water.
Fee per night: None.
Agency: Sierra National Forest, Kings River Ranger District, 209-855-8321.
Activities: Hiking, swimming, fishing, boating.
Finding the campground: From the town of Shaver Lake, drive east on Dinkey Creek Road for 12 miles, turn right onto McKinley Grove Road (FR 40), and drive 13 miles. Turn left onto Courtright Reservoir Road (FR 10S16) and drive north 8 miles to Marmot Rock Campground on the south side of the reservoir. Drive north for 3 miles on the east side of the lake, crossing the dam spillway. The last 1.5 miles is dirt road that sometimes requires a four-wheel-drive vehicle. Voyager Rock may also be reached by boat. The road is being allowed to deteriorate because the ranger district plans to make this a boat-in campground only.

About the campground: See Marmot Rock Campground (No. 26 above) for information about the attractions of the reservoir and surrounding area. A trail leads northeast from Voyager Rock into the John Muir Wilderness. Elevation 8,200 feet. Stay limit 14 days. Open June through October.

29 Sawmill Flat

Location: 26 miles southeast of Shaver Lake.
Sites: 10 sites for tents and RVs.
Facilities: Picnic tables, fire rings, vault toilets. No drinking water.
Fee per night: None.
Agency: Sierra National Forest, Kings River Ranger District, 209-855-8321.
Activities: Hiking.
Finding the campground: From the town of Shaver Lake, drive east on Dinkey Creek Road for 12 miles, turn right onto McKinley Grove Road (FR 40) and drive about 12 miles. Turn right onto FR 11S12 and drive about 2 miles.

About the campground: Elevation 6,700 feet. Stay limit 14 days. Open June through October.

30 Bretz

Location: 13 miles southwest of Shaver Lake.
Sites: 10 sites for tents and RVs.
Facilities: Picnic tables, fire rings, vault toilets. No drinking water.
Fee per night: None.
Agency: Sierra National Forest, Kings River Ranger District, 209-855-8321.
Activities: Hiking.

Finding the campground: From the town of Shaver Lake, drive southwest on California 168 for 5 miles, turn left onto Peterson Mill Road (which becomes FR 10S02) and drive 8 miles.

About the campground: Elevation 5,200 feet. Stay limit 14 days. Open May through October.

31 Lower Kings River: Kirch Flat

Location: 58 miles east of Fresno.
Sites: 17 sites for tents and RVs, plus 1 group site that accommodates up to 50 people.
Facilities: Picnic tables, fire rings, vault toilets. No drinking water.
Fee per night: None for individual sites, group site $50. Reservations required for group site; call ranger district below.
Agency: Sierra National Forest, Kings River Ranger District, 209-855-8321.
Activities: Hiking, swimming, fishing, kayaking, rafting.
Finding the campground: From the intersection of California 180 and CA 41 in Fresno, drive north on CA 41 for 1.1 miles to Belmont Road. Turn right and drive about 17 miles, to where Belmont becomes Trimmer Springs Road. Continue for 34 miles, around the north shore of Pine Flat Reservoir. Go another 6 miles east beyond the lake.

About the campground: Six minimum-facility campgrounds are located along the bank of the Kings River, east of Pine Flat Reservoir (see Central Valley, pages 69-71, for campgrounds in the Pine Flat area). These camps provide a base for exploring the attractions of the Kings River Special Management Area and the Kings River National Recreation Trail, which winds gently along the river beneath spectacular granite formations and ends at Garlic Falls. The portion of the river that has been designated a National Wild and Scenic River begins about 8 miles east of the campgrounds. Kayaking, whitewater rafting, and fishing are popular. Mountain biking is possible along several four-wheel-drive roads and some trails, and there are many hiking opportunities. Stay limit 14 days. Open all year.

32 Lower Kings River: Camp 4¹/₂

Location: 61 miles east of Fresno.
Sites: 5 sites for tents.
Facilities: Picnic tables, fire rings, vault toilet. No drinking water.
Fee per night: None.
Agency: Sequoia National Forest, Hume Lake Ranger District, 209-338-2251.
Activities: Hiking, fishing.
Finding the campground: From the intersection of California 180 and CA 41 in Fresno, drive north on CA 41 for 1.1 miles to Belmont Road. Turn right and drive about 17 miles, to where Belmont becomes Trimmer Springs Road. Continue for

34 miles, around the north shore of Pine Flat Reservoir. Go another 9 miles east beyond the lake on Trimmer Springs Road (FR 11S12) and Davis Road (FR 12S01).

About the campground: See Kirch Flat Campground (No. 31 above) for more information about the attractions of this area. Stay limit 14 days. Open all year.

33 Lower Kings River: Gravel Flat

Location: 61 miles east of Fresno.
Sites: 1 group site for tents or RVs that accommodates up to 200 people.
Facilities: Picnic tables, fire rings, vault toilet. No drinking water.
Fee per night: No fee, but reservations required; call 209-855-8321.
Agency: Sierra National Forest, Kings River Ranger District, 209-855-8321.
Activities: Hiking, fishing.
Finding the campground: Across the road from Camp 4½ (see above).

About the campground: See Kirch Flat Campground (No. 31 above) for more information about the attractions of this area. Stay limit 14 days. Open all year.

34 Lower Kings River: Camp 4

Location: 62 miles east of Fresno.
Sites: 5 sites for tents.
Facilities: Picnic tables, fire rings, vault toilet. No drinking water.
Fee per night: None.
Agency: Sequoia National Forest, Hume Lake Ranger District, 209-338-2251.
Activities: Hiking, fishing.
Finding the campground: From Camp 4½ (see No. 32 above), continue east on FR 12S01 for 1 mile.

About the campground: See Kirch Flat Campground (No. 31 above) for more information about the attractions of this area. Stay limit 14 days. Open all year.

35 Lower Kings River: Bear Wallow

Location: 62 miles east of Fresno.
Sites: 1 group site for tents or RVs that accommodates up to 50 people.
Facilities: Picnic tables, fire rings, vault toilet. No drinking water.
Fee per night: No fee, but reservations required; call 209-855-8321.
Agency: Sierra National Forest, Kings River Ranger District, 209-855-8321.
Activities: Hiking, fishing.
Finding the campground: From Camp 4 (see No. 34 above), continue east on FR 12S01 for 0.3 mile.

About the campground: See Kirch Flat Campground (No. 31 above) for more information about the attractions of this area. Stay limit 14 days. Open all year.

36 Lower Kings River: Mill Flat

Location: 63 miles east of Fresno.
Sites: 5 sites for tents.
Facilities: Picnic tables, fire rings, vault toilet. No drinking water.
Fee per night: None.
Agency: Sequoia National Forest, Hume Lake Ranger District, 209-338-2251.
Activities: Hiking, fishing.
Finding the campground: From Camp 4 (see No. 34 above), continue east on FR 12S01 for half a mile.

About the campground: See Kirch Flat Campground (No. 31 above) for more information about the attractions of this area. Stay limit 14 days. Open all year.

37 Black Rock

Location: 71 miles east of Fresno.
Sites: 6 sites for tents only, 4 sites for tents and RVs.
Facilities: Picnic tables, fire rings, drinking water, vault toilet.
Fee per night: $8.
Agency: Sierra National Forest, Kings River Ranger District, 209-855-8321.
Activities: Fishing.
Finding the campground: From the intersection of California 180 and CA 41 in Fresno, drive north on CA 41 for 1.1 miles to Belmont Road. Turn right and drive about 17 miles, to where Belmont becomes Trimmer Springs Road. Continue for 34 miles, around the north shore of Pine Flat Reservoir. Go another 8 miles east beyond the lake on Trimmer Springs Road, turn left (north) onto Black Rock Road (FR 11S12), and drive 11 miles.

About the campground: This campground is located on the shore of Black Rock Reservoir at an elevation of 4,600 feet. Stay limit 14 days. Open May through October.

38 Pleasant Valley

Location: 8 miles northwest of Bishop.
Sites: 22 sites for tents and RVs.
Facilities: Picnic tables, grills, drinking water, pit toilets.
Fee per night: $6.
Agency: Inyo County Department of Parks and Recreation, 760-878-0272.
Activities: Fishing.
Finding the campground: From the intersection of California 168 and U.S. Highway 395 in Bishop, drive north on U.S. 395 for 7 miles, turn right onto Pleasant Valley Road, and drive 1.2 miles.

About the campground: Pleasant Valley Campground is situated on the bank of a small stream at 4,200 feet. Stay limit 14 days. Open all year.

39　Horton Creek

Location: 13 miles northwest of Bishop.
Sites: 52 sites for tents and RVs.
Facilities: Picnic tables, grills, pit toilets. No drinking water.
Fee per night: None.
Agency: Bureau of Land Management, Bishop Resources Area, 760-872-4881.
Activities: Hiking, fishing.
Finding the campground: From the intersection of California 168 and U.S. Highway 395 in Bishop, drive north on U.S. 395 for 8 miles, turn left onto Round Valley Road, and drive 5 miles.

About the campground: This campground is situated on the bank of a small stream at 5,000 feet. Stay limit 14 days. Open May through October.

40　Millpond Recreation Area

Location: 6 miles west of Bishop.
Sites: 100 sites for tents and RVs, many with water and electrical hookups.
Facilities: Picnic tables, grills, drinking water, flush toilets, ball field, archery range, tennis courts, horseshoe pits.
Fee per night: $12-$15. For reservations, call 760-873-5342.
Agency: Inyo County Department of Parks and Recreation, 760-878-0272.
Activities: Hiking, swimming, canoeing, kayaking.
Finding the campground: From the intersection of California 168 and U.S. Highway 395 in Bishop, drive west on CA 168 about 5 miles, turn left at the Millpond Recreation Area sign, and drive 1 mile.

About the campground: No boats with motors are permitted on this small lake, situated at 4,900 feet. Stay limit 14 days. Open March through November.

41　Shober Lane

Location: 1 mile south of Bishop.
Sites: 100 sites for tents and RVs, most with water and electrical hookups, some with TV hookups.
Facilities: Picnic tables, grills, drinking water, showers, flush toilets.
Fee per night: $17. For reservations, call 760-873-5342.
Agency: Inyo County Department of Parks and Recreation, 760-878-0272.
Finding the campground: From the intersection of California 168 and U.S. Highway 395 in Bishop, drive south on US 395 for 1 mile.

About the campground: Shober Lane is best used as a base for exploring and sightseeing in the surrounding area. Elevation 4,800 feet. Stay limit 14 days. Open March through November.

42 Bishop Creek Canyon: Big Trees

Location: 13 miles southwest of Bishop.
Sites: 9 sites for tents and RVs.
Facilities: Picnic tables, fire rings, drinking water, flush toilets.
Fee per night: $11.
Agency: Inyo National Forest, White Mountain Ranger District, 760-873-2500.
Activities: Hiking, fishing.
Finding the campground: From the intersection of California 168 and U.S. Highway 395 in Bishop, drive southwest on CA 168 for 12 miles, turn left onto Big Trees Road, and drive 1.2 miles.

About the campgrounds: Bishop Creek Canyon features forests, creeks, and lakes surrounded by canyon walls of granite. Fishing and hiking are the major sports. Trails lead from the canyon to the John Muir and Sequoia/Kings Canyon Wilderness Areas over Bishop and Piute passes. A series of scenic lakes, including South Lake, North Lake, and Lake Sabrina, are backdropped by the steep escarpment of the eastern Sierra Nevada. Pack stations and boat-launching facilities are located throughout the area, including two public boat ramps at Lake Sabrina and South Lake. Eight public campgrounds serve this scenic, high canyon country. Big Trees is on the bank of Bishop Creek at an elevation of 7,500 feet. Stay limit 14 days. Open Memorial Day through Labor Day.

43 Bishop Creek Canyon: Forks

Location: 15 miles southwest of Bishop.
Sites: 8 sites for tents and RVs.
Facilities: Picnic tables, fire rings, drinking water, flush toilets.
Fee per night: $8.
Agency: Inyo National Forest, White Mountain Ranger District, 760-873-2500.
Activities: Hiking.
Finding the campground: From the intersection of California 168 and U.S. Highway 395 in Bishop, drive southwest on CA 168 for 14 miles, turn left onto South Lake Road (FR 8S01), and drive half a mile.

About the campground: See Big Trees Campground (No. 42 above) for more information about this popular area. Elevation 7,800 feet. Stay limit 14 days. Open May through October.

44 Bishop Creek Canyon: Four Jeffrey

Location: 15 miles southwest of Bishop.
Sites: 106 sites for tents and RVs.
Facilities: Picnic tables, fire rings, drinking water, flush toilets, dump station.
Fee per night: $11.
Agency: Inyo National Forest, White Mountain Ranger District, 760-873-2500.
Activities: Hiking, fishing.

Finding the campground: From the intersection of California 168 and U.S. Highway 395 in Bishop, drive southwest on CA 168 for 14 miles, turn left onto South Lake Road (FR 8S01), and drive 1 mile.

About the campground: Four Jeffrey is on the bank of the South Fork of Bishop Creek at an elevation of 8,100 feet. It is close to several small lakes. For more information about this popular area, see Big Trees Campground (No. 42 above). Stay limit 14 days. Open mid-April to mid-October.

45 Bishop Creek Canyon: Intake 2

Location: 14 miles southwest of Bishop.
Sites: 14 sites for tents and RVs.
Facilities: Picnic tables, fire rings, drinking water, flush toilets, boat launch.
Fee per night: $8.
Agency: Inyo National Forest, White Mountain Ranger District, 760-873-2500.
Activities: Hiking, fishing, boating.
Finding the campground: From the intersection of California 168 and U.S. Highway 395 in Bishop, drive southwest on CA 168 for 14 miles.

About the campground: This campground is on the bank of the Middle Fork of Bishop Creek at 7,500 feet, adjacent to a small lake. For more information about this popular area, see Big Trees Campground (No. 42 above). Stay limit 14 days. Open April through October.

46 Bishop Creek Canyon: Bishop Park

Location: 15 miles southwest of Bishop.
Sites: 21 sites for tents and RVs, plus 1 group site.
Facilities: Picnic tables, fire rings, drinking water, flush toilets.
Fee per night: $8 individual, $25 group.
Agency: Inyo National Forest, White Mountain Ranger District, 760-873-2500.
Activities: Hiking.
Finding the campground: From the intersection of California 168 and U.S. Highway 395 in Bishop, drive southwest on CA 168 for 15 miles.

About the campground: For more information about this popular area, see Big Trees Campground (No. 42 above). Elevation 7,500 feet. Stay limit 14 days. Open April through October.

47 Bishop Creek Canyon: Sabrina

Location: 17 miles southwest of Bishop.
Sites: 18 sites for tents and RVs.
Facilities: Picnic tables, fire rings, drinking water, vault toilets.
Fee per night: $8.
Agency: Inyo National Forest, White Mountain Ranger District, 760-873-2500.

Activities: Hiking.
Finding the campground: From the intersection of California 168 and U.S. Highway 395 in Bishop, drive southwest on CA 168 for 17 miles.

About the campground: Boating, fishing, and swimming can be enjoyed at Lake Sabrina, about half a mile south of this campground. A boat launch and rentals are available there. A 6-mile, round-trip trail to scenic Blue Lake begins near the campground; the trailhead is at the end of the road. For more information about this popular area, see Big Trees Campground (No. 42 above). Elevation 9,000 feet. Stay limit 14 days. Open June through September.

48 Bishop Creek Canyon: North Lake

Location: 18 miles southwest of Bishop.
Sites: 11 sites for tents.
Facilities: Picnic tables, fire rings, drinking water, vault toilets.
Fee per night: $11.
Agency: Inyo National Forest, White Mountain Ranger District, 760-873-2500.
Activities: Hiking, fishing, horseback riding.
Finding the campground: From the intersection of California 168 and U.S. Highway 395 in Bishop, drive southwest on CA 168 for 17 miles, turn right onto Forest Road 8S02 and drive 1.3 miles.

About the campground: This campsite is situated on the bank of the North Fork of Bishop Creek at 9,500 feet, close to a small lake. Lamarck Lake Trail begins at the far side of the campground. It is a scenic, 8-mile round trip leading to Lower and Upper Lamarck Lakes. A 4.6-mile round-trip hike from the same trailhead leads to Loch Leven Lake. Stay limit 14 days. Open July through September.

49 Bishop Creek Canyon: Willow

Location: 21 miles southwest of Bishop.
Sites: 7 sites for tents and RVs.
Facilities: Picnic tables, fire rings, pit toilets. No drinking water.
Fee per night: $8.
Agency: Inyo National Forest, White Mountain Ranger District, 760-873-2500.
Activities: Hiking, fishing, boating.
Finding the campground: From the intersection of California 168 and U.S. Highway 395 in Bishop, drive southwest on CA 168 for 15 miles, turn left onto South Lake Road, and drive 6 miles.

About the campground: Excellent day hikes to lovely, small lakes are possible from Willow Campground. The trailhead for Tyee Lakes is less than half a mile north of the campground, Green and Brown Lakes Trail begins about a mile south, and more than a dozen lakes line both sides of Bishop Pass Trail, which begins 2 miles south. Fishing and boating can be enjoyed at South Lake, 1 mile south of the campground, where there is a public boat ramp. Elevation 8,700 feet. Stay limit 14 days. Open July through September.

50 Ancient Bristlecone Scenic Byway: Grandview

Location: 16 miles northeast of Big Pine.
Sites: 26 sites for tents and RVs.
Facilities: Picnic tables, grills, pit toilets. No drinking water.
Fee per night: None.
Agency: Inyo National Forest, White Mountain Ranger District, 760-873-2500.
Activities: Hiking.
Finding the campground: From the intersection of U.S. Highway 395 and California 168 in Big Pine, drive 10.5 miles northeast on CA 168, turn left onto FR 4S01, and drive 5 miles.

About the campground: The Ancient Bristlecone Pine Forest contains the oldest known trees on earth. Some bristlecones are more than 4,600 years old—1,500 years older than the oldest known sequoia. The Ancient Bristlecone Scenic Byway traverses the forest from south to north, terminating at its northern border. It offers views of these strange trees, many of which look more dead than alive. They are actually hardy survivors of harsh, high-altitude conditions. Schulman Grove, at the beginning of the forest, has an interpretive center and several self-guided nature trails. The byway is closed in winter. Elevation 3,900 feet. Stay limit 14 days. Open April through November.

51 Ancient Bristlecone Scenic Byway: Pinon, Fossil, Poleta & Juniper

Location: 11 miles northeast of Big Pine.
Sites: Group sites for tents and RVs, located within a mile of each other.
Facilities: Picnic tables, grills, pit toilets. No drinking water.
Fee per night: None.
Agency: Inyo National Forest, White Mountain Ranger District, 760-873-2500.
Activities: Hiking.
Finding the campgrounds: From the intersection of U.S. Highway 395 and California 168 in Big Pine, take CA 168 northeast for 11 miles to the dirt access road.

About the campgrounds: These group campgrounds are located within a mile of each other on CA 168. For more information about the attractions of the area, see Grandview Campground (above). Elevation 3,900 feet. Stay limit 14 days. Open April through November.

KINGS CANYON NATIONAL PARK & VICINITY

This area includes Kings Canyon National Park and its immediate vicinity. The park offers wonderful vistas, giant sequoia groves, and scenic trails. However, it does not have a monopoly on such scenic attractions. The upper portion of Sequoia National Forest fits around the northern part of the park like a giant jigsaw-puzzle piece, adding to the area's appeal and augmenting its campgrounds. On the western slopes of the Sierra Nevada, high-country attractions such as the southernmost glacier in North America and the alpine lakes of Big Pine Creek Valley draw hikers, backpackers, and equestrians.

Only two small fractions of Kings Canyon National Park are accessible by car and RV: Grant Grove and Cedar Grove. The remainder of its 400,000 acres are accessible only to those willing to shoulder a pack and set off on foot into the wilderness. Grant and Cedar Groves are separated by part of the Sequoia National Forest but connected by California 180. Grant Grove features a visitor center and a series of trails to explore its giant trees, while Cedar Grove features trails and views into deeply incised Kings Canyon. Both have several campgrounds, but Cedar Grove is open only in the summer.

The northern portion of the Sequoia National Forest contains more than a dozen groves of giant sequoia, many of them accessible only by unimproved roads or on foot. The Boole Tree, in Converse Mountain Grove, is the largest sequoia in a national forest, and Hume Lake is a popular water-sports location. Thirteen national forest campgrounds supplement those at Grant and Cedar Groves.

KINGS CANYON NATIONAL PARK AREA MAP

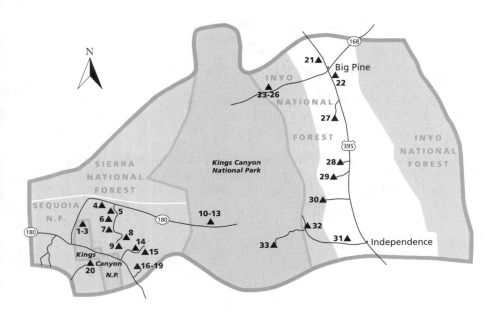

#	Name	Group sites	RV sites	Max. RV length	Hookups	Toilets	Showers	Drinking water	Dump station	Pets	Wheelchair	Recreation	Fee ($)	Season	Can reserve
1	Sunset	•	•	30		F		•		•		H	12	May–Oct	•
2	Azalea		•			F	•	•	•	•	•	H	12		
3	Crystal Spring		•			F		•		•		H	12	May–Oct	
4	Princess	•	•			V	•	•		•		H	12	Mem.Day–Labor Day	•
5	Hume Lake		•			F		•		•		HSF	14	May–Sep	•
6	Aspen Hollow	•	•			V		•		•		SF	115	Mem.Day–Labor Day	•
7	Logger Flat	•	•			V		•		•		HF	75	Mem.Day–Labor Day	•
8	Landslide		•			V		•		•		HF		May–Oct	
9	Tenmile		•			V				•		HF		May–Oct	
10	Sheep Creek		•			F	•	•		•		HR	12	June–Oct	
11	Sentinel		•			F	•	•	•	•	•	HR	12	Apr–Oct	
12	Canyon View	•	•			F	•	•		•		HR	12	As Req'd	•
13	Moraine		•			F		•		•		HR	12	As Req'd	
14	Buck Rock		•			V				•		H		June–Sep	
15	Big Meadows		•			V				•		HF		June–Oct	
16	Stony Creek		•			F		•		•		HF	12	May–Oct	•
17	Cove	•	•			V		•		•		HF	75	May–Oct	•
18	Fir	•	•			V		•		•		HF	112.50	Mem.Day–Labor Day	•
19	Upper Stony Creek		•			V		•		•		HF	12	May–Oct	•
20	Eshom Creek	•	•			V		•		•		F	10–12	May–Nov	
21	Baker Creek County Park		•			P				•		F	5	Apr–Nov	
22	Big Pine Triangle County Park		•			F		•		•			5	Apr–Nov	
23	Sage Flat		•			V		•		•		H	10	May–Oct	•
24	Upper Sage Flat		•			V		•		•		H	10	May–Oct	•
25	Palisade/Clyde	•	•			V		•		•		H	30	May–Oct	•
26	Big Pine Creek		•			V		•		•	•	H	10	May–Oct	•
27	Tinnemaha		•			P		•		•		F	5		
28	Taboose Creek		•			P				•		F	5		
29	Goodale Creek		•			P				•		F			
30	Oak Creek		•			F		•		•		H	11	June–Oct	•
31	Independence Creek		•			P		•		•		F	5		
32	Grays Meadow		•			F		•		•		F	11	Apr–Oct	•
33	Onion Valley					F		•		•		H	11	June–Sept	•

Hookups: W = Water E = Electric S = Sewer
Toilets: F = Flush V = Vault P = Pit C = Chemical
Recreation: H = Hiking S = Swimming F = Fishing B = Boating L = Boat Launch O = Off-highway Driving R = Horseback Riding
Maximum Trailer/RV Length given in feet. **Stay Limit** given in days. **Fee** given in dollars.
If no entry under **Season**, campground is open all year. If no entry under **Fee,** camping is free.

1 Kings Canyon National Park: Sunset

Location: At Grant Grove.
Sites: 184 sites for tents and RVs up to 30 feet long, plus 2 group sites for tents, each accommodating up to 27 people.
Facilities: Picnic tables, fire rings, drinking water, flush toilets.
Fee per night: $12 for individual sites, $27 for group sites. Latter must be reserved by writing Sunset Group Sites, PO Box 926, Kings Canyon National Park, CA 93633.
Agency: Kings Canyon National Park, 209-565-3341.
Activities: Hiking.
Finding the campground: From the Grant Grove Visitor Center, drive south on California 180 for 0.2 mile to the entrance on the right.

About the campground: Grant Grove lies at the western edge of Kings Canyon National Park and is the site of the General Grant Tree, which is 267 feet high and 107 feet in circumference at its base. Numerous trails thread through the grove, affording a full introduction to the giant sequoia and its environment. The trails are well marked and most are easy to moderate in difficulty. Trail guides are available at the visitor center. Trails not to be missed are the 0.6-mile General Grant Tree, 1-mile Big Stump, and 5-mile Sunset trails (all distances are round trip). Sunset is one of three campgrounds in Grant Grove; all are located within a half mile of the Grant Grove Visitor Center, which includes a grocery store, gas station, and restaurant. Showers are available at Grant Grove Lodge. Elevation 6,600 feet. Stay limit 15 days. Open May through October.

2 Kings Canyon National Park: Azalea

Location: At Grant Grove.
Sites: 113 sites for tents and RVs.
Facilities: Picnic tables, fire rings, drinking water, flush toilets, dump station.
Fee per night: $12.
Agency: Kings Canyon National Park, 209-565-3341.
Activities: Hiking.
Finding the campground: From the Grant Grove Visitor Center, drive half a mile north on California 180. The campground entrance is on the left.

About the campground: See Sunset Campground (No. 1 above) for more information about this fascinating destination. Elevation 6,600 feet. Stay limit 15 days. Open all year.

3 Kings Canyon National Park: Crystal Spring

Location: At Grant Grove.
Sites: 63 sites for tents and RVs.
Facilities: Picnic tables, fire rings, drinking water, flush toilets.
Fee per night: $12.

Agency: Kings Canyon National Park, 209-565-3341.
Activities: Hiking.
Finding the campground: From the Grant Grove Visitor Center, drive half a mile north on California 180. The campground entrance is on the right.

About the campground: See Sunset Campground (No. 1 above) for more information about this fascinating destination. Elevation 6,600 feet. Stay limit 15 days. Open May through October.

4 Princess

Location: 6 miles north of Grant Grove.
Sites: 88 sites for tents and RVs, plus 2 group sites.
Facilities: Picnic tables, fire rings, drinking water, vault toilets, dump station.
Fee per night: $12 for family units, $24 for multifamily units. For reservations, call 800-280-CAMP. Reservation fee, $8.65.
Agency: Sequoia National Forest, Hume Lake Ranger District, 209-338-2251.
Activities: Hiking.
Finding the campground: From the Grant Grove Visitor Center, drive north 6 miles on California 180.

About the campground: A trail near the campground leads to the Boole Tree, the largest giant sequoia in a national forest. To find the trailhead from the campground, go south on CA 180 for about 2 miles, make a sharp right onto FR 13S55 (where there is a sign to Boole Tree and Converse Basin), and drive about 2 miles. The trail is 2 miles round-trip. Another interesting short hike is to the Chicago Stump, about 5 miles southwest of the campground via CA 180, FR 13S03, and FR 13S65. A massive stump is all that remains of one of the world's largest trees, cut down in 1892 to provide a cross section for display at the Chicago World's Fair. Elevation 5,900 feet. Stay limit 14 days. Open Memorial Day to Labor Day weekend.

5 Hume Lake

Location: 9 miles northeast of Grant Grove.
Sites: 75 sites for tents and RVs.
Facilities: Picnic tables, fire rings, drinking water, flush toilets.
Fee per night: $14. For reservations, call 800-280-CAMP. Reservation fee, $8.65.
Agency: Sequoia National Forest, Hume Lake Ranger District, 209-338-2251.
Activities: Hiking, swimming, fishing.
Finding the campground: From the Grant Grove Visitor Center, drive north 6 miles on California 180, turn right onto Hume Lake Road (FR 13S09), and drive 3 miles.

About the campground: The closest lakeshore campground to Sequoia and Kings Canyon National Parks, Hume Lake offers good trout fishing in the spring. Elevation 5,200 feet. Stay limit 14 days. Open May through September.

6 Aspen Hollow

Location: 10 miles northeast of Grant Grove.
Sites: 1 group site for tents or RVs that accommodates up to 100 people.
Facilities: Picnic tables, fire circle, drinking water, vault toilets.
Fee per night: $115. Reservations required; call 800-280-CAMP. Reservation fee, $15.
Agency: Sequoia National Forest, Hume Lake Ranger District, 209-338-2251.
Activities: Swimming, fishing.
Finding the campground: From the Grant Grove Visitor Center, drive north 6 miles on California 180, turn right onto Hume Lake Road (FR 13S09), and drive about 4 miles.

About the campground: Aspen Hollow is about a mile from Hume Lake, where swimming and fishing are possible. Elevation 5,300 feet. Stay limit 14 days. Open Memorial Day through Labor Day weekend.

7 Logger Flat

Location: 11 miles northeast of Grant Grove.
Sites: 1 group site for tents or RVs that accommodates up to 50 people.
Facilities: Picnic tables, one grill, campfire circle, drinking water, vault toilets.
Fee per night: $75. Reservations required; call 800-280-CAMP. Reservation fee, $15.
Agency: Sequoia National Forest, Hume Lake Ranger District, 209-338-2251.
Activities: Hiking, fishing.
Finding the campground: From the Grant Grove Visitor Center, drive north 6 miles on California 180, turn right onto Hume Lake Road (FR 13S09), and drive about 4.5 miles.

About the campground: Logger Flat is located on the bank of Landslide Creek, at an elevation of 5,300 feet. Stay limit 14 days. Open Memorial Day through Labor Day weekend.

8 Landslide

Location: 12 miles northeast of Grant Grove.
Sites: 9 sites for tents and RVs.
Facilities: Picnic tables, fire rings, drinking water, vault toilets.
Fee per night: None.
Agency: Sequoia National Forest, Hume Lake Ranger District, 209-338-2251.
Activities: Hiking, fishing.
Finding the campground: From the Grant Grove Visitor Center, drive north 6 miles on California 180, turn right onto Hume Lake Road (FR 13S09), and drive about 6 miles.

About the campground: Landslide is located on the bank of Landslide Creek, at an elevation of 5,800 feet. Landslide Grove, an off-the-beaten-track sequoia stand, lies 1.5 miles southeast of the campground. Stay limit 14 days. Open May through October.

9 Tenmile

Location: 15 miles northeast of Grant Grove.
Sites: 13 sites for tents and RVs.
Facilities: Picnic tables, fire rings, vault toilets. No drinking water.
Fee per night: None.
Agency: Sequoia National Forest, Hume Lake Ranger District, 209-338-2251.
Activities: Hiking, fishing.
Finding the campground: From the Grant Grove Visitor Center, drive north 6 miles on California 180, turn right onto Hume Lake Road (FR 13S09), and drive about 9 miles.

About the campground: On the bank of Tenmile Creek, the campground is at an elevation of 5,800 feet. Bearskin Grove, one of the more remote sequoia stands, is a mile southwest of the campground, and Tenmile Grove lies about a mile east. Stay limit 14 days. Open May through October.

10 Kings Canyon National Park: Sheep Creek

Location: 30 miles northeast of Grant Grove, at Cedar Grove.
Sites: 111 sites for tents and RVs.
Facilities: Picnic tables, fire rings, drinking water, flush toilets, dump station.
Fee per night: $12.
Agency: Kings Canyon National Park, 209-565-3341.
Activities: Hiking, horseback riding.
Finding the campground: From Grant Grove Visitor Center, drive north and then east on California 180 for 30 miles.

About the campground: Cedar Grove is the easternmost section of Kings Canyon National Park that is accessible by car. Showers, a laundromat, a grocery store, and a gas station are available in Cedar Grove Village. Spectacular views are the hallmark of this part of the park, and many trails, long and short, take advantage of them. There is even a motor nature trail for those who prefer not to get out of their cars.

The Hotel Creek Trail leads to an overlook into Kings Canyon, the deepest canyon in the United States and the course of the South Fork of the Kings River. The view is impressive, though not as awesome as the Grand Canyon of the Colorado. This 5-mile round trip can be combined with a return via the Lewis Creek Trail, making an 8-mile loop. Other noteworthy trails include Roaring River Falls-River Trail Loop (5 miles), and Mist Falls (9 miles round trip). Elevation 4,600 feet. Stay limit 15 days. The entire Cedar Grove area, including the highway, closes for the winter.

11　Kings Canyon National Park: Sentinel

Location: 30 miles northeast of Grant Grove, at Cedar Grove.
Sites: 83 sites for tents and RVs.
Facilities: Picnic tables, fire rings, drinking water, flush toilets, dump station.
Fee per night: $12.
Agency: Kings Canyon National Park, 209-565-3341.
Activities: Hiking, horseback riding.
Finding the campground: From Sheep Creek Campground (see above), continue east for half a mile.

About the campground: See Sheep Creek Campground (above) for more information about the attractions of this area. Elevation 4,600 feet. Stay limit 15 days. Open April through October.

12　Kings Canyon National Park: Canyon View

Location: 31 miles northeast of Grant Grove, at Cedar Grove.
Sites: 37 sites for tents and RVs, plus 4 group sites for tents only, which accommodate a total of 40 people.
Facilities: Picnic tables, fire rings, drinking water, flush toilets, dump station.
Fee per night: $12 for individual sites; group sites $27 for first 20 people, $1 per person thereafter. Group sites must be reserved by writing Canyon View Group Sites, PO Box 926, Kings Canyon National Park, CA 93633.
Agency: Kings Canyon National Park, 209-565-3341.
Activities: Hiking, horseback riding.
Finding the campground: From Sheep Creek Campground (see above), continue east 0.7 mile.

About the campground: See Sheep Creek Campground (No. 10 above) for more information about the attractions of this area. Elevation 4,600 feet. Stay limit 15 days. Open when demand requires it.

13　Kings Canyon National Park: Moraine

Location: 31 miles northeast of Grant Grove, at Cedar Grove.
Sites: 120 sites for tents and RVs.
Facilities: Picnic tables, fire rings, drinking water, flush toilets.
Fee per night: $12.
Agency: Kings Canyon National Park, 209-565-3341.
Activities: Hiking, horseback riding.
Finding the campground: From Sheep Creek Campground (see No. 10, above), continue east 1 mile.

About the campground: See Sheep Creek Campground (No. 10 above) for more information about the attractions of this area. Elevation 4,600 feet. Stay limit 15 days. Open as required.

14 Buck Rock

Location: 10 miles southeast of Grant Grove.
Sites: 5 sites for tents and RVs.
Facilites: Picnic tables, fire rings, vault toilets. No drinking water.
Fee per night: None.
Agency: Sequoia National Forest, Hume Lake Ranger District, 209-338-2251.
Activities: Hiking.
Finding the campground: From the Grant Grove Visitor Center, drive southeast on Generals Highway for 7 miles, turn left onto Big Meadows Road, and drive 3 miles.

About the campground: Elevation 7,500 feet. Stay limit 15 days. Open June through September.

15 Big Meadows

Location: 13 miles southeast of Grant Grove.
Sites: 25 sites for tents and RVs.
Facilities: Picnic tables, fire rings, vault toilets. No drinking water.
Fee per night: None.
Agency: Sequoia National Forest, Hume Lake Ranger District, 209-338-2251.
Activities: Hiking, fishing.
Finding the campground: From Grant Grove Visitor Center, drive southeast on Generals Highway for 7 miles, turn left onto Big Meadows Road, and drive 6 miles.

About the campground: Big Meadows is located on the bank of a small creek at an elevation of 7,600 feet. Stay limit 15 days. Open June through October.

16 Stony Creek

Location: 14 miles southeast of Grant Grove.
Sites: 49 sites for tents and RVs.
Facilities: Picnic tables, fire rings, drinking water, flush toilets.
Fee per night: $12. For reservations, call 800-280-CAMP. Reservation fee, $8.65.
Agency: Sequoia National Forest, Hume Lake Ranger District, 209-338-2251.
Activities: Hiking, fishing.
Finding the campground: From the Grant Grove Visitor Center, drive southeast 14 miles on Generals Highway.

About the campground: Elevation 6,400 feet. Stay limit 14 days. Open May through October.

17 Cove

Location: 14 miles southeast of Grant Grove.
Sites: 1 group site for tents and RVs that accommodates up to 50 people.

Facilities: Picnic tables, fireplace, campfire ring, drinking water, vault toilets.
Fee per night: $75. For reservations, call 800-280-CAMP. Reservation fee, $15.
Agency: Sequoia National Forest, Hume Lake Ranger District, 209-338-2251.
Activities: Hiking, fishing.
Finding the campground: From the Grant Grove Visitor Center, drive southeast 14 miles on Generals Highway.

About the campground: Elevation 6,400 feet. Stay limit 14 days. Open May through October.

18 Fir

Location: 14 miles southeast of Grant Grove.
Sites: 1 group site for tents and RVs that accommodates up to 100 people.
Facilities: Picnic tables, fireplace, campfire ring, drinking water, vault toilets.
Fee per night: $112.50. For reservations, call 800-280-CAMP. Reservation fee, $15.
Agency: Sequoia National Forest, Hume Lake Ranger District, 209-338-2251.
Activities: Hiking, fishing.
Finding the campground: From the Grant Grove Visitor Center, drive southeast 14 miles on Generals Highway.

About the campground: Elevation 6,500 feet. Stay limit 14 days. Open Memorial Day through Labor Day weekend.

19 Upper Stony Creek

Location: 14 miles southeast of Grant Grove.
Sites: 18 sites for tents and RVs.
Facilities: Picnic tables, fire rings, drinking water, vault toilets.
Fee per night: $12. For reservations, call 800-280-CAMP. Reservation fee, $8.65.
Agency: Sequoia National Forest, Hume Lake Ranger District, 209-338-2251.
Activities: Hiking, fishing.
Finding the campground: From the Grant Grove Visitor Center, drive southeast 14 miles on Generals Highway.

About the campground: Elevation 6,400 feet. Stay limit 14 days. Open May through October.

20 Eshom Creek

Location: 50 miles northeast of Visalia.
Sites: 17 sites for tents and RVs, plus 7 group sites.
Facilities: Picnic tables, fire rings, drinking water, vault toilets.
Fee per night: $10 for individual sites, $12 for multifamily sites.
Agency: Sequoia National Forest, Hume Lake Ranger District, 209-338-2251.
Activities: Fishing.

Finding the campground: From the intersection of California 63 and CA 198 in Visalia, drive east 10.5 miles, turn left (north) onto CA 245 and drive 31 miles to Badger, turn right onto County Road 465 and drive northeast for 8 miles.

About the campground: Elevation 4,800 feet. Stay limit 14 days. Open May through November.

21 Baker Creek County Park

Location: Big Pine.
Sites: 70 sites for tents and RVs.
Facilities: Picnic tables, grills, pit toilets. No drinking water.
Fee per night: $5.
Agency: Inyo County Department of Parks and Recreation, 760-878-0272.
Activities: Fishing.
Finding the campground: At the intersection of U.S. Highway 395 and California 168 in Big Pine, turn west onto Baker Creek Road and drive 1 mile.

About the campground: This park is located on the bank of Baker Creek at an elevation of 4,000 feet. Stay limit 14 days. Open April through November.

22 Big Pine Triangle County Park

Location: Big Pine.
Sites: 40 sites for tents and RVs.
Facilities: Picnic tables, grills, drinking water, flush toilets.
Fee per night: $5.
Agency: Inyo County Department of Parks and Recreation, 760-878-0272.
Activities: Scenic driving.
Finding the campground: From Big Pine, drive north on U.S. Highway 395 for half a mile.

About the campground: Big Pine Triangle is located at the beginning of the Ancient Bristlecone Pine Scenic Byway, which provides views of the oldest trees on earth. (See Sierra & Inyo National Forests, page 103, for more campground information.) Some bristlecones are more than 4,600 years old—1,500 years older than the oldest known sequoia. The byway is closed in winter. Elevation 3,900 feet. Stay limit 14 days. Open April through November.

23 Big Pine Canyon: Sage Flat

Location: 9 miles west of Big Pine.
Sites: 28 sites for tents and RVs.
Facilities: Picnic tables, fire rings, drinking water, vault toilets.
Fee per night: $10. For reservations, call 800-280-CAMP. Reservation fee, $8.65.
Agency: Inyo National Forest, White Mountain Ranger District, 760-873-2500.
Activities: Hiking.

Finding the campground: From Big Pine, drive west about 9 miles on Glacier Lodge Road.

About the campground: Big Pine is a narrow, glacier-carved canyon and the site of Palisades Glacier, an Ice Age remnant and the southernmost glacier in the United States. Palisades can be reached by a strenuous 12-mile trail. Other trails lead from the canyon to lakes and streams in the John Muir Wilderness. Four public campgrounds are located near the western end of the canyon, all within half a mile of each other. Elevations vary from 7,400 to 7,700 feet. Stay limit 14 days. Open approximately May through October, depending upon snow conditions.

24 Big Pine Canyon: Upper Sage Flat

Location: 9.5 miles west of Big Pine.
Sites: 21 sites for tents and RVs.
Facilities: Picnic tables, fire rings, drinking water, vault toilets.
Fee per night: $10. For reservations, call 800-280-CAMP. Reservation fee, $8.65.
Agency: Inyo National Forest, White Mountain Ranger District, 760-873-2500.
Activities: Hiking.
Finding the campground: From Big Pine, drive west about 9.5 miles on Glacier Lodge Road.

About the campground: See Sage Flat Campground (above) for more information about this glacier-carved area. Stay limit 14 days. Open approximately May through October, depending upon snow conditions.

25 Big Pine Canyon: Palisade/Clyde

Location: 10 miles west of Big Pine.
Sites: 2 group sites for tents and RVs upper site holds 20 people, plus 2 RVs; and lower site holds 25 people, tents only.
Facilities: Picnic tables, fire rings, drinking water, vault toilets.
Fee per night: $30. Reservations required; call 800-280-CAMP. Reservation fee, $15.
Agency: Inyo National Forest, White Mountain Ranger District, 760-873-2500.
Activities: Hiking.
Finding the campground: From Big Pine, drive west about 10 miles on Glacier Lodge Road.

About the campground: See Sage Flat Campground (No. 23 above) for more information about this glacier-carved area. Stay limit 14 days. Open approximately May through October, depending upon snow conditions.

26 Big Pine Canyon: Big Pine Creek

Location: 10.5 miles west of Big Pine.
Sites: 30 sites for tents and RVs.
Facilities: Picnic tables, fire rings, drinking water, vault toilets.

Fee per night: $10. For reservations, call 800-280-CAMP. Reservation fee, $8.65.
Agency: Inyo National Forest, White Mountain Ranger District, 760-873-2500.
Activities: Hiking.
Finding the campground: From Big Pine, drive west about 10.5 miles on Glacier Lodge Road.

About the campground: An excellent 3-mile round-trip day hike begins nearby and leads to First and Second Falls. See Sage Flat Campground (No. 23 above) for more information about this glacier-carved area. Stay limit 14 days. Open approximately May through October, depending upon snow conditions.

27 Tinnemaha

Location: 10 miles south of Big Pine.
Sites: 55 sites for tents and RVs.
Facilities: Picnic tables, grills, drinking water (well), pit toilets.
Fee per night: $5.
Agency: Inyo County Department of Parks and Recreation, 760-878-0272.
Activities: Fishing.
Finding the campground: From the intersection of California 168 and U.S. Highway 395 in Big Pine, drive south 5.3 miles to Fish Springs Road, turn right, and drive 2.5 miles to Tinnemaha Road. Turn right again and drive 2 more miles.

About the campground: This campground is located on the bank of Tinnemaha Creek at an elevation of 4,400 feet. Stay limit 14 days. Open all year.

28 Taboose Creek

Location: 13 miles south of Big Pine.
Sites: 55 sites for tents and RVs.
Facilities: Picnic tables, pit toilets. No drinking water.
Fee per night: $5.
Agency: Inyo County Department of Parks and Recreation, 760-878-0272.
Activities: Fishing.
Finding the campground: From the intersection of California 168 and U.S. Highway 395 in Big Pine, drive south 10 miles to Taboose Creek Road, turn right, and drive 2.5 miles.

About the campground: The campground sits on the bank of Taboose Creek at an elevation of 3,900 feet. Stay limit 14 days. Open all year.

29 Goodale Creek

Location: 14 miles south of Big Pine.
Sites: 62 sites for tents and RVs.
Facilities: Picnic tables, fire rings, pit toilets. No drinking water.
Fee per night: None.

Agency: Bureau of Land Management, Bishop Resource Area, 760-872-4881.
Activities: Fishing.
Finding the campground: From the intersection of California 168 and U.S. Highway 395 in Big Pine, drive south 11.5 miles to Aberdeen Cut-Off Road, turn right, and drive 2 miles.

About the campground: Sites are located on the bank of Goodale Creek at an elevation of 4,100 feet. Stay limit 14 days. Open all year.

30 Oak Creek

Location: 5 miles northwest of Independence.
Sites: 21 sites for tents and RVs.
Facilities: Picnic tables, fire rings, drinking water, flush toilets.
Fee per night: $11. For reservations, call 800-280-CAMP. Reservation fee, $8.65.
Agency: Inyo National Forest, Mount Whitney Ranger District, 760-876-6200.
Activities: Hiking.
Finding the campground: From Independence, drive 2.2 miles north on U.S. Highway 395 to North Creek Road, turn left, and drive 3 miles.

About the campground: Elevation 5,000 feet. Stay limit 14 days. Open June to October 14, depending upon snow conditions.

31 Independence Creek

Location: 0.5 mile west of Independence.
Sites: 25 sites for tents and RVs.
Facilities: Picnic tables, drinking water, pit toilets.
Fee per night: $5.
Agency: Inyo County Department of Parks and Recreation, 760-878-0272.
Activities: Fishing.
Finding the campground: From Independence, drive west on Market Street for half a mile.

About the campground: Manzanar National Monument, a former World War II internment camp for Japanese-Americans, is located 5 miles south of the campground on U.S. 395. Elevation 3,900 feet. Stay limit 14 days. Open all year.

32 Grays Meadow

Location: 5.5 miles west of Independence.
Sites: 52 sites for tents and RVs, 17 in Lower Grays Meadow, 35 in Upper Grays Meadow.
Facilities: Picnic tables, fire rings, drinking water, flush toilets.
Fee per night: $11. For reservations, call 800-280-CAMP. Reservation fee, $8.65.
Agency: Inyo National Forest, Mount Whitney Ranger District, 760-876-6200.
Activities: Fishing.

Finding the campground: From Independence, drive west on Onion Valley Road for 5.5 miles.

About the campground: Elevation 6,000 feet. Stay limit 14 days. Open April 15 to October 15.

33 Onion Valley

Location: 12 miles west of Independence.
Sites: 29 sites for tents.
Facilities: Picnic tables, fire rings, drinking water, flush toilets.
Fee per night: $11. For reservations, call 800-280-CAMP. Reservation fee, $8.65.
Agency: Inyo National Forest, Mount Whitney Ranger District, 760-876-6200.
Activities: Hiking.
Finding the campground: From Independence, drive west on Onion Valley Road for about 12 miles.

About the campground: Onion Valley is the jump-off for many day hikes and backpack trips. Trails lead to several small lakes and also intersect the John Muir and Pacific Crest Trails via Kearsarge Pass. Elevation 9,200 feet. Stay limit 14 days. Open June 1 to September 30.

SEQUOIA NATIONAL PARK & VICINITY

According to National Geographic, a backpacker in Sequoia National Park can hike to a spot that is farther from roads than any other place in the contiguous 48 states. And, like Kings Canyon National Park to the north, only a small part of

SEQUOIA NATIONAL PARK AREA MAP

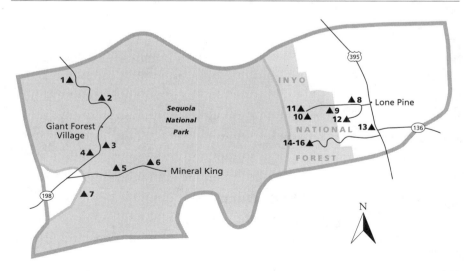

Sequoia is accessible by car and RV. But neither fact prevents easy access to magnificent examples of the trees for which the park is named.

Sequoia National Park and portions of the Sequoia and Inyo National Forests occupy almost the entire area described in this section. Although the national park is justifiably world famous for its stunning stands of giant sequoia, more than 30 groves of these unique trees can be found as well in Sequoia National Forest and Mountain Home State Demonstration Forest.

Mount Whitney, the highest peak in the contiguous United States, looms over the border between the national park and Inyo National Forest. Its campgrounds and trails provide access to the summit, the John Muir Wilderness, and some of the most popular equestrian and backpacking destinations in the United States. The North and South Forks of the Kern River have been designated Wild and Scenic Rivers, and knowledgeable kayakers and rafters challenge their whitewater and steep, narrow gorges. There is something for every outdoor enthusiast in this spectacularly scenic, high-country area.

	Group sites	RV sites	Max. RV length	Hookups	Toilets	Showers	Drinking water	Dump station	Pets	Wheelchair	Recreation	Fee ($)	Season	Can reserve
1 Dorst	•	•			F		•	•	•		H	14	June–Sep	•
2 Lodgepole		•			F	•	•	•	•	•	HR	12		•
3 Buckeye Flat					F		•		•		H	10	Apr–Sep	
4 Potwisha		•			F	•	•	•	•	•	H	10		
5 Atwel Mill		•			P		•		•		H	6	May–Sep	
6 Cold Springs		•			V	•	•		•		H	6	May–Sep	
7 South Fork					V		•		•		H	6	May–Sep	
8 Portagee Joe		•			P		•		•			6		
9 Lone Pine	•	•			V	•	•		•		HF	10		•
10 Whitney Portal	•	•			F		•		•		H	12	May–Oct	•
11 Whitney Trailhead					P		•		•		H	6	May–Oct	
12 Tuttle Creek		•			P				•		F		May–Nov	
13 Diaz Lake		•			F	•	•		•	•	SFB	8		
14 Golden Trout					P		•		•		HR	6	May–Oct	
15 Cottonwood Lakes					P		•		•		HR	6	May–Oct	
16 Equestrian					P		•		•		HR	12	May–Oct	

Hookups: W = Water E = Electric S = Sewer
Toilets: F = Flush V = Vault P = Pit C = Chemical
Recreation: H = Hiking S = Swimming F = Fishing B = Boating L = Boat Launch O = Off-highway Driving R = Horseback Riding
Maximum Trailer/RV Length given in feet. **Stay Limit** given in days. **Fee** given in dollars.
If no entry under **Season,** campground is open all year. If no entry under **Fee,** camping is free.

1 Sequoia National Park: Dorst

Location: 14 miles north of Giant Forest Village.
Sites: 218 sites for tents and RVs, plus 5 group sites that accommodate 12 to 50 people each.

Facilities: Picnic tables, fire rings, drinking water, flush toilets, dump station.
Fee per night: $14 individual, $38-$57 group. Group sites must be reserved; call Destinet, 800-365-CAMP. Reservation fee, $15.
Agency: Sequoia National Park, 209-565-3341.
Activities: Hiking.
Finding the campground: From Giant Forest Village, drive northeast and then west on Generals Highway for a total of 14 miles.

About the campground: A trail from the campground leads to Muir Grove, a sequoia stand accessible only on foot. Elevation 6,720 feet. Stay limit 14 days. Open June through September.

2 Sequoia National Park: Lodgepole

Location: 5 miles northeast of Giant Forest Village.
Sites: 250 sites for tents and RVs.
Facilities: Picnic tables, fire rings, drinking water, flush toilets, showers, dump station, riding stable.
Fee per night: $12. For reservations, call 800-365-CAMP.
Agency: Sequoia National Park, 209-565-3341.
Activities: Hiking, horseback riding.
Finding the campground: From Giant Forest Village, drive northeast on Generals Highway for 5 miles.

About the campground: Lodgepole is the closest campground to the Giant Forest area of Sequoia National Park, where four of the five largest sequoias in the park are located. The biggest of these, the General Sherman Tree, is the largest tree on earth at more than 274 feet high and 102 feet in circumference. There are more than 40 miles of walks and trails through the 5 square miles of the Giant Forest area. All are well marked and range in difficulty from easy to moderate. A grocery store and restaurant are located in Giant Forest Village. Elevation 6,700 feet. Stay limit 14 days. Open all year.

3 Sequoia National Park: Buckeye Flat

Location: 5 miles south of Giant Forest Village.
Sites: 28 sites for tents.
Facilities: Picnic tables, fire rings, drinking water, flush toilets.
Fee per night: $10.
Agency: Sequoia National Park, 209-565-3341.
Activities: Hiking.
Finding the campground: From Giant Forest Village, drive south 5 miles on Generals Highway.

About the campground: Elevation 2,800 feet. Stay limit 14 days. Open April through September, depending upon snow conditions.

4 Sequoia National Park: Potwisha

Location: 8 miles south of Giant Forest Village.
Sites: 44 sites for tents and RVs.
Facilities: Picnic tables, fire grills, drinking water, flush toilets, dump station.
Fee per night: $10.
Agency: Sequoia National Park, 209-565-3341.
Activities: Hiking.
Finding the campground: From Giant Forest Village, drive south 8 miles on Generals Highway.

About the campground: Elevation 2,080 feet. Stay limit 14 days. Open all year.

5 Sequoia National Park: Atwell Mill

Location: 32 miles south of Giant Forest Village.
Sites: 21 sites for tents and small RVs; no trailers.
Facilities: Picnic tables, fire rings, drinking water, pit toilets.
Fee per night: $6.
Agency: Sequoia National Park, 209-565-3341.
Activities: Hiking.
Finding the campground: From Giant Forest Village, drive south 13 miles on Generals Highway, turn left onto Mineral King Road, and drive 19 miles.

About the campground: The road to Atwell Mill is narrow, unpaved, rough in places, and open only during the summer. The Atwell-Hockett Trail leads south from the campground, and another leads north to Redwood Meadow and Bearpaw Meadow. Elevation 6,540 feet. Stay limit 14 days. Open approximately May 15 to September 15.

6 Sequoia National Park: Cold Springs

Location: 38 miles southeast of Giant Forest Village.
Sites: 37 sites for tents and small RVs; no trailers.
Facilities: Picnic tables, fire rings, drinking water, vault toilets, dump station.
Fee per night: $6.
Agency: Sequoia National Park, 209-565-3341.
Activities: Hiking.
Finding the campground: From Giant Forest Village, drive south 13 miles on Generals Highway, turn left (east) onto Mineral King Road, and drive 25 miles.

About the campground: The road to Cold Springs is narrow, unpaved, rough in places, and open only during the summer. A network of trails leading from the campground vicinity makes Cold Springs a major jumping-off point for backpack trips in almost any direction. The most frequent destinations are the many small lakes in the area. One popular loop trail visits the Franklin Lakes, ascends

Franklin Pass (11,680 feet), and returns via Sawtooth Pass (11,700 feet) and Monarch Lakes. Elevation 7,500 feet. Stay limit 14 days. Open approximately May 15 to September 15.

7 Sequoia National Park: South Fork

Location: 28 miles south of Giant Forest Village.
Sites: 13 sites for tents and pickup campers. Not recommended for trailers or RVs.
Facilities: Picnic tables, fire rings, drinking water, vault toilets.
Fee per night: $6.
Agency: Sequoia National Park, 209-565-3341.
Activities: Hiking.
Finding the campground: From Giant Forest Village, drive south 16 miles on Generals Highway, turn left onto South Fork Drive, and go about 12 miles.

About the campground: A trail leads east from the campground to Garfield Grove, a stand of sequoia accessible only on foot. Elevation 3,620 feet. Stay limit 14 days. Open approximately May 15 to September 15.

8 Portagee Joe

Location: 1 mile west of Lone Pine.
Sites: 15 sites for tents and RVs.
Facilities: Picnic tables, fire rings, drinking water, pit toilets.
Fee per night: $6.
Agency: Inyo County Department of Parks and Recreation, 760-878-0272.
Finding the campground: From the town of Lone Pine, drive west half a mile to Tuttle Creek Road, turn left, and drive 200 yards.

About the campground: Portagee Joe is a good alternative if the Whitney Portal Campground (see No. 10 below) is full. Manzanar National Monument, a former internment camp for Japanese-Americans during World War II, is 9 miles north of the campground on U.S. Highway 395. Elevation 3,700 feet. Stay limit 14 days. Open all year.

9 Lone Pine

Location: 7 miles west of the town of Lone Pine.
Sites: 43 sites for tents and RVs, plus 1 group site, which can accomodate up to 15 people.
Facilities: Picnic tables, fire rings, vault toilets, drinking water (May to October only). A store that also offers meals and showers is open during the summer.
Fee per night: $10 individual, $30 group. For reservations (required for group site), call 800-280-CAMP. Reservation fee, $8.65 individual, $15 group.
Agency: Inyo National Forest, Mount Whitney Ranger District, 760-876-6200.
Activities: Hiking, fishing.

Finding the campground: From the town of Lone Pine, drive west 7 miles on Whitney Portal Road.

About the campground: Used as a stopover for hikers headed for Mount Whitney, the campground has excellent views of the mountain. The lower trailhead for the Whitney Portal National Recreation Trail is located at the campground. The 4-mile trail ascends 2,720 feet to the Whitney Portal Campground (see below), providing spectacular views of Mount Whitney, Owens Valley, and the White Mountains en route. Elevation 6,000 feet. Stay limit 14 days. Open all year.

10 Whitney Portal

Location: 12 miles west of Lone Pine.
Sites: 44 sites for tents and RVs, plus 3 group sites, each accommodating 15 people.
Facilities: Picnic tables, fire rings, drinking water, flush toilets.
Fee per night: $12 individual, $30 group. For reservations (required for group sites), call 800-280-CAMP. Reservation fee, $8.65 individual, $15 group.
Agency: Inyo National Forest, Mount Whitney Ranger District, 760-876-6200.
Activities: Hiking.
Finding the campground: From the town of Lone Pine, drive west 12 miles on Whitney Portal Road.

About the campground: Whitney Portal is the main starting point for climbers of Mount Whitney, the highest peak in the contiguous United States (14,495 feet). A quota system is in effect for hiking to the summit of the mountain from May 22 to October 15; reservations must be made in advance by mail. Call the ranger district for details. The campground is also used by backpackers heading for the John Muir and Pacific Crest Trails. Because of the popularity of these trails, permits also are required for their use between the last weekend in June and September 15. The upper trailhead for the Whitney Portal National Recreation Trail (not the trail to the summit) is also located in the campground, near the fishing pond. Elevation 8,000 feet. Stay limit 7 days. Open April 23 to October 26.

11 Whitney Trailhead

Location: 13 miles west of Lone Pine.
Sites: 10 sites for tents.
Facilities: Picnic tables, fire rings, drinking water, pit toilets.
Fee per night: $6.
Agency: Inyo National Forest, Mount Whitney Ranger District, 760-876-6200.
Activities: Hiking.
Finding the campground: From the town of Lone Pine, drive west 13 miles on Whitney Portal Road.

About the campground: This is the closest campground to the Mount Whitney Trail (see Whitney Portal Campground [No. 10 above] for more information). Although designated as a walk-in campground, the campsites are located just a few yards from the parking lot. Elevation 8,300 feet. Stay limit 1 night. Open April 23 to October 26.

12 Tuttle Creek

Location: 6 miles southwest of Lone Pine.
Sites: 85 sites for tents and RVs.
Facilities: Picnic tables, fire rings, pit toilets. No drinking water.
Fee per night: None.
Agency: Bureau of Land Management, Bishop Resource Area, 760-872-4881.
Activities: Fishing nearby.
Finding the campground: From the town of Lone Pine, drive 3.5 miles west on Whitney Portal Road, turn left onto Horseshoe Meadow Road, and drive 1.6 miles. Turn right onto Tuttle Creek Road and drive 0.8 mile.

About the campground: Fishing is possible in nearby streams and at Diaz Lake. The campground is also a good alternative if the Whitney Portal and Whitney Trailhead campgrounds are full (see No. 10 above). Elevation 5,000 feet. Stay limit 14 days. Open May through November.

13 Diaz Lake

Location: 2 miles south of Lone Pine.
Sites: 200 sites for tents and RVs.
Facilities: Picnic tables, grills, drinking water (well), flush toilets, solar showers, boat ramp.
Fee per night: $8.
Agency: Inyo County Department of Parks and Recreation, 760-878-0272.
Activities: Fishing, swimming, boating, waterskiing.
Finding the campground: From the town of Lone Pine, drive south 2 miles on U.S. Highway 395.

About the campground: Situated on the shore of an 86-acre lake, the campground offers a range of water sports not found elsewhere for many miles. Boats are limited to 20 feet in length. Elevation 3,800 feet. Stay limit 14 days. Open all year.

14 Horseshoe Meadow: Golden Trout

Location: 22 miles southwest of Lone Pine.
Sites: 18 sites for tents.
Facilities: Picnic tables, fire rings, drinking water, pit toilets.
Fee per night: $6.
Agency: Inyo National Forest, Mount Whitney Ranger District, 760-876-6200.
Activities: Hiking, horseback riding.
Finding the campground: From the town of Lone Pine, drive 3.5 miles west on

Whitney Portal Road, turn left onto Horseshoe Meadow Road, and drive 18 miles.

About the campground: There are three campgrounds at this location, all within 1.5 miles of each other: Golden Trout is for tenters; Cottonwood Lakes (see No. 15 below) is for tenters and equestrians; and Equestrian (see No. 16, below) is for campers with horses. Trails from the area lead to Cottonwood Lakes, Trail Pass, and the Pacific Crest Trail. Elevation 10,000 feet. Stay limit 1 night. Open May 15 to October 15.

15 Horseshoe Meadow: Cottonwood Lakes

Location: 22 miles southwest of Lone Pine.
Sites: 12 sites for tents.
Facilities: Picnic tables, fire rings, drinking water, pit toilets.
Fee per night: $6, campers with horses $10.
Agency: Inyo National Forest, Mount Whitney Ranger District, 760-876-6200.
Activities: Hiking, horseback riding.
Finding the campground: From the town of Lone Pine, drive 3.5 miles west on Whitney Portal Road, turn left onto Horseshoe Meadow Road, and drive 18 miles.

About the campground: See Golden Trout Campground (No. 14 above) for more information about the three campgrounds in this area. Elevation 10,000 feet. Stay limit 1 night. Open May 15 to October 15.

16 Horseshoe Meadow: Equestrian

Location: 22 miles southwest of Lone Pine.
Sites: 10 sites for tents.
Facilities: Picnic tables, fire rings, drinking water, pit toilets.
Fee per night: $12.
Agency: Inyo National Forest, Mount Whitney Ranger District, 760-876-6200.
Activities: Hiking, horseback riding.
Finding the campground: From the town of Lone Pine, drive 3.5 miles west on Whitney Portal Road, turn left onto Horseshoe Meadow Road, and drive 18 miles.

About the campground: See Golden Trout Campground (No. 14 above) for more information about the three campgrounds in this area. Elevation 10,000 feet. Stay limit 1 night. Open May 15 to October 15.

SEQUOIA NATIONAL FOREST (NORTH)

A major feature of this area is Long Meadow, one of the finest sequoia groves in the national forest. The Trail of a Hundred Giants, a half-mile loop through this magnificent stand of trees, begins at the Redwood Meadow Campground (No. 16). The trail is relatively flat and wheelchair accessible. Unusual features of the grove are the density of the big trees, the number of "twins"—two sequoias

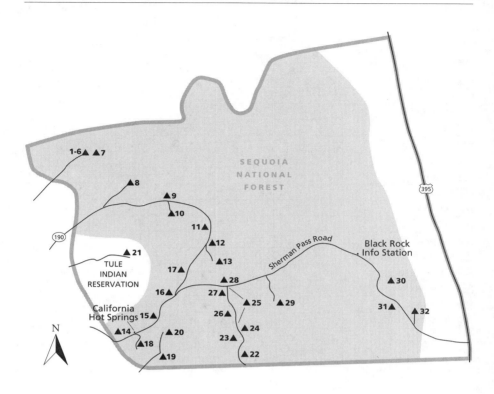

	Group sites	RV sites	Max. RV length	Hookups	Toilets	Showers	Drinking water	Dump station	Pets	Wheelchair	Recreation	Fee ($)	Season	Can reserve
1 Methuselah	•	•			V		•		•		HFR		May–Nov	•
2 Hedrick Pond		•			V		•		•		HFR		May–Nov	•
3 Frazier Mill		•			V		•		•		HFR		May–Nov	•
4 Shake Camp		•			V		•		•		HFR		May–Nov	•
5 Hidden Falls					V		•		•		HFR		May–Nov	•
6 Moses Gulch					V				•		HFR		May–Nov	•
7 Balch County Park		•	30		F	•			•	•	HF	8	May–Sep	
8 Wishon		•	24		V	•	•		•		HF	12		•
9 Belnap		•	22		V	•	•		•		HF	12	Apr–Nov	•
10 Coy Flat		•	24		V	•	•		•		H	10	Apr–Nov	•
11 Quaking Aspen	•	•	24		V	•	•		•		HF	12	May–Nov	•
12 Peppermint		•	24		P				•		HF			
13 Lower Peppermint		•			V	•	•		•		HF	12	May–Oct	
14 Leavis Flat		•	16		V	•	•		•		F	10		•

	Group sites	RV sites	Max. RV length	Hookups	Toilets	Showers	Drinking water	Dump station	Pets	Wheelchair	Recreation	Fee ($)	Season	Can reserve
15 Holey Meadow		•	16		V		•		•		F	10	May–Nov	•
16 Redwood Meadow		•	16		V		•		•		H	12	May–Nov	•
17 Long Meadow			16		V				•		H	6	May–Nov	•
18 White River		•	16		V		•		•		HF	10	May–Oct	•
19 Panorama		•			V				•		H			
20 Frog Meadow					V				•		H		June–Nov	
21 Cholollo		•			C		•		•		HF	10		
22 Headquarters		•	27		V		•		•		F	12		•
23 Camp 3		•	30		V		•		•		F	12		•
24 Hospital Flat		•	30		V		•		•		F	12	May–Sep	•
25 Kern River		•			C				•		F			
26 Gold Ledge		•	30		V		•		•		F	12		•
27 Fairview		•	45		V		•		•		F	12		•
28 Limestone		•	30		V				•		F	8	Apr–Nov	•
29 Horse Meadow		•	22		V		•		•		HF	5	May–Nov	
30 Troy Meadow		•	20		V		•		•		HFO		May–Nov	
31 Fish Creek		•	27		V		•		•		HFO		May–Nov	
32 Kennedy Meadows		•	30		V		•		•		HF			

Hookups: W = Water E = Electric S = Sewer
Toilets: F = Flush V = Vault P = Pit C = Chemical
Recreation: H = Hiking S = Swimming F = Fishing B = Boating L = Boat Launch O = Off-highway Driving R = Horseback Riding
Maximum Trailer/RV Length given in feet. **Stay Limit** given in days. **Fee** given in dollars.
If no entry under **Season,** campground is open all year. If no entry under **Fee,** camping is free.

growing close together and sharing ground resources—and a "sequedar," a sequoia and a cedar that have grown together.

A 25-mile stretch of the North Fork of the Kern River, designated a Wild and Scenic River, runs from north to south through the region. It offers fishing and challenging kayaking and whitewater rafting. And Cholollo Campground (No. 21) provides an unusual opportunity to camp on the Tule River Indian Reservation.

1 Mountain Home State Forest: Methuselah

Location: 20 miles northeast of Springville.
Sites: 1 large group site for tents or RVs.
Facilities: Picnic tables, camp stoves, vault toilets, drinking water.
Fee per night: None. Reservations required; call the state forest.
Agency: Mountain Home State Forest, 209-539-2321 (summer), 209-539-2855 (winter).
Activities: Hiking, fishing, horseback riding.
Finding the campground: From Springville, drive north on Springville-Milo Road (J37) for 8 miles, turn right onto Balch Park Road, and drive about 11 miles to the state forest headquarters. Methuselah is half a mile southeast of head-

quarters. A shorter but steeper route to the campgrounds is to drive 3 miles north of Springville on J37, turn right onto Bear Creek Drive, and drive 14 miles to the forest headquarters. This route is not suitable for larger RVs or trailers.

About the campground: Established in 1946 to preserve huge old-growth redwoods once described by naturalist John Muir as the finest in the Sierra Nevada, Mountain Home State Forest encompasses more than 5,200 such trees within its 4,807 acres. Points of interest include the Adams Tree, which is 240 feet tall and 85 feet in circumference; the Hercules Tree, which has a large room cut into its base; and the Indian Bathtubs, which are deep basins carved in solid granite and used by ancient inhabitants. Many trails traverse the area, leading to these and other features of the forest. Three ponds are stocked with rainbow trout, and native rainbow, brook, and brown trout can be caught in the forks of the Tule River and its tributary streams. Horses may be rented at the Pack Station near Shake Camp (see No. 4, below). Elevations in the forest range from 4,800 to 7,600 feet. Stay limit 15 days. Open May through November, depending upon snow conditions.

2 Mountain Home State Forest: Hedrick Pond

Location: 21 miles northeast of Springville.
Sites: 14 sites for tents and RVs.
Facilities: Picnic tables, camp stoves, vault toilets, drinking water.
Fee per night: None. Reservations required; call the state forest.
Agency: Mountain Home State Forest, 209-539-2321 (summer), 209-539-2855 (winter).
Activities: Hiking, fishing, horseback riding.
Finding the campground: From Springville, drive north on Springville-Milo Road (J37) for 8 miles, turn right onto Balch Park Road, and drive about 11 miles to the state forest headquarters. Hedrick Pond is 2 miles north of headquarters. A shorter but steeper route to the campgrounds is to drive 3 miles north of Springville on J37, turn right onto Bear Creek Drive, and drive 14 miles to the forest headquarters. This route is not suitable for larger RVs or trailers.

About the campground: Fishing is permitted in nearby Hedrick Pond. For more information about the state forest and its attractions, see Methuselah Campground (No. 1 above). Stay limit 15 days. Open May through November, depending upon snow conditions.

3 Mountain Home State Forest: Frazier Mill

Location: 24 miles northeast of Springville.
Sites: 46 sites for tents and RVs.
Facilities: Picnic tables, camp stoves, vault toilets, drinking water.
Fee per night: None. Reservations required; call the state forest.
Agency: Mountain Home State Forest, 209-539-2321 (summer), 209-539-2855 (winter).

Activities: Hiking, fishing, horseback riding.
Finding the campground: From Springville, drive north on Springville-Milo Road (J37) for 8 miles, turn right onto Balch Park Road, and drive about 11 miles to the state forest headquarters. Frazier Mill is 5 miles north of headquarters. A shorter but steeper route to the campgrounds is to drive 3 miles north of Springville on J37, turn right onto Bear Creek Drive, and drive 14 miles to the forest headquarters. This route is not suitable for larger RVs or trailers.

About the campground: For more information about the state forest and its attractions, see Methuselah Campground (No. 1 above). Stay limit 15 days. Open May through November, depending upon snow conditions.

4 Mountain Home State Forest: Shake Camp

Location: 26 miles northeast of Springville.
Sites: 11 sites for tents and RVs.
Facilities: Picnic tables, camp stoves, vault toilets, drinking water.
Fee per night: None. Reservations required; call the state forest.
Agency: Mountain Home State Forest, 209-539-2321 (summer), 209-539-2855 (winter).
Activities: Hiking, fishing, horseback riding.
Finding the campground: From Springville, drive north on Springville-Milo Road (J37) for 8 miles, turn right onto Balch Park Road, and drive about 11 miles to the state forest headquarters. Shake Camp is 7 miles north of headquarters. A shorter but steeper route to the campgrounds is to drive 3 miles north of Springville on J37, turn right onto Bear Creek Drive, and drive 14 miles to the forest headquarters. This route is not suitable for larger RVs or trailers.

About the campground: For more information about the state forest and its attractions, see Methuselah Campground (No. 1 above). Stay limit 15 days. Open May through November, depending upon snow conditions.

5 Mountain Home State Forest: Hidden Falls

Location: 27 miles northeast of Springville.
Sites: 8 sites for tents.
Facilities: Picnic tables, camp stoves, vault toilets, drinking water.
Fee per night: None. Reservations required; call the state forest.
Agency: Mountain Home State Forest, 209-539-2321 (summer), 209-539-2855 (winter).
Activities: Hiking, fishing, horseback riding.
Finding the campground: From Springville, drive north on Springville-Milo Road (J37) for 8 miles, turn right onto Balch Park Road, and drive about 11 miles to the state forest headquarters. Hidden Falls Campground is 8 miles north of headquarters. A shorter but steeper route to the campgrounds is to drive 3 miles north of Springville on J37, turn right onto Bear Creek Drive, and drive 14 miles to the forest headquarters. This route is not suitable for larger RVs or trailers.

About the campground: Hidden Falls Campground is on the bank of the Wishon Fork of the Tule River. For more information about the state forest and its attractions, see Methuselah Campground (No. 1 above). Stay limit 15 days. Open May through November, depending upon snow conditions.

6 Mountain Home State Forest: Moses Gulch

Location: 28 miles northeast of Springville.
Sites: 10 sites for tents.
Facilities: Picnic tables, camp stoves, vault toilets. No drinking water.
Fee per night: None. Reservations required; call the state forest.
Agency: Mountain Home State Forest, 209-539-2321 (summer), 209-539-2855 (winter).
Activities: Hiking, fishing, horseback riding.
Finding the campground: From Springville, drive north on Springville-Milo Road (J37) for 8 miles, turn right onto Balch Park Road, and drive about 11 miles to the state forest headquarters. Moses Gulch Campground is 9 miles north of headquarters. A shorter but steeper route to the campgrounds is to drive 3 miles north of Springville on J37, turn right onto Bear Creek Drive, and drive 14 miles to the forest headquarters. This route is not suitable for larger RVs or trailers.

About the campground: Moses Gulch Campground is on the bank of the Wishon Fork of the Tule River. For more information about the state forest and its attractions, see Methuselah Campground (No. 1 above). Stay limit 15 days. Open May through November, depending upon snow conditions.

7 Balch County Park

Location: 20 miles northeast of Springville.
Sites: 80 sites for tents and RVs up to 30 feet long.
Facilities: Picnic tables, grills, drinking water, flush toilets.
Fee per night: $8, pets $1.
Agency: Tulare County General Services, 209-539-3896 (summer), 209-733-6612 (winter).
Activities: Hiking, fishing.
Finding the campground: From Springville, drive north on Springville-Milo Road (J37) for 8 miles, turn right onto Balch Park Road, and drive about 12 miles (1 mile past the state forest headquarters). A shorter but steeper route to the campgrounds is to drive 3 miles north of Springville on J37, turn right onto Bear Creek Drive, and drive 14 miles to the forest headquarters. This route is not suitable for larger RVs or trailers.

About the campground: The park is located within Mountain Home State Forest. For more information about the forest and its attractions, see Methuselah Campground (No. 1 above). Elevation 6,400 feet. Stay limit 14 days. Open May through September, depending on snow conditions.

8 Wishon

Location: 12 miles northeast of Springville.
Sites: 33 family sites and 4 double-family sites for tents and RVs up to 24 feet long.
Facilities: Picnic tables, grills, fire rings, drinking water, vault toilets.
Fee per night: $12. For reservations, call 800-280-CAMP. Reservation fee, $8.65.
Agency: Sequoia National Forest, Tule River Ranger District, 209-539-2607.
Activities: Hiking, fishing.
Finding the campground: From Springville, drive 7.7 miles northeast on California 190, turn left onto Wishon Drive (County Road 208), and drive 4 miles.

About the campground: Year-round fishing is possible in the North Fork of the Tule River. Elevation 4,000 feet. Stay limit 14 days. Open all year, depending on snow conditions.

9 Belnap

Location: 19 miles east of Springville.
Sites: 15 sites for tents and RVs up to 22 feet long; no trailers.
Facilities: Picnic tables, grills, fire rings, drinking water, vault toilets.
Fee per night: $12. For reservations, call 800-280-CAMP. Reservation fee, $8.65.
Agency: Sequoia National Forest, Tule River Ranger District, 209-539-2607.
Activities: Hiking, fishing.
Finding the campground: From Springville, drive 18 miles northeast on California 190 to Camp Nelson, turn right onto Nelson Drive, and drive 1 mile.

About the campground: Belnap offers a special treat: the opportunity to camp right in a grove of giant sequoia trees. Fishing is open year-round. Elevation 5,000 feet. Stay limit 14 days. Open April through November.

10 Coy Flat

Location: 19 miles east of Springville.
Sites: 20 sites for tents and RVs up to 24 feet long.
Facilities: Picnic tables, grills, fire rings, drinking water, vault toilets.
Fee per night: $10. For reservations, call 800-280-CAMP. Reservation fee, $8.65.
Agency: Sequoia National Forest, Tule River Ranger District, 209-539-2607.
Activities: Hiking.
Finding the campground: From Springville, drive northeast 18 miles on California 190 to Camp Nelson, turn right onto FR 21S94, and drive 1 mile.

About the campground: Elevation 5,000 feet. Stay limit 14 days. Open April through November.

11 Quaking Aspen

Location: 27 miles east of Springville.
Sites: 16 sites for tents, 16 sites for RVs up to 24 feet long, plus 7 group sites that

accommodate a total of up to 50 people.

Facilities: Picnic tables, grills, fire rings, drinking water, vault toilets.

Fee per night: $12 for individual sites, $37.50 for 25-person sites, $75 for 50-person sites. For reservations, call 800-280-CAMP. Reservation fee, $8.65 for individuals, $15 for groups.

Agency: Sequoia National Forest, Tule River Ranger District, 209-539-2607.

Activities: Hiking, fishing.

Finding the campground: From Springville, drive northeast on California 190 for 27 miles. CA 190 becomes Western Divide Highway just beyond Camp Nelson.

About the campground: Quaking Aspen has been listed by *Sunset* as one of the 100 best campgrounds in the western United States. The Needles Lookout Trail, leading to a series of monolithic rock formations, is one of the best short hikes (5 miles round trip) in the Sequoia National Forest. Offering majestic views of Kern River Canyon and the Golden Trout Wilderness, it begins 3.5 miles east of the campground. Drive half a mile south on Western Divide Highway, turn left onto FR 21S05, and drive 3 miles to the trailhead. Elevation 7,000 feet. Stay limit 14 days. Open May through November.

12 Peppermint

Location: 31 miles east of Springville.

Sites: Open camping for tents and RVs up to 24 feet long.

Facilities: Some picnic tables and fire rings, 1 pit toilet. No drinking water.

Fee per night: None.

Agency: Sequoia National Forest, Tule River Ranger District, 209-539-2607.

Activities: Hiking, fishing.

Finding the campground: From Springville, drive 30 miles northeast on California 190, which becomes Western Divide Highway just beyond Camp Nelson. Turn left onto FR 21S07 and drive 1 mile.

About the campground: Situated on the bank of Peppermint Creek, the campground is less than 2 miles from Dome Rock, a granite monolith that provides a panoramic overlook of the Kern River Canyon. Elevation 7,100 feet. Stay limit 14 days. Open all year, depending on snow conditions.

13 Lower Peppermint

Location: 10 miles north of Johnsondale.

Sites: 17 sites for tents and RVs.

Facilities: Picnic tables, fire rings, drinking water, vault toilets.

Fee per night: $12.

Agency: Sequoia National Forest, Hot Springs Ranger District, 805-548-6503.

Activities: Hiking, fishing.

Finding the campground: From Johnsondale, drive 10 miles north on FR 22S82 (Lloyd Meadow Road).

About the campground: This campground is on the bank of Peppermint Creek, at an altitude of 5,300 feet. Stay limit 14 days. Open May through October.

14 Leavis Flat

Location: In California Hot Springs.
Sites: 9 sites for tents and RVs up to 16 feet long.
Facilities: Picnic tables, fire rings, drinking water, vault toilets.
Fee per night: $10. For reservations, call 800-280-CAMP. Reservation fee, $8.65.
Agency: Sequoia National Forest, Hot Springs Ranger District, 805-548-6503.
Activities: Fishing.
Finding the campground: Leavis Flat is on County Road J22 (Hot Springs Road), just west of the center of California Hot Springs.

About the campground: Deer Creek Mill Grove, the southernmost stand of sequoia trees in the world, is east of California Hot Springs, about 5 miles from the campground. Elevation 3,100 feet. Stay limit 14 days. Open all year.

15 Holey Meadow

Location: 12 miles north of California Hot Springs.
Sites: 10 sites for tents and RVs up to 16 feet long.
Facilities: Picnic tables, fire rings, drinking water, vault toilets.
Fee per night: $10. For reservations, call 800-280-CAMP. Reservation fee, $8.65.
Agency: Sequoia National Forest, Hot Springs Ranger District, 805-548-6503.
Activities: Fishing.
Finding the campground: From California Hot Springs, drive east 2 miles on Hot Springs Road, turn left onto Parker Pass Road (County SM50), and drive north for 9 miles. Turn left onto Western Divide Highway and drive 0.7 mile.

About the campground: Elevation 6,400 feet. Stay limit 14 days. Open May through November.

16 Redwood Meadow

Location: 15 miles north of California Hot Springs.
Sites: 15 sites for tents and RVs up to 16 feet long.
Facilities: Picnic tables, fire rings, drinking water, vault toilets.
Fee per night: $12. For reservations, call 800-280-CAMP. Reservation fee, $8.65.
Agency: Sequoia National Forest, Hot Springs Ranger District, 805-548-6503.
Activities: Hiking.
Finding the campground: From California Hot Springs, drive east 2 miles on Hot Springs Road, turn left onto Parker Pass Road (County SM50), and drive north for 9 miles. Turn left onto Western Divide Highway and drive 3.7 miles.

About the campground: The campground is at the trailhead to the Trail of a Hundred Giants, a half-mile loop trail through Long Meadow Sequoia Grove, which is one of the finest sequoia stands in the national forest. Elevation 6,500 feet. Stay limit 14 days. Open May through October.

17   Long Meadow

Location: 16 miles north of California Hot Springs.
Sites: 6 sites for tents and RVs up to 16 feet long.
Facilities: Picnic tables, fire rings, vault toilets. No drinking water.
Fee per night: $6. For reservations, call 800-280-CAMP. Reservation fee, $8.65.
Agency: Sequoia National Forest, Hot Springs Ranger District, 805-548-6503.
Activities: Hiking.
Finding the campground: From California Hot Springs, drive east 2 miles on Hot Springs Road, turn left onto Parker Pass Road (SM50), and drive north for 9 miles. Turn left onto Western Divide Highway and drive 4.7 miles.

About the campground: The campground is less than a mile from the Long Meadow Giant Sequoia Grove and the Trail of a Hundred Giants (see section introduction, page 124). Elevation 5,300 feet. Stay limit 14 days. Open May through November.

18   White River

Location: 7 miles southeast of California Hot Springs.
Sites: 12 spaces for tents and RVs up to 16 feet long.
Facilities: Picnic tables, fire rings, drinking water, vault toilets.
Fee per night: $10. For reservations, call 800-280-CAMP. Reservation fee, $8.65.
Agency: Sequoia National Forest, Hot Springs Ranger District, 805-548-6503.
Activities: Hiking, fishing.
Finding the campground: From California Hot Springs, drive east 2 miles to Hot Springs Ranger Station, turn right onto County Road SM56, and drive 2 miles through Pine Flat to the Tulare County Fire Station. Continue south on FR 23S05 for 2.5 miles.

About the campground: Elevation 4,000 feet. Stay limit 14 days. Open May through October.

19   Panorama

Location: 17 miles northeast of Glennville.
Sites: 10 sites for tents and RVs; no trailers.
Facilities: Picnic tables, fire rings, vault toilets. No drinking water.
Fee per night: None.
Agency: Sequoia National Forest, Hot Springs Ranger District, 805-548-6503.
Activities: Hiking.
Finding the campground: From the intersection of California 155 and Linns Valley Road just west of Glennville, take Linns Valley Road (County Road M3, later M9) and drive northeast about 8 miles. Bear left on Sugarloaf Drive, and drive about 4 miles to Guernsey Mill. Continue south on FR 23S16 for about 5 miles.

About the campground: Elevation 6,800 feet. Stay limit 14 days. Open all year.

20 Frog Meadow

Location: 20 miles northeast of Glennville.
Sites: 10 sites for tents.
Facilities: Picnic tables, fire rings, vault toilets. No drinking water.
Fee per night: None.
Agency: Sequoia National Forest, Hot Springs Ranger District, 805-548-6503.
Activities: Hiking.
Finding the campground: From the intersection of California 155 and Lynn Valley Road just west of Glennville, take Lynn Valley Road (County Road M3, later M9) and drive northwest about 8 miles. Bear left on Sugarloaf Drive, and drive about 4 miles to Guernsey Mill. Continue south on FR 23S16 for about 5 miles. Turn left onto FR 24S50 and drive about 3 miles.

About the campground: Elevation 7,500 feet. Stay limit 14 days. Open June through November.

21 Cholollo

Location: 35 miles east of Porterville on the Tule Indian Reservation.
Sites: 100 sites for tents and RVs.
Facilities: Picnic tables, grills, fire rings at most locations, drinking water, portable toilets.
Fee per night: $10 for up to 6 people.
Agency: Tule River Tribal Council, 209-781-4271.
Activities: Hiking, fishing.
Finding the campground: From the intersection of California 65 and CA 190 in Porterville, drive east on CA 190 for 5.7 miles. Turn right onto Road 284 and drive half a mile, and then turn left onto Reservation Road (J42) and drive 18 miles to the Tule Indian Reservation entrance. Continue to where the pavement ends and drive 11 more miles.

About the campground: One of the few campgrounds on an Indian reservation, Cholollo is popular with anglers and visitors to the Native American festivals that are held at various times of the year. Call the tribal council for information. Stay limit 14 days. Open all year.

22 Headquarters

Location: 4 miles north of Kernville.
Sites: 44 sites for tents and RVs up to 27 feet long.
Facilities: Picnic tables, fire rings, drinking water, vault toilets.
Fee per night: $12. For reservations, call 800-280-CAMP. Reservation fee, $8.65.
Agency: Sequoia National Forest, Cannel Meadow Ranger District, 760-376-3781.
Activities: Fishing, kayaking.
Finding the campground: From Kernville, drive 4 miles north on Sierra Way (SM99).

About the campground: Headquarters is on the bank of the Kern River at an elevation of 2,800 feet. Stay limit 14 days. Open all year.

23 Camp 3

Location: 5 miles north of Kernville.
Sites: 52 sites for tents and RVs up to 30 feet long.
Facilities: Picnic tables, fire rings, drinking water, vault toilets.
Fee per night: $12. For reservations, call 800-280-CAMP. Reservation fee, $8.65.
Agency: Sequoia National Forest, Cannel Meadow Ranger District, 760-376-3781.
Activities: Fishing, kayaking.
Finding the campground: From Kernville, drive 5 miles north on Sierra Way (SM99).

About the campground: Camp 3 is on the bank of the Kern River at an elevation of 2,800 feet. Stay limit 14 days. Open all year.

24 Hospital Flat

Location: 6.5 miles north of Kernville.
Sites: 40 sites for tents and RVs up to 30 feet long.
Facilities: Picnic tables, fire rings, drinking water, vault toilets.
Fee per night: $12. For reservations, call 800-280-CAMP. Reservation fee, $8.65.
Agency: Sequoia National Forest, Cannel Meadow Ranger District, 760-376-3781.
Activities: Fishing, kayaking.
Finding the campground: From Kernville, drive 6.5 miles north on Sierra Way (SM99).

About the campground: This campground is situated on the bank of the Kern River at an elevation of 3,000 feet. Stay limit 14 days. Open May through September.

25 Kern River

Location: Between 3 and 19 miles north of Kernville.
Sites: 7 undeveloped, open camping areas for tents and RVs.
Facilities: Pit or chemical toilets. No drinking water.
Fee per night: None.
Agency: Sequoia National Forest, Cannel Meadow Ranger District, 760-376-3781.
Activities: Fishing, kayaking.
Finding the campgrounds: All these areas lie along Sierra Way (SM99) north of Kernville as follows: Riverkern, 3 miles; Halfway, 4.7 miles; Thunderbird, 5.5 miles; Chico Flat, 5.7 miles; Corral Creek, 8.5 miles; Spring Hill, 9 miles; Brush Creek Flat, 19 miles.

About the campgrounds: These areas are mostly large, open, dirt fields, with some grass and a few trees. Their advantage is that they provide a wide range of camping opportunities along the bank of the North Fork of the Kern River, which has been designated a National Wild and Scenic River. This stretch of the Kern is famous for its excellent kayaking. Campsites must be at least 25 feet from the water's edge, and campers must obtain campfire permits, which are available from any Forest Service office. These sites are best suited for self-contained units. Elevation from 2,800 to 3,800 feet. Stay limit 14 days. Open all year, as weather permits.

26 Gold Ledge

Location: 10 miles north of Kernville.
Sites: 37 sites for tents and RVs up to 30 feet long.
Facilities: Picnic tables, fire rings, drinking water, vault toilets.
Fee per night: $12. For reservations, call 800-280-CAMP. Reservation fee, $8.65.
Agency: Sequoia National Forest, Cannel Meadow Ranger District, 760-376-3781.
Activities: Fishing, kayaking.
Finding the campground: From Kernville, drive 10 miles north on Sierra Way (SM99).

About the campground: Gold Ledge is on the bank of the Kern River at an elevation of 3,200 feet. Stay limit 14 days. Open all year.

27 Fairview

Location: 16 miles north of Kernville.
Sites: 55 sites for tents and RVs up to 45 feet long.
Facilities: Picnic tables, fire rings, drinking water, vault toilets.
Fee per night: $12. For reservations, call 800-280-CAMP. Reservation fee, $8.65.
Agency: Sequoia National Forest, Cannel Meadow Ranger District, 760-376-3781.
Activities: Fishing, kayaking.
Finding the campground: From Kernville, drive 16 miles north on Sierra Way (SM99).

About the campground: Fairview is on the bank of the Kern River at an elevation of 3,500 feet. Stay limit 14 days. Open all year, with reduced services from December through April.

28 Limestone

Location: 19 miles north of Kernville.
Sites: 22 sites for tents and RVs up to 30 feet long.
Facilities: Picnic tables, fire rings, vault toilets. No drinking water.
Fee per night: $8. For reservations, call 800-280-CAMP. Reservation fee, $8.65.
Agency: Sequoia National Forest, Cannel Meadow Ranger District, 760-376-3781.
Activities: Fishing, kayaking.
Finding the campground: From Kernville, drive 19 miles north on Sierra Way (SM99).

About the campground: Limestone is on the bank of the Kern River at an elevation of 3,800 feet. Stay limit 14 days. Open April through November.

29 Horse Meadow

Location: 35 miles north of Kernville.
Sites: 41 sites for tents and RVs up to 22 feet long.
Facilities: Picnic tables, fire rings, drinking water (dependent on weather conditions; no water in dry periods), vault toilets.
Fee per night: $5.
Agency: Sequoia National Forest, Cannel Meadow Ranger District, 760-376-3781.
Activities: Hiking, fishing.
Finding the campground: From Kernville, drive north on Sierra Way (SM 99) for 20 miles, turn right onto Sherman Pass Road (FR 22S05), and drive 6 miles. Turn right onto Cherry Hill Road (FR 22S12) and drive about 9 miles.

About the campground: Fishing season is from May 1 to November 15. A 9-mile, round-trip trail leads from the campground along Salmon Creek to the top of Salmon Creek Falls. Elevation 7,400 feet. Stay limit 14 days. Open late May through November.

30 Troy Meadow

Location: About 53 miles northeast of Kernville.
Sites: 73 sites for tents and RVs up to 20 feet long.
Facilities: Picnic tables, fire rings, drinking water (dependent on weather conditions; no water in dry periods), vault toilets.
Fee per night: None.
Agency: Sequoia National Forest, Cannel Meadow Ranger District, 760-376-3781.
Activities: Hiking, fishing, off-highway driving.
Finding the campground: From Kernville, drive north on Sierra Way (SM 99) for 20 miles, turn right onto Sherman Pass Road (FR 22S05), and drive about 30 miles, then turn right onto FR 22S05 and drive 2.5 miles.

About the campground: The area surrounding the campground contains 155 miles of trails suitable for off-highway driving, most of it for trail/backcountry motorcycles. Fishing season is May 1 to November 15. Elevation 7,800 feet. Stay limit 14 days. Open late May through November.

31 Fish Creek

Location: About 55 miles northeast of Kernville.
Sites: 33 sites for tents and RVs up to 27 feet long, 3 sites for RVs up to 40 feet long.
Facilities: Picnic tables, fire rings, drinking water (dependent on weather conditions; no water in dry periods), vault toilets.

Fee per night: None.
Agency: Sequoia National Forest, Cannel Meadow Ranger District, 760-376-3781.
Activities: Hiking, fishing, off-highway driving.
Finding the campground: From Troy Meadow Campground (see No. 30 above), continue 2 miles southeast on Forest Road 22S05.

About the campground: The area surrounding the campground contains 155 miles of trails suitable for OHV driving, most of it for trail/backcountry motorcycles. Fishing season is May 1 to November 15. The Jackson Creek National Recreation Trail begins at the campground and proceeds north 5 miles to the summit of Jackson Peak (9,245 feet). Elevation 7,400 feet. Stay limit 14 days. Open late May through November.

32 Kennedy Meadows

Location: 66 miles northeast of Kernville.
Sites: 38 sites for tents and RVs up to 30 feet long, plus 3 overflow areas for any size RV.
Facilities: Picnic tables, fire rings, drinking water (dependent on weather conditions; no water in dry periods), vault toilets.
Fee per night: None.
Agency: Inyo National Forest, Lone Pine Ranger District, 760-876-6200.
Activities: Hiking, fishing, kayaking.
Finding the campground: From Troy Meadow Campground (see No. 30 above), continue southeast on Forest Road 22S05 for 8 miles. Turn left (north) onto Kennedy Meadows Road and drive 3 miles.

About the campground: Kennedy Meadows is situated along the bank of the South Fork of the Kern River, which has been designated a National Wild and Scenic River. Fishing season is May 1 to November 15. The Pacific Crest Trail passes by the campground, allowing hikers to sample the trail north or south. Elevation 6,100 feet. Stay limit 14 days. Open all year.

SEQUOIA NATIONAL FOREST (SOUTH)

Isabella Lake is the centerpiece of this area. Nine miles long and with 40 miles of shoreline, it is one of the largest lakes in Southern California. It offers a full range of water sports, including swimming, fishing, boating, waterskiing, jet skiing, and sailboarding. Fishing for bass and trout is usually best in the spring; waterskiing is usually limited to the summer months. As Isabella is a manmade reservoir, it is subject to seasonal drawdowns. The landscape surrounding the lake is not as attractive as that around other large lakes in the foothills of the Sierra Nevada. The hills are mostly brown and treeless, and the shoreline is relatively barren.

Other activities in the area include fishing, kayaking, and canoeing in the Kern River, a large portion of which has been designated a National Wild and Scenic River.

Sequoia National Forest (South) Area Map

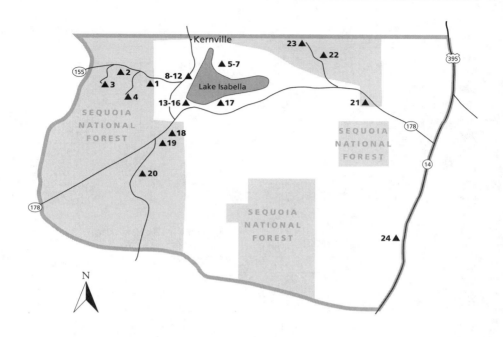

1 Greenhorn Mountain County Park

Location: 7 miles west of Wofford Heights.
Sites: 70 sites for tents and RVs up to 25 feet long.
Facilities: Picnic tables, fire rings, grills, drinking water, flush toilets, showers, playground.
Fee per night: $6, pets $2.
Agency: Kern County Parks Department, 760-376-6780.
Activities: Hiking.
Finding the campground: From Wofford Heights, drive 7 miles west on California 155 to the entrance on the left.

About the campground: Elevation 6,000 feet. Stay limit 14 days. Open April through October.

2 Cedar Creek

Location: 10 miles west of Wofford Heights.
Sites: 10 sites for tents.
Facilities: Picnic tables, fire rings, drinking water (May through October only), vault toilets.
Fee per night: None.

	Group sites	RV sites	Max. RV length	Hookups	Toilets	Showers	Drinking water	Dump station	Pets	Wheelchair	Recreation	Fee ($)	Season	Can reserve
1 Greenhorn Mountain		•	25		F	•	•		•		H	6	Apr–Oct	
2 Cedar Creek					V	•			•		F			
3 Alder Creek		•	20		V				•		HF		May–Oct	
4 Evans Flat		•	20		C				•		HR		May–Sep	
5 Camp 9		•			F	•	•	•	•		SFBL	6–10		•
6 Stine Cove Rec Area		•			C				•		SFB			
7 Hanning Flat		•			C				•		SFB			
8 Live Oak North/South	•	•	30		F	•	•		•		SFB	14	See entry	
9 Live Oak	•	•	30		F	•	•		•		SFB	80		•
10 Tillie Creek	•	•	45		F	•	•	•	•	•	SFB	14		•
11 Boulder Gulch		•	45		F	•	•		•		SFB	14	May–Sep	
12 Hungry Gulch		•	30		F	•	•		•		SFB	14	May–Sep	
13 French Gulch	•	•			F	•	•		•		SFB	150		•
14 Pioneer Point		•	30		F	•	•		•		SFB	14		
15 Main Dam		•	45		F		•	•	•		SFB	12	May–Sep	
16 Auxiliary Dam		•			F			•	•		SFB			
17 Paradise Cove		•			F	•	•	•	•		SFB	14		
18 Sandy Flat		•	24		V	•			•	•	F	12	May–Oct	•
19 Hobo		•	24		V	•			•		F	12	May–Sep	•
20 Breckenridge					C				•		H		May–Oct	
21 Walker Pass		•			P	•			•		H			
22 Long Valley		•			P	•			•		HSF			
23 Chimney Creek		•	25		P	•			•		H			
24 Red Rock Canyon		•	30		P	•	•	•	•		H	10–12		

Hookups: W = Water E = Electric S = Sewer
Toilets: F = Flush V = Vault P = Pit C = Chemical
Recreation: H = Hiking S = Swimming F = Fishing B = Boating L = Boat Launch O = Off-highway Driving R = Horseback Riding
Maximum Trailer/RV Length given in feet. **Stay Limit** given in days. **Fee** given in dollars.
If no entry under **Season,** campground is open all year. If no entry under **Fee,** camping is free.

Agency: Sequoia National Forest, Greenhorn Ranger District, 760-379-5646.
Activities: Fishing.
Finding the campground: From Wofford Heights, drive west 10 miles on California 155.

About the campground: Elevation 4,800 feet. Stay limit 14 days. Open all year.

3 Alder Creek

Location: 16 miles west of Wofford Heights.
Sites: 12 sites for tents and RVs up to 20 feet long.

Facilities: Picnic tables, fire rings, vault toilets. No drinking water.
Fee per night: None.
Agency: Sequoia National Forest, Greenhorn Ranger District, 760-379-5646.
Activities: Hiking, fishing.
Finding the campground: From Wofford Heights, drive 12.5 miles west on California 155, turn left onto FR 25S04, and drive 3 miles.

About the campground: Elevation 3,900 feet. Stay limit 14 days. Open May through October.

4 Evans Flat

Location: 15 miles southwest of Wofford Heights.
Sites: 16 sites for tents and RVs up to 20 feet long.
Facilities: Picnic tables, fire rings, portable toilet, corrals. No drinking water.
Fee per night: None.
Agency: Sequoia National Forest, Greenhorn Ranger District, 760-379-5646.
Activities: Hiking, horseback riding.
Finding the campground: From Wofford Heights, drive 7 miles west on California 155 to Greenhorn Summit, turn left onto Rancheria Road, and drive south for 8 miles.

About the campground: Evans Flat has a pasture and four corrals, but water for horses is not always available. Stay limit 14 days. Elevation 6,200 feet. Open May through September.

5 Isabella Lake: Camp 9

Location: 5 miles south of Kernville.
Sites: 109 sites for tents and RVs.
Facilities: Drinking water, flush toilets, dump station, boat launch, fish-cleaning station.
Fee per night: $6-$10. For reservations, call 800-280-CAMP. Reservation fee, $8.65.
Agency: Sequoia National Forest, Greenhorn Ranger District, 760-379-5646.
Activities: Swimming, fishing, boating, waterskiing, jet skiing, sailboarding.
Finding the campground: From Kernville, drive south 5 miles on Sierra Way.

About the campground: Camp 9 is on the north shore of Isabella Lake. Several marinas in the area offer boat rental and services, and outfitters offer kayak rental and instruction, as well as whitewater rafting trips. Supplies can be purchased in Kernville, Wofford Heights, Lake Isabella, Kernvale, and Mountain Mesa. Reservations are recommended for all the campgrounds in the Isabella Lake area, especially for holiday and summer weekends. Stay limit 14 days. Open all year.

In addition to the established campgrounds on Isabella Lake, open camping is available at no charge in the 2-mile stretch of undeveloped shoreline from the auxiliary dam to South Fork Recreation Area. There are no facilities, and the area is best suited for self-contained vehicles. Access is best from the auxiliary dam and old Isabella Road.

6 Isabella Lake: Stine Cove Recreation Area

Location: 7 miles south of Kernville.
Sites: Open camping for tents and RVs.
Facilities: Chemical toilets, no water.
Fee: None.
Agency: Sequoia National Forest, Greenhorn Ranger District, 760-379-5646.
Activities: Swimming, fishing, boating, waterskiing, jet skiing, sailboarding.
Finding the campground: From Kernville, drive south on Sierra Way, about 2 miles past Camp 9 (see above).

About the campground: Stine Cove is situated on the water and resembles a large parking lot, with some grass and a few trees. It is best suited for self-contained units. For more about the attractions of the area, see Camp 9 (No. 5 above). Stay limit 14 days. Open all year.

7 Isabella Lake: Hanning Flat

Location: 8 miles south of Kernville.
Sites: Open camping for tents and RVs.
Facilities: Chemical toilets, no water.
Fee: None.
Agency: Sequoia National Forest, Greenhorn Ranger District, 760-379-5646.
Activities: Swimming, fishing, boating, waterskiing, jet skiing, sailboarding.
Finding the campground: From Kernville, drive south on Sierra Way, about 1 mile past Stine Cove (see above).

About the campground: Hanning Flat is situated on the water. For more information about the attractions of the area, see Camp 9 (No. 5 above). Stay limit 14 days. Open all year.

8 Isabella Lake: Live Oak North & South

Location: Half mile south of Wofford Heights.
Sites: 60 sites (North) and 90 sites (South) for tents and RVs up to 30 feet long, plus 1 group site that accommodates up to 100 people.
Facilities: Picnic tables, grills, fire rings, flush toilets, showers, drinkingwater.
Fee per night: $14 individual sites, $150 group site.
Agency: Sequoia National Forest, Greenhorn Ranger District, 760-379-5646.
Activities: Swimming, fishing, boating, waterskiing, jet skiing, sailboarding.
Finding the campgrounds: From Wofford Heights, drive south on California 155 for half a mile.

About the campgrounds: These campgrounds are only open on holiday weekends to accommodate overflow. See Camp 9 (No. 5 above) for more information about the attractions of this area.

9 | Isabella Lake: Live Oak Group

Location: Half mile south of Wofford Heights.
Sites: 1 group site for tents or RVs up to 30 feet long, accommodating up to 80 people.
Facilities: Picnic tables, grills, fire rings, flush toilets, showers, drinking water.
Fee per night: $80. Reservations required; call 800-280-CAMP. Reservation fee, $15.
Agency: Sequoia National Forest, Greenhorn Ranger District, 760-379-5646.
Activities: Swimming, fishing, boating, waterskiing, jet skiing, sailboarding.
Finding the campground: From Wofford Heights, drive south on California 155 for half a mile.

About the campground: For more information about the attractions of this area, see Camp 9 (No. 5 above). Stay limit 14 days. Open all year.

10 | Isabella Lake: Tillie Creek

Location: 1 mile south of Wofford Heights.
Sites: 159 sites for tents and RVs up to 45 feet long, including 80 sites with pull-thrus, plus 4 group sites.
Facilities: Picnic tables, fire rings, drinking water, flush toilets, showers, dump station, playground, fish-cleaning station.
Fee per night: $14 individuals, $75-$120 groups. Reservations required for group sites; call 800-280-CAMP. Reservation fee, $15.
Agency: Sequoia National Forest, Greenhorn Ranger District, 760-379-5646.
Activities: Swimming, fishing, boating, waterskiing, jet skiing, sailboarding.
Finding the campground: From Wofford Heights, drive south on California 155 for 1 mile.

About the campground: Tillie Creek is located on the water on the west shore of the lake. See Camp 9 (No. 5 above) for more about the attractions of this area. Stay limit 14 days. Open all year.

11 | Isabella Lake: Boulder Gulch

Location: 2.6 miles south of Wofford Heights.
Sites: 78 sites for tents and RVs up to 45 feet long, including 35 sites with pull-thrus.
Facilities: Picnic tables, fire rings, grills, drinking water, flush toilets, showers, fish-cleaning station.
Fee per night: $14.
Agency: Sequoia National Forest, Greenhorn Ranger District, 760-379-5646.
Activities: Swimming, fishing, boating, waterskiing, jet skiing, sailboarding.
Finding the campground: From Wofford Heights, drive south on California 155 for 2.6 miles.

About the campground: Boulder Gulch is situated on the water on the west shore of Isabella Lake. It is aptly named, as large boulders, including a huge centerpiece, occupy most of the free space in the campground. For more about the attractions of this area, see Camp 9 (No. 5 above). Stay limit 14 days. Open May 15 through September.

12 Isabella Lake: Hungry Gulch

Location: 2.6 miles south of Wofford Heights.
Sites: 78 sites for tents and RVs up to 30 feet long, including 40 sites with pull-thrus.
Facilities: Picnic tables, fire rings, grills, drinking water, flush toilets, showers, playground.
Fee per night: $14.
Agency: Sequoia National Forest, Greenhorn Ranger District, 760-379-5646.
Activities: Swimming, fishing, boating, waterskiing, jet skiing, sailboarding.
Finding the campground: From Wofford Heights, drive south on California 155 for 2.6 miles. Hungry Gulch is across the highway from Boulder Gulch Campground (see above).

About the campground: See Camp 9 (No. 5 above) for more about the attractions of this area. Stay limit 14 days. Open May 15 through September.

13 Isabella Lake: French Gulch

Location: 4 miles south of Wofford Heights.
Sites: 1 group site for tents or RVs that accommodates up to 100 people.
Facilities: Picnic tables, fire rings, grills, drinking water, flush toilets, showers.
Fee per night: $150. Reservations required, call 800-280-CAMP. Reservation fee, $15.
Agency: Sequoia National Forest, Greenhorn Ranger District, 760-379-5646.
Activities: Swimming, fishing, boating, waterskiing, jet skiing, sailboarding.
Finding the campground: From Wofford Heights, drive south 4 miles on California 155.

About the campground: French Gulch is on the water on the western shore of Isabella Lake. See Camp 9 (No. 5 above) for more about the attractions of this area. Stay limit 14 days. Open all year.

14 Isabella Lake: Pioneer Point

Location: 5 miles south of Wofford Heights.
Sites: 78 sites for tents and RVs up to 30 feet long, including 50 sites with pull-thrus.
Facilities: Picnic tables, fire rings, grills, drinking water, flush toilets, showers, playground, fish-cleaning station, marina access.
Fee per night: $14.

Pioneer Point Marina is just across the highway from one of the many campgrounds on Isabella Lake.

Agency: Sequoia National Forest, Greenhorn Ranger District, 760-379-5646.
Activities: Swimming, fishing, boating, waterskiing, jet skiing, sailboarding.
Finding the campground: From Wofford Heights, drive 5 miles south on California 155.

About the campground: Pioneer Point Campground is across the highway from the Pioneer Point Marina. See Camp 9 (No. 5 above) for more about the attractions of this area. Stay limit 14 days. Open all year.

15 Isabella Lake: Main Dam

Location: 1.5 miles north of the town of Lake Isabella.
Sites: 82 sites for tents and RVs up to 45 feet long.
Facilities: Picnic tables, fire rings, grills, drinking water, flush toilets, dump station.
Fee per night: $12.
Agency: Sequoia National Forest, Greenhorn Ranger District, 760-379-5646.
Activities: Swimming, fishing, boating, waterskiing, jet skiing, sailboarding.
Finding the campground: From the town of Lake Isabella, drive 1.5 miles north on California 155.

About the campground: The campground is adjacent to Main Dam, the westernmost of two dams on Isabella Lake. See Camp 9 (No. 5 above) for more about the attractions of this area. Stay limit 14 days. Open May through September.

16 Isabella Lake: Auxiliary Dam

Location: 1 mile northeast of the town of Lake Isabella.
Sites: Open camping area for tents and RVs.
Facilities: Flush and chemical toilets, dump station.
Fee per night: None.
Agency: Sequoia National Forest, Greenhorn Ranger District, 760-379-5646.
Activities: Swimming, fishing, boating, waterskiing, jet skiing, sailboarding.
Finding the campground: From the town of Lake Isabella, drive 1 mile northeast on California 178.

About the campground: The campground is on the water on the southwest shore of Isabella Lake, just east of the auxiliary dam, the easternmost of two dams on the lake. It resembles a large, dirt parking lot, with no grass and no trees. It is best suited for self-contained units. See Camp 9 (No. 5 above) for more about the attractions of this area. Stay limit 14 days. Open all year.

17 Isabella Lake: Paradise Cove

Location: 4 miles northeast of the town of Lake Isabella.
Sites: 58 sites for tents and RVs, plus 80 open campsites for self-contained RVs.
Facilities: Picnic tables, fire rings, grills, drinking water, flush toilets, showers, dump station, fish-cleaning station.
Fee per night: $14.
Agency: Sequoia National Forest, Greenhorn Ranger District, 760-379-5646.
Activities: Swimming, fishing, boating, waterskiing, jet skiing, sailboarding.
Finding the campground: From the town of Lake Isabella, take California 178 northeast for 4 miles.

About the campground: Paradise Cove campsites are tiered in several levels, from the highway to the shoreline. The open sites for self-contained RVs are arranged close together, parking-lot style, but they are closest to the water. For more about the attractions of this area, see Camp 9 (No. 5 above). Stay limit 14 days. Open all year.

18 Sandy Flat

Location: 5 miles southwest of the town of Lake Isabella.
Sites: 35 sites for tents and RVs up to 24 feet long.
Facilities: Picnic tables, fire rings, drinking water, vault toilets.
Fee per night: $12. For reservations, call 800-280-CAMP. Reservation fee, $8.65.
Agency: Sequoia National Forest, Greenhorn Ranger District, 760-379-5646.
Activities: Fishing, rafting.
Finding the campground: From the town of Lake Isabella, drive 4 miles southwest on California 178 to Borel Road. Turn left and drive 0.3 mile to Old Kern Canyon Road, turn right, and drive about half a mile.

About the campground: Sandy Flat is on the bank of the Kern River at an elevation of 2,300 feet. It has launch sites for rafts to enter the river. Stay limit 14 days. Open May through October.

19 Hobo

Location: 6 miles southwest of the town of Lake Isabella.
Sites: 35 sites for tents, 10 sites for RVs up to 24 feet long; no trailers.
Facilities: Picnic tables, fire rings, drinking water, vault toilets.
Fee per night: $12. For reservations, call 800-280-CAMP. Reservation fee, $8.65.
Agency: Sequoia National Forest, Greenhorn Ranger District, 760-379-5646.
Activities: Fishing.
Finding the campground: From the town of Lake Isabella, drive 4 miles southwest on California 178 to Borel Road, turn left, and drive 0.3 mile to Old Kern Canyon Road. Turn right and drive 2 miles.

About the campground: Hobo is situated on the bank of the Kern River at an elevation of 2,300 feet. Stay limit 14 days. Open May through September.

20 Breckenridge

Location: 25 miles southwest of the town of Lake Isabella.
Sites: 8 sites for tents.
Facilities: Picnic tables, fire rings, portable toilets. No drinking water.
Fee per night: None.
Agency: Sequoia National Forest, Greenhorn Ranger District, 760-379-5646.
Activities: Hiking.
Finding the campground: From the intersection of California 178 and Lake Isabella Boulevard in the town of Lake Isabella, take Lake Isabella Boulevard (which becomes Caliente Bodfish Road) south for 12 miles to Havilah. Continue on Caliente Bodfish Road for 2.5 miles, turn right onto FR 28S06, and drive 10 miles.

About the campground: Elevation 7,100 feet. Stay limit 14 days. Open May through October.

21 Walker Pass

Location: 16 miles west of Ridgecrest.
Sites: 10 sites for tents and RVs.
Facilities: Drinking water, pit toilets.
Fee per night: None.
Agency: Bureau of Land Management, Caliente Resource Area, 805-861-4236.
Activities: Hiking.
Finding the campground: From the intersection of U.S. Highway 395 and California 178 west of Ridgecrest, drive west on CA 178 for 16 miles. Upon reaching the top of Walker Pass, continue slowly, watching for the campground sign about 100 yards farther on the left.

About the campground: Walker Pass is a trailhead for the Pacific Crest Trail, which passes less than a quarter of a mile away. Elevation 5,200 feet. Stay limit 14 days. Open all year.

22 Long Valley

Location: 36 miles northwest of Ridgecrest.
Sites: 13 sites for tents and RVs.
Facilities: Picnic tables, fire rings, drinking water, pit toilets.
Fee per night: None.
Agency: Bureau of Land Management, Caliente Resource Area, 805-861-4236.
Activities: Hiking, swimming, and fishing nearby.
Finding the campground: From the intersection of U.S. Highway 395 and California 178 west of Ridgecrest, drive west 26 miles on CA 178, turn right onto Canebreak Road, and follow the signs about 10 miles to the campground.

About the campground: Elevation 5,200 feet. Stay limit 14 days. Open all year.

23 Chimney Creek

Location: 38 miles northwest of Ridgecrest.
Sites: 36 sites for tents and RVs up to 25 feet long.
Facilities: Picnic tables, fire rings, drinking water, pit toilets.
Fee per night: None.
Agency: Bureau of Land Management, Caliente Resource Area, 805-861-4236.
Activities: Hiking.
Finding the campground: From the intersection of U.S. Highway 395 and California 178 west of Ridgecrest, drive west 26 miles on CA 178, turn right onto Canebreak Road, and follow the signs about 12 miles to the campground.

About the campground: Chimney Creek is located on the Pacific Crest Trail. Elevation 5,900 feet. Stay limit 14 days. Open all year.

24 Red Rock Canyon State Park

Location: 25 miles northeast of Mojave.
Sites: 50 sites for tents and RVs up to 30 feet long.
Facilities: Picnic tables, grills, drinking water, pit toilets, dump station.
Fee per night: $10-$12, pets $1.
Agency: California Department of Parks and Recreation, 805-942-0662.
Activities: Hiking, four-wheel-drive exploring.
Finding the campground: From the intersection of California 58 and CA 14 north of Mojave, take CA 14 northeast for 25 miles.

About the campground: This 28,000-acre park is noted for its scenic red sandstone cliffs, including the Red Cliffs Natural Preserve, which is visible on the east side of the highway. Other interesting rock formations include outcroppings

Many campsites in Red Rock Canyon State Park are located dramatically close to the scenic red sandstone cliffs for which the park is known.

of orange sandstone, pink tuff, and brown lava. Several short trails and a nature loop begin within a mile of the campground, and a 3-mile round trip through the Red Cliffs Natural Preserve begins 2 miles from a parking lot off the highway. Many campsites are set dramatically close to twisted rock cliffs and fluted walls, providing a unique setting for tents and RVs. While scattered Joshua trees dot the park, the campground has no shade to help ameliorate the heat of summer days. But the night sky is magnificent year-round. A visitor center is open on weekends. Elevation 2,600 feet. Stay limit 14 days. Open all year.

LOS ANGELES COUNTY

The City of Angels could just as easily be called the City of Cinema, the City of Museums, or the City of World-Class Shopping. Among its tourist attractions are Universal Studios Hollywood, the *Queen Mary*, and Six Flags Magic

LOS ANGELES COUNTY AREA MAP

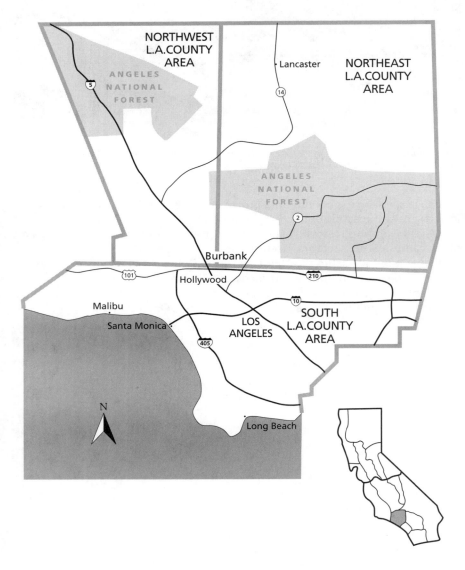

Mountain. The J. Paul Getty Museum, the newer Getty Center, the Museum of Contemporary Art, and the Southwest Museum are just four of its many museums.

But Los Angeles County offers much more than the lights and lure of the big city. The Angeles National Forest and the San Gabriel Mountains provide an outdoor environment for virtually every summer and winter outdoor activity. And its coastline also presents year-round opportunities. Scenic Malibu has ten public-access paths to the shoreline, where its star-studded beach homes are on display. Santa Monica Pier, Third Street Promenade, and the Venice Beach Boardwalk contribute musicians, mimes, sidewalk artists, and eccentrics to the scene. For those who prefer to get away from the commercialism, 15 miles of sand stretches from Marina del Rey to Redondo Beach and includes Manhattan and Hermosa Beaches.

Year-round fine weather has attracted tourists and residents to the Los Angeles area since before the turn of the twentieth century. From the coastal region to the edge of the mountains, mild winters and cool summers are the norm. Average maximum/minimum temperatures range in summer from 82 to 62 degrees F and in winter from 68 to 48 degrees. Spring brings temperatures from 71 to 53 degrees F, and fall from 78 to 58 degrees F. The percentage of average days of sunshine is fairly consistent year-round: 77 percent in summer, 75 in fall, 71 in winter, and 70 in the spring.

This book divides Los Angeles County into three parts: the Northwest, Northeast, and South.

NORTHWEST L.A. COUNTY

Most of the campgrounds described in this section of the book are in the Angeles National Forest, 1,000 square miles of wilderness running almost the entire width of northern Los Angeles County. As the backyard of the nation's second largest city, the forest hosts millions of visitors every year. A landscape of rugged mountains, canyons, streams, and lakes, it attracts outdoor enthusiasts year-round. More than 500 miles of trails, 60 campgrounds, and dozens of fishing streams lure diverse groups seeking to hike, fish, swim, hunt, ride horseback, mountain bike, backpack, drive off-highway-vehicles, and camp. Winter sports enthusiasts can enjoy the facilities of nine major ski areas. Many campgrounds serve as excellent bases or starting points for wilderness adventures in this diverse region, although many are closed or inaccessible during the winter.

Three major lakes in the region provide year-round water sports. Castaic and Pyramid Lakes, north of Santa Clarita, feature well-developed state park facilities. Smaller Bouquet Reservoir provides a more isolated experience. For an experience of a different kind, the world-famous Six Flags Magic Mountain Amusement Park lies just west of Santa Clarita.

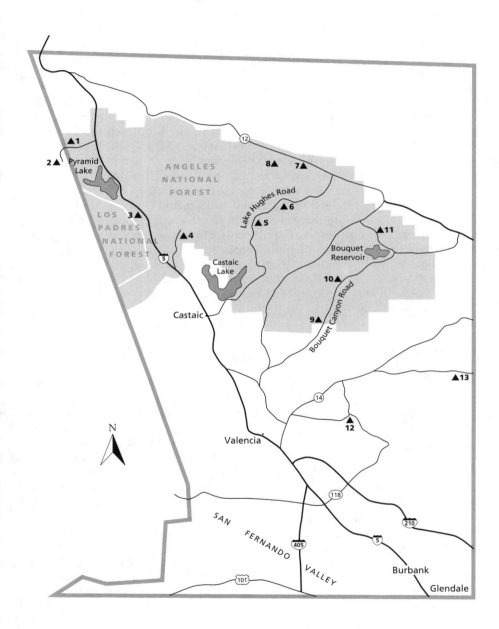

	Group sites	RV sites	Max. RV length	Hookups	Toilets	Showers	Drinking water	Dump station	Pets	Wheelchair	Recreation	Fee ($)	Season	Can reserve
1 Los Almos	•	•	26		F		•	•	•	•	HSFB	10		
2 Hardluck		•	25		P				•		HS			
3 Oak Flat		•	18		V				•		HF			
4 Cienaga					V				•		HS		May–Dec	
5 Prospect		•	18		V				•		HS			
6 Cottonwood		•	16		V				•		HS			
7 Upper Shake					V				•		H		May–Dec	
8 Sawmill		•	16		V				•		H			
9 Zuni					V				•		HF			
10 Streamside					V				•		HF			
11 Spunky					V				•		H		May–Nov	
12 Live Oak		•	30		V		•		•		H	10		
13 Soledad		•	25		V		•		•		H	10		

Hookups: W = Water   E = Electric   S = Sewer
Toilets: F = Flush   V = Vault   P = Pit   C = Chemical
Recreation: H = Hiking   S = Swimming   F = Fishing   B = Boating   L = Boat Launch   O = Off-highway Driving   R = Horseback Riding
Maximum Trailer/RV Length given in feet.   **Stay Limit** given in days.   **Fee** given in dollars.
If no entry under **Season,** campground is open all year. If no entry under **Fee,** camping is free.

1 Los Alamos

Location: 8 miles south of Gorman.
Sites: 93 sites for tents and RVs up to 26 feet long, plus 3 group sites that accommodate a total of 75 people.
Facilities: Picnic tables, fire rings, drinking water, flush toilets, dump station, store.
Fee per night: $10.
Agency: Angeles National Forest, Saugus District Office, 805-296-9710.
Activities: Hiking, swimming, fishing, boating nearby.
Finding the campground: From Gorman, take Interstate 5 south for 7 miles, exiting at Smokey Bear Road. Drive west for 1 mile, watching for campground signs.

About the campground: Pyramid Lake Recreation Area, 1.5 miles southeast of the campground, offers a myriad of water sports. Elevation 2,600 feet. Stay limit 14 days. Open all year.

2 Hardluck

Location: 11 miles south of Gorman.
Sites: 26 sites for tents and RVs up to 25 feet long.
Facilities: Picnic tables, fire rings, pit toilets. No drinking water.

Fee per night: None.
Agency: Los Padres National Forest, Mount Pinos Ranger District, 805-245-3731.
Activities: Hiking, swimming.
Finding the campground: From Gorman, take Interstate 5 south for 7 miles, exiting at Smokey Bear Road. Drive west for 1.7 miles to a dirt road that leads left. Take this road for 2 miles.

About the campground: Although situated just across the border in Ventura County, Hardluck can be reached by vehicle only from Los Angeles County. The campground lies along the bank of the Smith Fork of Piru Creek, and swimming is usually possible in spring and fall. The campground is a little more than 3 miles from the Pyramid Lake Recreation Area. Elevation 2,800 feet. Stay limit 14 days. Open all year.

3 | Oak Flat

Location: 9 miles north of Castaic.
Sites: 27 sites for tents and RVs up to 18 feet long.
Facilities: Picnic tables, fire rings, vault toilets. No drinking water.
Fee per night: None.
Agency: Angeles National Forest, Saugus District Office, 805-296-9710.
Activities: Hiking, fishing.
Finding the campground: From Castaic, take Interstate 5 north for 6 miles to the next exit (Templin Highway). Take Templin northwest for 3 miles.

About the campground: Elevation 2,800 feet. Stay limit 14 days. Open all year.

4 | Cienaga

Location: 12 miles north of Castaic.
Sites: 12 sites for tents.
Facilities: Picnic tables, fire rings, vault toilets. No drinking water.
Fee per night: None.
Agency: Angeles National Forest, Saugus District Office, 805-296-9710.
Activities: Hiking, seasonal swimming.
Finding the campground: From Castaic, take Interstate 5 north for 6 miles to the next exit (Templin Highway). Take Templin northwest for about 6 miles.

About the campground: Elevation 2,100 feet. Stay limit 14 days. Open May through December.

5 | Prospect

Location: 15 miles north of Castaic.
Sites: 22 sites for tents and RVs up to 18 feet long.
Facilities: Picnic tables, fire rings, vault toilets. No drinking water.
Fee per night: None.

Agency: Angeles National Forest, Saugus District Office, 805-296-9710.
Activities: Hiking, seasonal swimming.
Finding the campground: From Castaic, drive north on Lake Hughes Road for about 15 miles.

About the campground: Elevation 2,150 feet. Stay limit 14 days. Open all year.

6 Cottonwood

Location: 19 miles northeast of Castaic.
Sites: 22 sites for tents and RVs up to 16 feet long.
Facilities: Picnic tables, fire rings, vault toilets. No drinking water.
Fee per night: None.
Agency: Angeles National Forest, Saugus District Office, 805-296-9710.
Activities: Hiking, seasonal swimming.
Finding the campground: From Castaic, drive north then northeast on Lake Hughes Road for about 19 miles.

About the campground: Elevation 2,600 feet. Stay limit 14 days. Open all year.

7 Upper Shake

Location: 28 miles northeast of Castaic.
Sites: 18 sites for tents.
Facilities: Picnic tables, fire rings, vault toilets. No drinking water.
Fee per night: None.
Agency: Angeles National Forest, Saugus District Office, 805-296-9710.
Activities: Hiking.
Finding the campground: From Castaic, drive north on Lake Hughes Road for about 24 miles to Lake Hughes. Turn left onto Pine Canyon Road (N2) and drive 4.3 miles.

About the campground: Elevation 4,400 feet. Stay limit 14 days. Open May through December.

8 Sawmill

Location: 32 miles north of Castaic.
Sites: 8 sites for tents and RVs up to 16 feet long.
Facilities: Picnic tables, fire rings, vault toilets. No drinking water.
Fee per night: None.
Agency: Angeles National Forest, Saugus District Office, 805-296-9710.
Activities: Hiking.
Finding the campground: From Castaic, drive north on Lake Hughes Road for about 24 miles to Lake Hughes. Turn left onto Pine Canyon Road (N2) and drive 4.7 miles to FR 7N23 (unpaved). Turn left and drive 3.5 miles.

About the campground: The campground is located along the Pacific Crest Trail, providing the opportunity to hike a portion of this National Scenic Trail. Elevation 5,200 feet. Stay limit 14 days. Open all year.

9 Zuni

Location: 18.5 miles east of Castaic.
Sites: 10 sites for tents.
Facilities: Picnic tables, fire rings, vault toilets. No drinking water.
Fee per night: None.
Agency: Angeles National Forest, Saugus District Office, 805-296-9710.
Activities: Hiking, fishing.
Finding the campground: From Interstate 5, 6 miles south of Castaic, take the Magic Mountain Road exit and drive east for 2.5 miles to Bouquet Canyon Road. Turn left and drive about 10 miles.

About the campground: Stay limit 14 days. Open all year.

10 Streamside

Location: 22 miles east of Castaic.
Sites: 9 sites for tents.
Facilities: Picnic tables, fire rings, vault toilets. No drinking water.
Fee per night: None.
Agency: Angeles National Forest, Saugus District Office, 805-296-9710.
Activities: Hiking, fishing.
Finding the campground: From Interstate 5, 6 miles south of Castaic, take the Magic Mountain Road exit and drive east for 2.5 miles to Bouquet Canyon Road. Turn left and drive about 13 miles.

About the campground: Elevation 2,500 feet. Stay limit 14 days. Open all year.

11 Spunky

Location: 30 miles northeast of Castaic.
Sites: 10 sites for tents.
Facilities: Picnic tables, vault toilets. No drinking water.
Fee per night: None.
Agency: Angeles National Forest, Saugus District Office, 805-296-9710.
Activities: Hiking.
Finding the campground: From Interstate 5, 6 miles south of Castaic, take the Magic Mountain Road exit and drive east for 2.5 miles to Bouquet Canyon Road. Turn left and drive about 18 miles to Spunky Canyon Road at the eastern end of Bouquet Reservoir. Turn left and drive about 3 miles.

About the campground: Elevation 3,300 feet. Stay limit 14 days. Open May through November.

12 Live Oak

Location: 8 miles north of San Fernando.
Sites: 7 sites for tents and RVs up to 30 feet long.
Facilities: Picnic tables, fire rings, drinking water, vault toilets.
Fee per night: $10.
Agency: Angeles National Forest, Tujunga District Office, 818-899-1900.
Activities: Hiking, mountain biking.
Finding the campground: From the intersection of Interstate 5 and California 14 northwest of San Fernando, drive north on CA 14 for 3 miles to the exit for Placerita Canyon State Park (Placerita Canyon Road). Drive east on Placerita Canyon Road for about 5 miles, passing the state park en route.

About the campground: Elevation 2,000 feet. Stay limit 14 days. Open all year.

13 Soledad

Location: 15 miles northeast of San Fernando.
Sites: 6 sites for tents and RVs up to 25 feet.
Facilities: Picnic tables, fire rings, drinking water, vault toilets.
Fee per night: $10.
Agency: Angeles National Forest, Tujunga District Office, 818-899-1900.
Activities: Hiking.
Finding the campground: From the intersection of Interstate 5 and California 14 northwest of San Fernando, drive north on CA 14 for 10 miles to the exit for Soledad Canyon Road. Turn east onto Soledad Canyon Road and drive about 5 miles.

About the campground: Elevation 2,000 feet. Stay limit 14 days. Open all year.

NORTHEAST L.A. COUNTY

As in Northwest L.A. County, the Angeles National Forest dominates the landscape, along with the San Gabriel Mountains. The Angeles Crest Scenic Byway (California 2), which runs 66 miles from LaCanada to Wrightwood, climbs to the crest of the San Gabriels, where mile after mile of scenic vistas unfold. Two visitor centers and four campgrounds are located along the route, with more campgrounds a short distance off the highway. A worthwhile side trip is Mount Wilson, where one of the world's largest telescopes is located. It provides sweeping views across the Los Angeles basin to the Pacific Ocean.

1 Saddleback Butte State Park

Location: 17 miles east of Lancaster.
Sites: 50 sites for tents and RVs up to 30 feet long, plus 1 group site that accommodates up to 30 people.

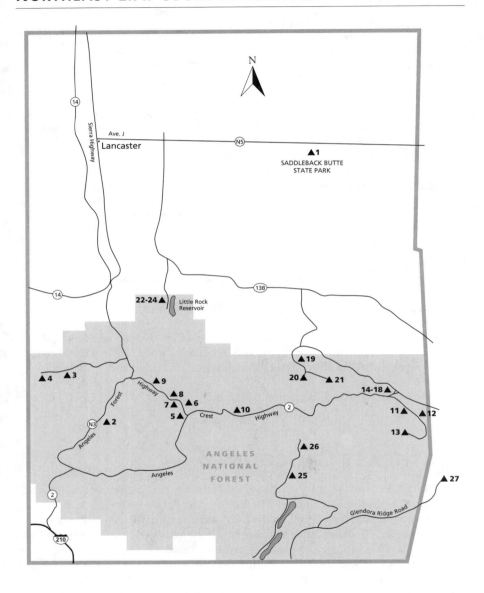

Facilities: Picnic tables, barbecue grills, drinking water, flush toilets, dump station.

Fee per night: $13 for individual sites, $45 for group site. To reserve group site only, call Parknet, 800-444-7275. Reservation fee, $13.50.

Agency: California Department of Parks and Recreation, 805-942-0662.

Activities: Hiking.

Finding the campground: From the intersection of California 14/138 and CA

		Group sites	RV sites	Max. RV length	Hookups	Toilets	Showers	Drinking water	Dump station	Pets	Wheelchair	Recreation	Fee ($)	Season	Can reserve
1	Saddleback Butte State Park	•	•	30		F		•	•	•	•	H	13		•
2	Monte Cristo		•	30		V		•		•	•	H	10		
3	Lightning Point	•				F		•		•		HR	30	Apr–Oct	•
4	Messenger Flat					V		•		•		HR	8	Apr–Nov	
5	Chilao Rec Area	•	•	40		V		•		•	•	H	12		•
6	Bandido	•	•	40		V		•				HR	50	Apr–Nov	•
7	Horse Flats		•	36		V		•		•	•	HR	10	Apr–Nov	
8	Sulphur Springs	•	•	18		V		•				H	100	Apr–Sep	•
9	Mount Pacifico					V				•		HR		May–Nov	
10	Buckhorn		•	22		V		•		•		H	12	Apr–Nov	
11	Blue Ridge		•	20		V				•		H		May–Nov	
12	Guffy					V				•		H		May–Nov	
13	Lupine					V				•		H		May–Nov	
14	Table Mountain		•	32		V		•		•		H	12	May–Nov	
15	Apple Tree					V		•		•		H	8		
16	Lake		•	20		V		•		•		HSFBL	10	May–Nov	
17	Mountain Oak		•	24		F		•		•		H	10	May–Nov	
18	Jackson Flat	•				F		•		•		H	75–90	May–Nov	•
19	Sycamore Flats		•	18		V		•		•		HF	5		
20	South Fork		•	16		V		•		•		HS	5	May–Nov	
21	Big Rock					V				•		H	5	May–Nov	
22	Rocky Point					V		•		•	•	HOSFBL	10		
23	Sage					V		•		•	•	HOSFB	10		
24	Basin		•	28		V		•		•		HOSFB	10		
25	Coldbrook		•	22		V		•		•		HF	8		
26	Crystal Lake Rec Area	•	•	22		F		•		•	•	HF	12		•
27	Manker Flats		•	22		F		•		•		H	8	May–Sep	

Hookups: W = Water   E = Electric   S = Sewer
Toilets: F = Flush   V = Vault   P = Pit   C = Chemical
Recreation: H = Hiking   S = Swimming   F = Fishing   B = Boating   L = Boat Launch   O = Off-highway driving   R = Horseback Riding
Maximum Trailer/RV Length given in feet.   **Stay Limit** given in days.   **Fee** given in dollars.
If no entry under **Season,** campground is open all year. If no entry under **Fee,** camping is free.

N5 (Avenue J) in Lancaster, drive east on CA N5 for 17 miles.

About the campground: Formerly called Joshua Tree State Park, this 2,955-acre desert preserve offers a half-mile nature trail and a 5.2-mile loop trail to the summit of Saddleback Butte (elevation 3,651 feet). The trail climbs about 950 feet. Sweeping views, rock formations, and an open Joshua tree forest make the park well worth a visit. Except for ramadas over a few tables in the picnic area, there is no shade in the park. Elevation 2,700 feet. Stay limit 15 days. Open all year.

2 Monte Cristo

Location: 19 miles north of Pasadena.
Sites: 19 sites for tents and RVs up to 30 feet long.
Facilities: Picnic tables, fire rings, drinking water, vault toilets.
Fee per night: $10.
Agency: Angeles National Forest, Tujunga District Office, 818-899-1900.
Activities: Hiking, mountain biking.
Finding the campground: From the intersection of Interstate 210 and California 2 (Angeles Crest Highway) north of Pasadena, drive north on CA 2 for about 10 miles to Angeles Forest Highway (N3). Turn left and drive about 9 miles.

About the campground: Elevation 3,600 feet. Stay limit 14 days. Open all year.

3 Lightning Point

Location: 31 miles north of Pasadena.
Sites: 6 group sites accommodating a total of 210 people. Tents only.
Facilities: Picnic tables, fire rings, drinking water, flush toilets, 25 horse corrals.
Fee per night: $30. Reservations required; call 818-899-1900.
Agency: Angeles National Forest, Tujunga District Office, 818-899-1900.
Activities: Hiking, horseback riding.
Finding the campground: From the intersection of Interstate 210 and California 2 (Angeles Crest Highway) north of Pasadena, drive north on CA 2 for about 10 miles to Angeles Forest Highway (N3). Turn left and drive about 13 miles to FR 3N17. Turn left and drive 8 miles.

About the campground: Elevation 6,200 feet. Stay limit 14 days. Open April through October.

4 Messenger Flat

Location: 32 miles north of Pasadena.
Sites: 10 sites for tents.
Facilities: Picnic tables, fire rings, drinking water, vault toilets.
Fee per night: $8.
Agency: Angeles National Forest, Tujunga District Office, 818-899-1900.
Activities: Hiking, mountain biking, horseback riding.
Finding the campground: From the intersection of Interstate 210 and California 2 (Angeles Crest Highway) north of Pasadena, drive north on CA 2 for about 10 miles to Angeles Forest Highway (N3). Turn left and drive about 13 miles to FR 3N17. Turn left and drive 9 miles.

About the campground: A trail from the campground leads to the summit of Mount Gleason. Elevation 5,500 feet. Stay limit 14 days. Open April through November.

5 Chilao Recreation Area

Location: 26 miles north of Pasadena.
Sites: 111 sites for tents and RVs up to 40 feet long, plus 1 large group campground that accommodates up to 50 people.
Facilities: Picnic tables, fire rings, drinking water, vault toilets. A dump station is located at nearby Charlton Flat Picnic Area, near the visitor center.
Fee per night: $12 for individual sites, $100 for group site. Reservations required for groups; call 818-449-1749.
Agency: Angeles National Forest, Arroyo Seco District Office, 818-790-1151.
Activities: Hiking, mountain biking.
Finding the campground: From the intersection of Interstate 210 and California 2 (Angeles Crest Highway) north of Pasadena, drive north on CA 2 for about 26 miles.

About the campground: Chilao has four separate camping loops, all within half a mile of each other. Three of them—Meadow Loop, Manzanita Loop, and Little Pine Loop—are for individual tents and RVs. The group campground is called Coulter. Three nature loop trails and other hiking trails are in the area. A visitor center offers displays, books, brochures, and ranger presentations. Across the highway from the visitor center, Devil's Canyon Vista provides a broad panorama of the San Gabriel Wilderness and Twin Peaks. Elevation 5,300 feet. Stay limit 14 days. Individual sites open all year; group campground open April through November.

6 Bandido

Location: 30.5 miles north of Pasadena.
Sites: 2 group sites for tents and RVs up to 40 feet long, accommodating a total of 120 people.
Facilities: Picnic tables, fire rings, drinking water, vault toilets.
Fee per night: $50. Reservations required; call 818-449-1749.
Agency: Angeles National Forest, Arroyo Seco District Office, 818-790-1151.
Activities: Hiking, mountain biking, horseback riding.
Finding the campground: From the intersection of Interstate 210 and California 2 (Angeles Crest Highway) north of Pasadena, drive north on CA 2 for about 29 miles to FR 3N17. Turn left and drive about 1.5 miles.

About the campground: A short nature loop trail begins at the campground. The Chilao Visitor Center is only 1 mile away by trail, 4 miles by road. Elevation 5,700 feet. Stay limit 14 days. Open April through November.

7 Horse Flats

Location: 32 miles north of Pasadena.
Sites: 25 sites for tents and RVs up to 36 feet long.
Facilities: Picnic tables, fire rings, drinking water, vault toilets.
Fee per night: $10.

Agency: Angeles National Forest, Arroyo Seco District Office, 818-790-1151.
Activities: Hiking, mountain biking, horseback riding.
Finding the campground: From the intersection of Interstate 210 and California 2 (Angeles Crest Highway) north of Pasadena, drive north on CA 2 for about 29 miles to FR 3N17. Turn left and drive about 2.5 miles.

About the campground: The Chilao Visitor Center is only 1 mile away by trail, 4 miles by road. Elevation 5,700 feet. Stay limit 14 days. Open April through November.

8 Sulphur Springs

Location: 35 miles north of Pasadena.
Sites: 10 group sites for tents and RVs up to 18 feet long, accommodating a total of 80 people.
Facilities: Picnic tables, fire rings, drinking water, vault toilets.
Fee per night: $100. Reservations required; call 818-790-9523.
Agency: Angeles National Forest, Arroyo Seco District Office, 818-790-1151.
Activities: Hiking, mountain biking.
Finding the campground: From the intersection of Interstate 210 and California 2 (Angeles Crest Highway) north of Pasadena, drive north on CA 2 for about 29 miles to FR 3N17. Turn left and drive about 4.5 miles north to FR 5N04. Turn right and drive 1.5 miles.

About the campground: Elevation 5,200 feet. Stay limit 14 days. Open April through September.

9 Mount Pacifico

Location: 36 miles north of Pasadena.
Sites: 8 sites for tents.
Facilities: Picnic tables, fire rings, vault toilets. No drinking water.
Fee per night: None.
Agency: Angeles National Forest, Arroyo Seco District Office, 818-790-1151.
Activities: Hiking, mountain biking, horseback riding.
Finding the campground: From the intersection of Interstate 210 and California 2 (Angeles Crest Highway) north of Pasadena, drive north on CA 2 for about 29 miles to FR 3N17. Turn left and drive about 6.5 miles to a signed road, which leads right about half a mile to the campground.

About the campground: The campground is situated along the Pacific Crest Trail at an elevation of 7,100 feet. Stay limit 14 days. Open May through November.

10 Buckhorn

Location: 33 miles north of Pasadena.
Sites: 40 sites for tents and RVs up to 22 feet long.

Facilities: Picnic tables, fire rings, drinking water, vault toilets.
Fee per night: $12.
Agency: Angeles National Forest, Arroyo Seco District Office, 818-790-1151.
Activities: Hiking.
Finding the campground: From the intersection of Interstate 210 and California 2 (Angeles Crest Highway) north of Pasadena, drive north on CA 2 for about 33 miles.

About the campground: Situated in a forest of large, mature pines and some cedars, Buckhorn is a good base for hikers. The Burkhardt Trail to Cooper Canyon Falls (2 miles) starts near site 18 in the campground. This trail also crosses the Pacific Crest Trail after 1.5 miles. The High Desert Recreational Trail can also be accessed from Burkhardt Trail. Elevation 6,300 feet. Stay limit 14 days. Open April through November.

11 Blue Ridge

Location: 13 miles west of Wrightwood.
Sites: 8 sites for tents and RVs up to 20 feet long.
Facilities: Picnic tables, fire rings, vault toilets. No drinking water.
Fee per night: None.
Agency: Angeles National Forest, Valyermo District Office, 805-944-2187.
Activities: Hiking, mountain biking.
Finding the campground: From the intersection of California 138 and CA 2 northeast of Wrightwood, take CA 2 (Angeles Crest Highway) west about 11 miles to Inspiration Point. Turn left onto Blue Ridge Road (FR 3N06) and drive about 2 miles.

About the campground: The Pacific Crest Trail passes right by the campground. Elevation 8,000 feet. Stay limit 14 days. Open May through November.

12 Guffy

Location: 16 miles west of Wrightwood.
Sites: 6 sites for tents.
Facilities: Picnic tables, fire rings, vault toilets. No drinking water.
Fee per night: None.
Agency: Angeles National Forest, Valyermo District Office, 805-944-2187.
Activities: Hiking.
Finding the campground: From the intersection of California 138 and CA 2 northeast of Wrightwood, take CA 2 (Angeles Crest Highway) west about 11 miles to Inspiration Point. Turn left onto Blue Ridge Road (FR 3N06) and drive east about 5 miles.

About the campground: A short connecting trail joins the campground with the Pacific Crest Trail. Elevation 8,300 feet. Stay limit 14 days. Open May through November.

13 Lupine

Location: 18 miles west of Wrightwood.
Sites: 11 sites for tents.
Facilities: Picnic tables, fire rings, vault toilets. No drinking water.
Fee per night: None.
Agency: Angeles National Forest, Valyermo District Office, 805-944-2187.
Activities: Hiking.
Finding the campground: From the intersection of California 138 and CA 2 northeast of Wrightwood, take CA 2 (Angeles Crest Highway) west about 11 miles to Inspiration Point. Turn left onto Blue Ridge Road (FR 3N06) and drive about 5 miles. Near Guffy Campground (see above), turn south onto FR 3N39 and go about 2 miles.

About the campground: Only two short trails are accessible here, plus a four-wheel-drive road that leads to isolated Cabin Flat Campground. Hiking opportunities are better at the other campgrounds in the area. Stay limit 14 days. Open May through November.

14 Big Pines Recreation Area: Table Mountain

Location: 6 miles northwest of Wrightwood.
Sites: 115 sites for tents and RVs up to 32 feet long.
Facilities: Picnic tables, fire rings, drinking water, vault toilets.
Fee per night: $12.
Agency: Angeles National Forest, Valyermo District Office, 805-944-2187
Activities: Hiking.
Finding the campground: Drive 5 miles northwest of Wrightwood on California 2 (Angeles Crest Highway) to the Big Pines Visitor Center. There, at the 3-way intersection of CA 2, Big Pines Highway (N4), and FR 4N21, follow 4N21 just over a mile to an unpaved road (FR 4N03). Turn left onto FR 4N03 and drive 0.4 mile.

About the campground: The Big Pines Recreation Area lies astride the Angeles Crest Scenic Byway (CA 2) in the San Gabriel Mountains. It features three picnic areas and five campgrounds: Table Mountain, Apple Tree, Lake, Mountain Oak, and Jackson Flats Group Campground (see below). There is a visitor center at the intersection of CA 2 and Big Pines Highway. Inspiration Point, located on Blue Ridge 1.5 miles west of the center, provides an impressive view of the San Gabriel Mountains, including Mount Baden-Powell, Mount Baldy, Iron Mountain, and other rugged peaks of the Sheep Mountain Wilderness. Hiking is the main activity in the area, and information about trails can be obtained at the visitor center. The Pacific Crest National Scenic Trail passes not far to the south. Elevation 7,000 feet. Stay limit 14 days. Open May through November.

15 Big Pines Recreation Area: Apple Tree

Location: 7 miles northwest of Wrightwood.
Sites: 8 sites for tents.
Facilities: Picnic tables, fire rings, drinking water, vault toilets.
Fee per night: $8.
Agency: Angeles National Forest, Valyermo District Office, 805-944-2187.
Activities: Hiking.
Finding the campground: Drive 5 miles west of Wrightwood on California 2 (Angeles Crest Highway) to the Big Pines Visitor Center. There, at the 3-way intersection of CA 2, Big Pines Highway (N4), and FR 4N21, follow Big Pines Highway west for 2 miles.

About the campground: For more information about the recreation area, see Table Mountain (No. 14 above). Elevation 6,200. Stay limit 14 days. Open all year.

16 Big Pines Recreation Area: Lake

Location: 8 miles northwest of Wrightwood.
Sites: 8 sites for tents and RVs up to 20 feet long.
Facilities: Picnic tables, fire rings, drinking water, vault toilets, boat ramp.
Fee per night: $10.
Agency: Angeles National Forest, Valyermo District Office, 805-944-2187.
Activities: Hiking, boating, swimming, fishing.
Finding the campground: Drive 5 miles west of Wrightwood on California 2 (Angeles Crest Highway) to the Big Pines Visitor Center. There, at the 3-way intersection of CA 2, Big Pines Highway (N4), and FR 4N21, follow Big Pines Highway west for 3 miles.

About the campground: For more information about the recreation area, see Table Mountain (No. 14 above). Elevation 6,100. Stay limit 14 days. Open May through November.

17 Big Pines Recreation Area: Mountain Oak

Location: 9 miles northwest of Wrightwood.
Sites: 17 sites for tents and RVs up to 24 feet long.
Facilities: Picnic tables, fire rings, drinking water, flush toilets.
Fee per night: $10.
Agency: Angeles National Forest, Valyermo District Office, 805-944-2187.
Activities: Hiking.
Finding the campground: Drive 5 miles west of Wrightwood on California 2 (Angeles Crest Highway) to the Big Pines Visitor Center. There, at the 3-way intersection of CA 2, Big Pines Highway (N4), and FR 4N21, follow Big Pines Highway west for 3.6 miles.

About the campground: For more information about the recreation area, see

Table Mountain (No. 14 above). Elevation 6,100. Stay limit 14 days. Open May through November.

18 Big Pines Recreation Area: Jackson Flat

Location: 9 miles northwest of Wrightwood.
Sites: 5 group sites for tents, each accommodating up to 40 people.
Facilities: Picnic tables, fire rings, drinking water, flush toilets.
Fee per night: $75-$90. Reservations required; call 805-944-2187.
Agency: Angeles National Forest, Valyermo District Office, 805-944-2187.
Activities: Hiking.
Finding the campground: Drive 5 miles northwest of Wrightwood on California 2 (Angeles Crest Highway) to the Big Pines Visitor Center. There, at the 3-way intersection of CA 2, Big Pines Highway (N4), and FR 4N21, continue west on CA 2 for about 2 miles. Then bear right on FR 3N26.2 for about 1.5 miles.

About the campground: For more information about the recreation area, see Table Mountain (No. 14 above). Elevation 7,500. Stay limit 14 days. Open May through November.

19 Sycamore Flats

Location: 16 miles west of Wrightwood.
Sites: 12 sites for tents and RVs up to 18 feet long.
Facilities: Picnic tables, fire rings, drinking water, vault toilets.
Fee per night: $5.
Agency: Angeles National Forest, Valyermo District Office, 805-944-2187.
Activities: Hiking, fishing.
Finding the campground: From the intersection of California 2 and Big Pines Highway (N4) 5 miles west of Wrightwood, take Big Pines Highway west for about 9 miles to FR 4N11. Turn left (south) onto FR 4N11 and drive for 2 miles.

About the campground: Sycamore Flats Campground is on the bank of Big Rock Creek, at an elevation of 4,250 feet. Stay limit 14 days. Open all year.

20 South Fork

Location: 18 miles west of Wrightwood.
Sites: 21 sites for tents and RVs up to 16 feet long.
Facilities: Picnic tables, fire rings, vault toilets. No drinking water.
Fee per night: $5.
Agency: Angeles National Forest, Valyermo District Office, 805-944-2187.
Activities: Hiking, swimming.
Finding the campground: From the intersection of California 2 and Big Pines Highway (N4) 5 miles west of Wrightwood, take Big Pines Highway west for about 9 miles to FR 4N11. Turn left (south) onto FR 4N11 and drive for 2.5 miles to FR 4N11A. Turn right and drive another mile.

About the campground: The High Desert National Recreation Trail passes by the campground, making for hikes in either an eastern or western direction. Swimming is often possible in the South Fork of Big Rock Creek. Elevation 4,450 feet. Stay limit 14 days. Open May to November.

21 Big Rock

Location: 20 miles west of Wrightwood.
Sites: 8 sites for tents.
Facilities: Picnic tables, fire rings, vault toilets. No drinking water.
Fee per night: $5.
Agency: Angeles National Forest, Valyermo District Office, 805-944-2187.
Activities: Hiking.
Finding the campground: From the intersection of California 2 and Big Pines Highway (N4) 5 miles west of Wrightwood, take Big Pines Highway west for about 9 miles to FR 4N11. Turn left (south) onto FR 4N11 and drive for 6 miles.

About the campground: The campground is on the bank of Big Rock Creek, just north of the High Desert Recreation Trail. Elevation 4,500 feet. Stay limit 14 days. Open May to November.

22 Little Rock Canyon Recreation Area: Rocky Point

Location: 13 miles southeast of Palmdale.
Sites: 3 sites for tents.
Facilities: Picnic tables, fire rings, drinking water, vault toilets, boat ramp.
Fee per night: $10.
Agency: Angeles National Forest, Valyermo District Office, 805-944-2187.
Activities: Hiking, swimming, fishing, boating, mountain biking, off-highway driving.
Finding the campground: From the intersection of California 14 and CA 138 in Palmdale, take CA 138 east for 8 miles to Cheeseboro Road. Turn right and drive south for 3 miles to the Little Rock Entrance Station. The campground is 2 miles south of the entrance station.

About the campground: The recreation area is on the southwest shore of Little Rock Reservoir, providing a range of water sports. It contains two picnic areas and three campgrounds: Rocky Point, Sage, and Basin. Elevation 3,400 feet. Stay limit 14. Open all year.

23 Little Rock Canyon Recreation Area: Sage

Location: 13 miles southeast of Palmdale.
Sites: 4 sites for tents.
Facilities: Picnic tables, fire rings, drinking water, vault toilets.
Fee per night: $10.
Agency: Angeles National Forest, Valyermo District Office, 805-944-2187.

Activities: Hiking, swimming, fishing, boating, mountain biking, off-highway driving.
Finding the campground: From Rocky Point Campground (see above), continue south 0.2 mile.

About the campground: See Rocky Point (No. 22 above) for more about this recreation area. Elevation 3,400 feet. Stay limit 14 days. Open all year.

24 Little Rock Canyon Recreation Area: Basin

Location: 14 miles southeast of Palmdale.
Sites: 15 sites for tents and RVs up to 28 feet long.
Facilities: Picnic tables, fire rings, drinking water, vault toilets.
Fee per night: $10.
Agency: Angeles National Forest, Valyermo District Office, 805-944-2187.
Activities: Hiking, swimming, fishing, boating, mountain biking, off-highway driving.
Finding the campground: From Rocky Point Campground (see No. 22, above), continue south 1 mile.

About the campground: See Rocky Point Campground (No. 22 above) for more about this recreation area. Elevation 3,400 feet. Stay limit 14 days. Open all year.

25 Coldbrook

Location: 18 miles north of Azusa.
Sites: 25 sites for tents and RVs up to 22 feet long.
Facilities: Picnic tables, fire rings, drinking water, vault toilets.
Fee per night: $8.
Agency: Angeles National Forest, Mount Baldy District Office, 818-335-1251.
Activities: Hiking, fishing.
Finding the campground: From the intersection of Interstate 210 and California 39 in Azusa, take CA 39 (San Gabriel Canyon Road) north for 18 miles.

About the campground: The North Fork of the San Gabriel River flows through the campground, and trout fishing is popular in late spring. Elevation 3,350 feet. Stay limit 14 days. Open all year.

26 Crystal Lake Recreation Area

Location: 24 miles north of Azusa.
Sites: 176 sites for tents and RVs up to 22 feet long, plus 9 group sites that accommodate a total of 300 people.
Facilities: Picnic tables, fire rings, drinking water, flush toilets, food service, store.
Fee per night: $12 individual sites, group rates vary by size of group. Reservations required for groups; call 800-280-CAMP. Reservation fee, $15.50.
Agency: Angeles National Forest, Mount Baldy District Office, 818-335-1251.

Activities: Hiking, fishing, mountain biking.
Finding the campground: From the intersection of Interstate 210 and California 39 in Azusa, take CA 39 (San Gabriel Canyon Road) north for 24 miles.

About the campground: The recreation area includes a group campground (Deer Flat) and three separate family campground loops less than a quarter of a mile apart. Six interpretive trails begin near the campgrounds, as does a mile-long trail that circles Crystal Lake. Another trail leads north to intersect the Pacific Crest Trail. Rainbow trout can be caught in Crystal Lake. Elevation 5,800 feet. Stay limit 14 days. Open all year for individual campgrounds, May through October for group campground.

27 Manker Flats

Location: 12 miles north of Upland.
Sites: 22 sites for tents and RVs up to 22 feet long.
Facilities: Picnic tables, fire rings, drinking water, flush toilets.
Fee per night: $8.
Agency: Angeles National Forest, Mount Baldy District Office, 818-335-1251.
Activities: Hiking.
Finding the campground: From the intersection of California 66 and Mills Avenue in Upland, take Mills Avenue 2 miles north to Mount Baldy Road. Continue north on Mount Baldy for about 10 miles (3 miles past the Mount Baldy Visitor Center).

About the campground: Although Manker Flats is just across the county line in San Bernardino County, it is included here because it can only be reached by vehicle from Los Angeles County. It is situated in an attractive open pine forest, and there are several hiking trails in the vicinity. A half-mile trail starting 100 yards north of the campground leads to an overlook of San Bernardino Falls, which appears at its best in early spring. Elevation 6,300 feet. Stay limit 14 days. Open May through September.

SOUTH L.A. COUNTY

This area encompasses the most heavily populated section of the city of Los Angeles, including some of its most famous locations. Hollywood, Beverly Hills, Long Beach, Santa Monica, and Malibu all add their distinctive flavor to the area, and each has its own attractions for the visitor. Universal Studios in Hollywood, the *Queen Mary* in Long Beach, Santa Monica Pier, and the Venice Boardwalk are just a few examples. The new Getty Center highlights the area's many famous museums and El Pueblo de Los Angeles features 27 buildings of architectural and historical importance.

East of Santa Monica, 30 miles of beaches line the Pacific Coast Highway, including Topanga, Malibu, Point Dume, and Leo Carrillo State Beach. Inland, the Santa Monica Mountains offer beautiful Malibu Creek and Topanga State Parks, with miles of hiking, cycling, and equestrian trails.

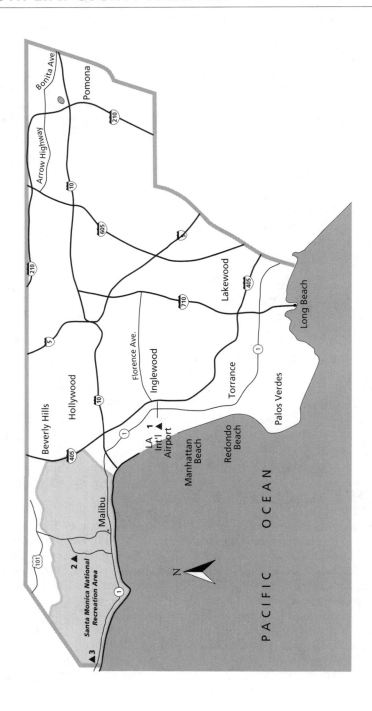

	Group sites	RV sites	Max. RV length	Hookups	Toilets	Showers	Drinking water	Dump station	Pets	Wheelchair	Recreation	Fee ($)	Season	Can reserve
1 Dockweiler State Beach		•	35		F	•	•	•	•		S	16-26		
2 Malibu Creek State Park	•	•	30		F	•	•	•	•	•	HFR	17		•
3 Leo Carrillo State Beach		•	31		F		•	•	•	•	HSF	14–18		•

Hookups: W = Water E = Electric S = Sewer
Toilets: F = Flush V = Vault P = Pit C = Chemical
Recreation: H = Hiking S = Swimming F = Fishing B = Boating L = Boat Launch O = Off-highway Driving R = Horseback Riding
Maximum Trailer/RV Length given in feet. **Stay Limit** given in days. **Fee** given in dollars.
If no entry under **Season**, campground is open all year. If no entry under **Fee**, camping is free.

1 Dockweiler State Beach

Location: 3 miles west of Inglewood.
Sites: 118 sites for RVs up to 35 feet long.
Facilities: Picnic tables, barbecue grills, drinking water, showers, flush toilets, laundromat, dump station.
Fee per night: $16 without hookups, $26 with full hookups.
Agency: California Department of Parks and Recreation, 310-322-4951.
Activities: Swimming, fishing, cycling.
Finding the campground: From the intersection of Interstates 405 and 105 in Los Angeles (Inglewood), take I-105 (Imperial Highway) west for 3 miles to Vista del Mar.

About the campground: Dockweiler is the only campground on the 15-mile-long sandy beach that stretches from Redondo Beach to Marina del Rey. However, it has one major disadvantage: It lies at the end of the runway for the Los Angeles International Airport. A 19-mile, paved bicycle trail runs past the campground, connecting Will Rogers State Beach and Redondo State Beach. Grunion runs occur during high tides in summer. Stay limit 15 days. Open all year.

2 Malibu Creek State Park

Location: 6 miles north of Malibu.
Sites: 60 sites for tents and RVs up to 30 feet long, plus 1 group site for tents that accommodates up to 60 people and 10 vehicles.
Facilities: Picnic tables, grills, drinking water, flush toilets, showers, dump station.
Fee per night: $17 individual sites, $90 group site. For reservations, call Parknet, 800-444-7275. Reservation fee, $7.50.
Agency: California Department of Parks and Recreation, 818-880-0350.
Activities: Hiking, fishing, mountain biking, horseback riding.
Finding the campground: From the intersection of California 1 and CA N1 (Malibu Canyon Road) in Malibu, drive north about 6 miles.

About the campground: The park is spread over 6,600 acres of scenic, rugged

The rugged Santa Monica Mountains loom over Malibu Creek State Park, which features miles of trails for hikers, bikers, and horseback riders.

terrain in the Santa Monica Mountains. It offers a visitor center, 15 miles of hiking and biking trails, a small lake, and good bird and small animal viewing along wooded Malibu Creek. Stay limit 7 days from June through September, 15 days from October through May. Open all year.

3 Leo Carrillo State Beach

Location: 28 miles northwest of Santa Monica.
Sites: 138 sites for tents and RVs up to 31 feet long, plus 1 group site for tents.
Facilities: Picnic tables, barbecue grills, drinking water, flush toilets, dump station. A store and snack bar are open during the summer months.
Fee per night: $14-$18 individual sites, $75 group site, pets $1. Reservations required for groups; call Parknet, 800-444-7275. Reservation fee, $13.50.
Agency: California Department of Parks and Recreation, 818-880-0350.
Activities: Hiking, swimming, fishing, surfing, snorkeling, scuba diving, whale watching.
Finding the campground: From Santa Monica, drive 28 miles northwest on California 1.

About the campground: This 1,600-acre park ranges from the shoreline to backdrop hills 1,000 feet high. CA 1 separates the beach from the inland portions of the park, and an underpass connects the two sections. Of the 138 campsites, 32 are beachfront sites on a concrete pad for self-contained RVs under 8 feet high (to negotiate the underpass). The remaining sites are across the highway in Arroyo Sequit Canyon. The coastal portion of the park consists of three separate beaches. South Beach is the most scenic and has the best facilities. North Beach, although host to the RV beachfront campground, is quieter and not as crowded. Yerba Buena Beach, the northernmost, is separated from North Beach by a strip of private property. Its well-shaped waves attract surfers. Stay limit 7 days from June through September, 15 days from October through May. Open all year.

ORANGE COUNTY

Once the domain of a single powerful ranching family, then a kingdom of orange groves, Orange County has undergone a dramatic transformation since the 1960s. Still the dominion of the rich and the powerful, the citrus groves and the ranches are mostly gone, replaced by costly coastal mansions, affluent suburbs, fancy yacht clubs, and world-famous theme parks. For those accustomed to thinking of the county as a southern suburb of Los Angeles, surprises are in store. For although the northeastern portion is heavily urbanized, much of the county still retains a natural, unspoiled character.

Year-round fine weather has been a major contributor to the popularity of Orange County, both as a place to visit and a place to live. The county enjoys a Mediterranean climate, particularly along the coastal strip, where mild winters and cool summers are the norm. Average maximum/minimum temperatures range in summer from 82 to 62 degrees F and in winter from 68 to 48 degrees F.

ORANGE COUNTY AREA MAP

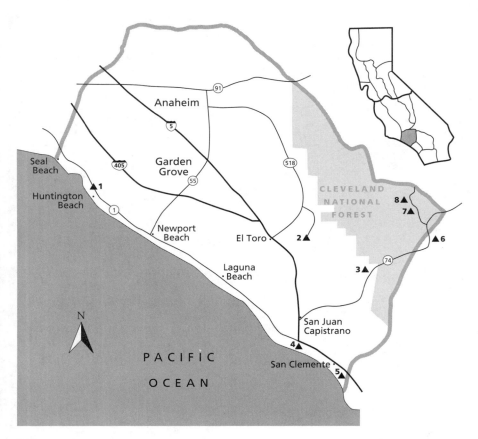

Spring brings temperatures from 71 to 53 degrees F and fall, 78 to 58 degrees F. The percentage of average days of sunshine is almost consistent year-round: 77 percent in summer, 75 in fall, 71 in winter, and 70 in spring.

Orange County can be divided into three distinct regions. The first of these is the northeast—Anaheim and its surroundings. This is the province of Disneyland, Knott's Berry Farm, and other meccas that bring tourists flocking by the thousands. The second region is the "Gold Coast," 42 miles of dark blue water and some of the most beautiful white sand beaches to be found anywhere. It is often called the "American Riviera," and it presents an almost uninterrupted playland from Seal Beach to San Clemente. Finally, in the mountainous southeast, the Santa Ana Mountains and the Cleveland National Forest guard a nearly pristine wilderness, where trees grow tall, streams run clear, and wildlife flourishes. Fortunately for RVers and tenters, campgrounds are located in all three regions. They are described in the following pages.

1 Bolsa Chica State Beach

Location: Huntington Beach.
Sites: 50 sites for self-contained RVs up to 40 feet long.
Facilities: Restrooms, cold showers, picnic area, fire rings, snack bar all available in public park.
Fee per night: $14-$18. For reservations, call Parknet, 800-444-7275. Reservation fee, $7.50.
Agency: California Department of Parks and Recreation, 714-536-1454.
Activities: Hiking, swimming, fishing, surfing, cycling, bird watching.
Finding the campground: In Huntington Beach on California 1 (Pacific Coast Highway), between Golden West Street and Warner Avenue.

About the campground: This campground is little more than a parking lot for self-contained RVs, but it provides direct access to a beautiful, 6-mile-long sandy

		Group sites	RV sites	Max. RV length	Hookups	Toilets	Showers	Drinking water	Dump station	Pets	Wheelchair	Recreation	Fee ($)	Season	Can reserve
1	Bolsa Chica State Beach		•	40		F				•	•	SFH	14–18		•
2	O'Neill Regional Park		•	35	W	F	•	•	•	•	•	HF	12		
3	Caspers Wilderness Park		•			F	•	•	•		•	HR	12		•
4	Doheny State Beach		•	28		F	•	•	•	•	•	SF	14–23		•
5	San Clemente State Beach		•	30	WES	F	•	•		•	•	HSF	14–24		•
6	Upper San Juan		•	32		V	•					H	10	Apr–Sep	
7	Blue Jay	•	•	40		V	•		•			H	10	Apr–Sep	
8	Falcon	•	•	40		V	•		•			H	35–70	May–Sep	•

Hookups: W = Water E = Electric S = Sewer
Toilets: F = Flush V = Vault P = Pit C = Chemical
Recreation: H = Hiking S = Swimming F = Fishing B = Boating L = Boat Launch O = Off-highway Driving R = Horseback Riding
Maximum Trailer/RV Length given in feet. **Stay Limit** given in days. **Fee** given in dollars.
If no entry under **Season,** campground is open all year. If no entry under **Fee,** camping is free.

beach. The Bolsa Chica Ecological Reserve, which adjoins the park on the north, is a 500-acre salt marsh with interpretive displays, a 3-mile loop trail, and a mile-long nature trail. A 10-mile coastal trail leads from the park to Newport Beach Pier. A paved bike path, 20 miles long, runs south to Dana Point. The area is a paradise for bird watchers, as it is a rest stop along the Pacific Flyway for migrating shore birds and water fowl. Stay limit 7 days from June through September, 14 days from October through May. Open all year.

2 O'Neill Regional Park

Location: 10 miles northeast of Laguna Hills.
Sites: 90 sites for tents and RVs up to 35 feet long, including 45 sites with water hookups.
Facilities: Picnic tables, fire rings, barbecue grills, drinking water, flush toilets, showers, dump station, playground.
Fee per night: $12, pets $2.
Agency: Orange County Parks Department, 714-858-9365.
Activities: Hiking, fishing.
Finding the campground: From the intersection of Interstate 5 and County Road S18 (El Toro Road) in Laguna Hills, drive northeast on CR S18 for 7.2 miles to CR S19 (Live Oak Canyon Road). Turn right and drive 3.2 miles.

About the campground: O'Neill is a 1,700-acre park in the foothills of the Santa Ana Mountains. The campground is about 75 percent shaded by oak and sycamore trees. It offers two self-guided nature walks and a nature center. The Trabuco Creek Trail follows a shaded stream from the campground south to Mission Viejo. Fishing is possible in Trabuco Creek. The trailhead for the Holy Jim Historic Trail is located 2 miles east of the campground. Trail guides for this 1.5-hour, self-guided trip are available at the El Cariso Visitor Information Center and the Silverado Fire Station. Stay limit 15 days. Open all year.

3 Caspers Wilderness Park

Location: 10 miles northeast of San Juan Capistrano.
Sites: 42 sites for tents and RVs, 10 overflow sites, 30 sites for campers with horses.
Facilities: Picnic tables, fire rings, barbecue grills, drinking water, flush toilets, showers, dump station, playground, horse corrals.
Fee per night: $12, horses $3. For reservations, call the park.
Agency: Orange County Parks Department, 714-831-2174.
Activities: Hiking, horseback riding, mountain biking.
Finding the campground: From the intersection of Interstate 5 and California 74 in San Juan Capistrano, drive northeast on CA 74 for about 10 miles.

About the campground: More than 30 miles of trails wind through the park for hikers, mountain bikers, and horseback riders. Hikers and equestrians share the same trails, but mountain bikers have their own. The trail network in Bell Canyon offers the best paths for hikers, and maps are available at the park visitor center. Because horses are permitted in the park, no pets are allowed. Stay limit 15 days. Open all year.

4 Doheny State Beach

Location: 5 miles northwest of San Clemente.
Sites: 120 sites for tents and RVs up to 28 feet long.
Facilities: Picnic tables, barbecue grills, drinking water, flush toilets, showers, dump station. A snack bar is open during the summer.
Fee per night: $14-$23, pets $1. For reservations, call Parknet, 800-444-7275. Reservation fee, $7.50.
Agency: California Department of Parks and Recreation, 714-496-6171.
Activities: Swimming, fishing, surfing, scuba diving.
Finding the campground: Follow Interstate 5 north of San Clemente for 5 miles, to its intersection with California 1. The park is at the entrance of Dana Point Harbor.

About the campground: *Sunset* has named Doheny one of the 100 best campgrounds in the western United States. A large grassy lawn with picnic areas and shade trees backs a very attractive sandy beach. Surfing is best at the north end of the beach, and an off-shore marine refuge attracts scuba divers. A full-service marina is located at Dana Point Harbor, which borders the beach on the north. The mission of San Juan Capistrano is only about 5 miles away. Stay limit 7 days from June through September, 15 days from October through May. Open all year.

5 San Clemente State Beach

Location: In San Clemente.
Sites: 157 sites for tents and RVs up to 30 feet long, including 72 sites with full hookups.
Facilities: Picnic tables, barbecue grills, drinking water, showers, flush toilets.
Fee per night: $14-$24. For reservations, call Parknet, 800-444-7275. Reservation fee, $7.50.
Agency: California Department of Parks and Recreation, 714-492-3156.
Activities: Hiking, swimming, fishing, surfing.
Finding the campground: On Interstate 5, drive to the south end of San Clemente and take the Avenida Calafia exit.

About the campground: The campground is located on a bluff overlooking a long, narrow beach. Railroad tracks parallel the shoreline between the campsites and the beach. Several hiking trails follow the coast. Stay limit 7 days from June through September, 15 days from October through May. Open all year.

6 Upper San Juan

Location: 16 miles northeast of San Juan Capistrano.
Sites: 18 sites for tents and RVs up to 32 feet long.

Facilities: Picnic tables, fire rings, drinking water, vault toilets.
Fee per night: $10.
Agency: Cleveland National Forest, Trabuco Ranger District, 909-736-1811.
Activities: Hiking.
Finding the campground: From the intersection of Interstate 5 and California 74 in San Juan Capistrano, take CA 74 northeast for about 16 miles.

About the campground: Although Upper San Juan lies just across the line in Riverside County, it is an integral part of the scenic Ortega Highway drive in Orange County and a good base for trails in the area. For that reason it is shown here in addition to its primary listing under the Inland Empire (page 201). Stay limit 14 days. Open April through September.

7 Blue Jay

Location: 20 miles northeast of San Juan Capistrano.
Sites: 50 sites for tents and RVs up to 40 feet long, plus 5 group sites.
Facilities: Picnic tables, fire rings, drinking water, vault toilets.
Fee per night: $10.
Agency: Cleveland National Forest, Trabuco District Office, 909-736-1811.
Activities: Hiking.
Finding the campground: From the intersection of Interstate 5 and California 74 in San Juan Capistrano, take CA 74 northeast for about 18 miles to Long Canyon Road (FR 6S05). Turn left onto Long Canyon Road and drive another 2 miles.

About the campground: The Ortega Highway (CA 74) between San Juan Capistrano and Lake Elsinore offers fine panoramic views of the ocean and surrounding mountains. The campground is the trailhead for several major trails into the Santa Ana Mountains. Stay limit 14 days. Open April through September.

8 Falcon

Location: 20 miles northeast of San Juan Capistrano.
Sites: 3 group sites for tents and RVs up to 20, 30, and 40 feet long respectively.
Facilities: Picnic tables, fire rings, drinking water, vault toilets.
Fee per night: $35-$70. Reservations required; call 800-280-CAMP. Reservation fee, $17.35.
Agency: Cleveland National Forest, Trabuco District Office, 909-736-1811.
Activities: Hiking.
Finding the campground: From the intersection of Interstate 5 and California 74 in San Juan Capistrano, take CA 74 northeast for about 18 miles to Long Canyon Road (FR 6S05). Turn left onto Long Canyon Road and drive another 2 miles. Falcon is just west of Blue Jay Campground (see above) on Long Canyon Road.

About the campground: Stay limit 14 days. Open May through September.

INLAND EMPIRE

Between the coastal beaches of Orange County and the great deserts of southeastern California, the Inland Empire serves as a transition zone. Only a 15-minute aerial tram ride separates the desert community of Palm Springs from 2.5-mile-high San Jacinto State Park, and the change is dramatic as well as swift. One steps out of the gondola car into an alpine world of tall pines and cool breezes, with the hot desert sands still visible far below. Elsewhere, the transition is more gradual. In the north, at Victorville, the desert yields more slowly, receding by degrees until it surrenders entirely to the San Bernardino National Forest. And in the west, the urban sprawl of Los Angeles finally fades away east of Ontario.

INLAND EMPIRE AREA MAP

The Inland Empire, with its mountains, forests, and lakes, is a welcome refuge for those seeking relief from the congestion of Los Angeles or the searing heat of the desert. When people say that it is possible in Southern California to water-ski and snow ski in the same day, they are speaking of the Inland Empire. The proximity of soaring mountains to alpine lakes makes it possible. Big Bear, just one of several large lakes, offers year-round recreation: water sports from spring to fall and snow play in winter, when snow in the vicinity can get up to 6 feet deep.

The region is also rich in history, museums, and other cultural opportunities. The Temecula Valley is the gateway to California's southernmost wine country, with more than half a dozen wineries offering tastings and retail sales.

Weather is more nearly temperate here than in other parts of Southern California. The average summer temperature ranges from a high of 97 to a low of 63 degrees F, while winter brings highs of 65 and lows of 41 degrees F. Spring sees readings of between 83 and 53 degrees F, and in the fall temperatures average highs of 76 and lows of 47 degrees F. On average, 91 percent of summer days are sunny, 89 percent of fall, 79 percent of winter, and 89 percent of spring.

This book divides the Inland Empire into two areas: San Bernardino County and Riverside County.

SAN BERNARDINO COUNTY

The San Bernardino Mountains span the county from east to west, dividing it roughly in half. The southern part of the county is fertile and populated, while the north is sparsely inhabited desert. In between, the mountains provide a welcome, forested alternative to both. Three large lakes—Big Bear, Arrowhead, and Silverwood—embellish the mountains and the San Bernardino National Forest, the region's most prominent outdoor recreation area.

In the eastern part of the county, the Rim of the World Scenic Byway follows the crest of the mountains, offering spectacular views at almost every turn. Beginning as California 38 at Mill Creek Ranger Station about 9 miles east of San Bernardino, the byway climbs and winds its way through marvelous scenery for 107 miles, including along the shores of Big Bear and Silverwood Lakes. Becoming CA 18 at the west end of Big Bear Lake and CA 138 at Crestline, the drive comes to an end shortly after it intersects with Interstate 15.

1 Mojave Narrows Regional Park

Location: 9 miles south of Victorville.
Sites: 110 sites for tents and RVs, including 38 sites with full hookups.
Facilities: Picnic tables, barbecue grills, fire rings, drinking water, showers, flush toilets, dump station, playground, snack bar, boat rentals, public phone.
Fee per night: $10-$15, pets $1.
Agency: San Bernardino County Regional Parks, 760-245-2226.
Activities: Hiking trails, fishing, boating, horseback riding.
Finding the campground: From Victorville, drive south on Interstate 15 for 2 miles to the Bear Valley Cutoff exit. Drive east on Bear Valley Cutoff for 4 miles,

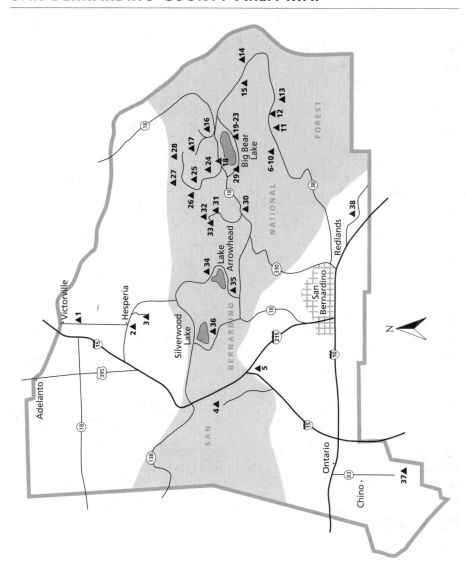

turn left onto Ridgecrest Road, and drive 3 miles.

About the campground: Mojave Narrows is located along the bank of the Mojave River, with several sites on the water. It is adjacent to a small lake, which is stocked with rainbow trout for the November–April fishing season and stocked with catfish for the May–September season. The campground affords a pleasant oasis in a desert environment. It is close to railroad tracks, and trains go by with relative frequency. Stay limit 14 days. Open all year.

	Group sites	RV sites	Max. RV length	Hookups	Toilets	Showers	Drinking water	Dump station	Pets	Wheelchair	Recreation	Fee ($)	Season	Can reserve
1 Mojave Narrows Park		•		WES	F	•	•	•	•	•	HFBR	10–15		
2 Hesperia Lake Park		•		WE	F	•	•	•	•	•	F	10–13		
3 Mojave River Forks		•		WES	F	•	•	•	•	•	H	13–19		•
4 Applewhite		•	30		F		•	•	•	•	F	10		
5 Glen Helen Park		•			F	•	•	•	•	•	HSF	10–12		•
6 Barton Flats: Council	•				V		•				HF	25–100	May–Oct	•
7 Barton Flats: Barton Flats		•	45		F	•	•	•			HF	10	May–Oct	•
8 Barton Flats: San Gorgonio		•	43		F	•	•				HF	10	May–Oct	•
9 Barton Flats: Oso and Lobo	•	•			F		•				HF	25–100	May–Oct	•
10 Barton Flats: South Fork		•	30		V		•				HF	10	May–Oct	•
11 Heart Bar		•	50		V		•		•	•	H	10	May–Oct	•
12 Heart Bar Equestrian	•	•			F	•	•		•		R	65	May–Oct	•
13 Coon Creek Cabin	•				V				•		H	30–45	May–Oct	•
14 Juniper Springs	•				V		•		•		H	50	May–Oct	•
15 Green Canyon	•				V		•		•		H	35	May–Oct	•
16 Tanglewood	•	•			V				•		H	35	May–Oct	•
17 Holcomb Valley		•	25		V				•		H	10		
18 Serrano		•	55	WES	F	•	•	•	•	•	HFS	12–24	May–Oct	•
19 Pineknot		•	45		F	•			•	•	HFB	12	May–Oct	•
20 Buttercup	•	•			C	•			•		HFBS	50	May–Oct	
21 Cold Brook		•	25		V		•		•		HFSB	12		
22 Boulder	•	•			V				•		HSFB	25–50	May–Oct	•
23 Deer	•	•			V				•		HSFB	25–50	May–Oct	•
24 Gray's Peak	•	•			V				•		H	25–50	May–Oct	•
25 Hanna Flat		•	40		V		•		•		H	12	May–Oct	•
26 Ironwood	•				V				•			35	May–Oct	•
27 Big Pine Horse Camp	•				V		•		•		R	35	May–Oct	•
28 Big Pine Flat		•	30		V		•		•		H	10	May–Oct	•
29 Bluff Mesa	•	•			V				•		H	25	May–Oct	•
30 Shady Cove	•				V		•		•		H	55–100	May–Oct	•
31 Green Valley		•	22		V		•		•		F	10	May–Oct	•
32 Crab Flat		•	15		V		•		•		H	10	May–Oct	•
33 Tent Peg	•				V				•		H	30	May–Oct	•
34 North Shore		•	22		F	•			•	•	FO	10	May–Oct	•
35 Dogwood		•	22		F	•	•	•	•		O	12–16	May–Oct	•
36 Silverwood Lake SRA	•	•	34		F	•	•	•	•	•	HSFB	12–18		•
37 Prado Regional Park	•	•		WES	F	•	•	•	•	•	HFBR	15		•
38 Yucaipa Regional Park	•	•		WES	F	•	•		•	•	SFB	11–18		

Hookups: W = Water E = Electric S = Sewer
Toilets: F = Flush V = Vault P = Pit C = Chemical
Recreation: H = Hiking S = Swimming F = Fishing B = Boating L = Boat Launch O = Off-highway Driving R = Horseback Riding
Maximum Trailer/RV Length given in feet. **Stay Limit** given in days. **Fee** given in dollars.
If no entry under **Season**, campground is open all year. If no entry under **Fee**, camping is free.

2 Hesperia Lake Park

Location: 2 miles southeast of Hesperia.
Sites: 86 sites for tents and RVs, including 30 sites with water and electrical hookups.
Facilities: Picnic tables, fire rings, drinking water, showers, playground, ball field, horseshoe pits, public phone.
Fee per night: $10-$13 for two people.
Agency: City of Hesperia, 800-521-6332.
Activities: Fishing.
Finding the campground: From Interstate 15, take the Hesperia exit (Main Street) and drive east 7 miles. Bear right on Arrowhead Lake Road and drive 2 miles south to the campground entrance on the left.

About the campground: The small lake is stocked weekly with 1,000 pounds of catfish. No fishing license is required, but a fishing fee is charged. Stay limit 14 days. Open all year.

3 Mojave River Forks Regional Park

Location: 7 miles southeast of Hesperia.
Sites: 75 sites for tents and RVs, including 25 sites with full hookups and 8 sites with pull-thrus.
Facilities: Picnic tables, barbecue grills, fire rings, drinking water, showers, flush toilets, dump station, store, ball field, playground, public phone.
Fee per night: $13-$19. Reservations accepted for RV sites.
Agency: San Bernardino County Regional Parks, 760-389-2322.
Activities: Hiking.
Finding the campground: From Interstate 15, take the Hesperia exit (Main Street) and drive east 7 miles. Bear right on Arrowhead Lake Road and drive 5.5 miles south. Then turn left onto California 173 and drive 1 mile.

About the campground: Situated on the northern rim of the Cleveland National Forest, the campground is 7 miles northeast of popular Silverwood Lake. Stay limit 14 days. Open all year.

4 Applewhite

Location: 16 miles northwest of Rancho Cucamonga.
Sites: 42 sites for tents and RVs up to 30 feet long.
Facilities: Picnic tables, fire rings, drinking water, flush toilets.
Fee per night: $10.
Agency: San Bernardino National Forest, Cajon Ranger District, 909-887-2576.
Activities: Fishing in Lytle Creek.
Finding the campground: From the intersection of California 66 and Interstate 15 in Rancho Cucamonga, take the Sierra Avenue exit and drive northwest on Lytle Creek Road for 9 miles.

About the campground: Elevation 3,300 feet. Stay limit 14 days. Open all year.

5 Glen Helen Regional Park

Location: 10 miles northwest of San Bernardino.
Sites: 45 sites for tents and RVs.
Facilities: Picnic tables, barbecue grills, fire rings, drinking water, showers, flush toilets, playground, snack bar, ball field, volleyball court, horseshoe pits, public phone.
Fee per night: $10-$12. Reservations accepted.
Agency: San Bernardino County Regional Parks, 909-880-2522.
Activities: Swimming, fishing.
Finding the campground: From the intersection of California 259 and Interstate 215 in San Bernardino, drive 8 miles northwest on I-215 to the Devore Road exit. Drive southwest on Devore Road about 2 miles.

About the campground: Glen Helen is a county "water park." It features a half-acre swimming pool; a 350-foot, double-flume water slide; a small lake stocked with catfish and bass; and pedal boat rental. Stay limit 14 days. Open all year.

6 Barton Flats Recreation Area: Council

Location: 27 miles northeast of Redlands.
Sites: 1 group site for tents that accommodates up to 50 people and 10 vehicles.
Facilities: Picnic tables, fire rings, drinking water, vault toilets.
Fee per night: $25-$100. For reservations, call 800-280-CAMP. Reservation fee, $17.35.
Agency: San Bernardino National Forest, San Gorgonio Ranger District, 909-794-1123.
Activities: Hiking, fishing.
Finding the campground: From the intersection of Interstate 10 and California 38 in Redlands, take CA 38 east and then northeast for 27 miles.

About the campgrounds: Situated along the Rim of the World Scenic Byway, Barton Flats campgrounds offer some of the best facilities in the San Bernardino National Forest and some of its best hiking trails. Most of the trails into the San Gorgonio Wilderness begin here, and access to the Pacific Crest Trail is nearby. The Santa Ana River Trail passes through the park, as does the Lost Creek Trail. A visitor center is open during the summer months. Fishing is possible in the Santa Ana River at South Fork Campground (see below). Elevation 6,100 feet. Stay limit 14 days. Open approximately May through October.

7 Barton Flats Recreation Area: Barton Flats

Location: 28 miles northeast of Redlands.
Sites: 47 sites for tents and RVs up to 45 feet long.
Facilities: Picnic tables, fire rings, drinking water, showers, flush toilets, dump station.
Fee per night: $10. For reservations, call 800-280-CAMP. Reservation fee, $8.65.
Agency: San Bernardino National Forest, San Gorgonio Ranger District, 909-794-1123.

Activities: Hiking, fishing.
Finding the campground: From the intersection of Interstate 10 and California 38 in Redlands, take CA 38 east and then northeast for 27.5 miles.

About the campground: See Council Campground (No. 6 above) for more about the attractions of this recreation area. Elevation 6,300 feet. Stay limit 14 days. Open approximately May through October.

8 Barton Flats Recreation Area: San Gorgonio

Location: 28 miles northeast of Redlands.
Sites: 55 sites for tents and RVs up to 43 feet long.
Facilities: Picnic tables, fire rings, drinking water, showers, flush toilets.
Fee per night: $10. For reservations, call 800-280-CAMP. Reservation fee, $8.65.
Agency: San Bernardino National Forest, San Gorgonio Ranger District, 909-794-1123.
Activities: Hiking, fishing.
Finding the campground: From the intersection of Interstate 10 and California 38 in Redlands, take CA 38 east and then northeast for 28 miles.

About the campground: See Council Campground (No. 6 above) for more about the attractions of this recreation area. Elevation 6,400 feet. Stay limit 14 days. Open approximately May through October.

9 Barton Flats Recreation Area: Oso & Lobo

Location: 28 miles northeast of Redlands.
Sites: 2 adjacent group sites for tents or RVs (Oso accommodates up to 100 people and 20 vehicles; Lobo takes up to 75 people and 15 vehicles).
Facilities: Picnic tables, fire rings, drinking water, flush toilets.
Fee per night: $25-$100. For reservations, call 800-280-CAMP. Reservation fee, $17.35.
Agency: San Bernardino National Forest, San Gorgonio Ranger District, 909-794-1123.
Activities: Hiking, fishing.
Finding the campground: From the intersection of Interstate 10 and California 38 in Redlands, take CA 38 east and then northeast for 28.3 miles.

About the campground: See Council Campground (No. 6 above) for more about the attractions of this recreation area. Elevation 6,600 feet. Stay limit 14 days. Open approximately May through October.

10 Barton Flats Recreation Area: South Fork

Location: 31 miles northeast of Redlands.
Sites: 24 sites for tents and RVs up to 30 feet long.
Facilities: Picnic tables, fire rings, drinking water, vault toilets.

Fee per night: $10. For reservations, call 800-280-CAMP. Reservation fee, $8.65.
Agency: San Bernardino National Forest, San Gorgonio Ranger District, 909-794-1123.
Activities: Hiking, fishing.
Finding the campground: From the intersection of Interstate 10 and California 38 in Redlands, take CA 38 east and then northeast for 31 miles.

About the campground: See Council Campground (No. 6 above) for more about the attractions of this recreation area. Elevation 6,400 feet. Stay limit 14 days. Open approximately May through October.

11 Heart Bar

Location: 33 miles northeast of Redlands.
Sites: 94 sites for tents and RVs up to 50 feet long.
Facilities: Picnic tables, fire rings, drinking water, vault toilets.
Fee per night: $10. For reservations, call 800-280-CAMP. Reservation fee, $8.65.
Agency: San Bernardino National Forest, San Gorgonio Ranger District, 909-794-1123.
Activities: Hiking.
Finding the campground: From the intersection of Interstate 10 and California 38 in Redlands, southeast of San Bernardino, take CA 38 east and then northeast for 32 miles. Turn left onto FR 1N02 and drive 1 mile.

About the campground: Elevation 6,900 feet. Stay limit 14 days. Open approximately May through October.

12 Heart Bar Equestrian

Location: 34 miles northeast of Redlands.
Sites: 1 group site for tents or RVs that accommodates up to 65 people and 21 vehicles.
Facilities: Picnic tables, fire rings, drinking water, showers, flush toilets, corrals.
Fee per night: $65. For reservations, call 800-280-CAMP. Reservation fee, $17.35.
Agency: San Bernardino National Forest, San Gorgonio Ranger District, 909-794-1123.
Activities: Horseback riding.
Finding the campground: From Heart Bar Campground (see No. 11 above), continue on FR1N02 for half a mile.

About the campground: The camp is for equestrian use only. Elevation 7,000 feet. Stay limit 14 days. Open approximately May through October.

13 Coon Creek Cabin

Location: 37 miles east of Redlands.
Sites: 1 group site for tents accommodating up to 40 people and 14 cars; no RVs.

Facilities: Picnic tables, fire rings, vault toilets. No drinking water.
Fee per night: $30-$45. For reservations, call 800-280-CAMP. Reservation fee, $17.35.
Agency: San Bernardino National Forest, San Gorgonio Ranger District, 909-794-1123.
Activities: Hiking.
Finding the campground: From Heart Bar Campground (see No. 11 above), continue east on FR1N02 for 4 miles.

About the campground: The Pacific Crest Trail runs alongside the campground, which is situated at 8,200 feet. Stay limit 14 days. Open approximately May through October.

14 Juniper Springs

Location: 9 miles southeast of Big Bear City.
Sites: 1 group site for tents or RVs that accommodates up to 40 people and 8 vehicles.
Facilities: Picnic tables, fire rings, drinking water, vault toilets.
Fee per night: $50. Reservations required; call 800-280-CAMP. Reservation fee, $17.35.
Agency: San Bernardino National Forest, Big Bear Ranger District, 909-866-3437.
Activities: Hiking.
Finding the campground: From Big Bear City, drive southeast on California 38 for about 6 miles to unpaved FR 2N04. Turn left and drive 2.5 miles, and then continue straight ahead on FR 2N64Y for half a mile.

About the campground: Elevation 7,700 feet. Stay limit 14 days. Open approximately May through October.

15 Green Canyon

Location: 3 miles southeast of Big Bear City.
Sites: 1 group site for tents that accommodates up to 40 people and 8 vehicles; no RVs.
Facilities: Picnic tables, fire rings, drinking water, vault toilets.
Fee per night: $35. For reservations, call 800-280-CAMP. Reservation fee, $17.35.
Agency: San Bernardino National Forest, Big Bear Ranger District, 909-866-3437.
Activities: Hiking.
Finding the campground: From Big Bear City, drive southeast on California 38 for about 3 miles to the unpaved entrance road on the right.

About the campground: Elevation 7,200 feet. Stay limit 14 days. Open approximately May through October.

16 Tanglewood

Location: 6 miles northwest of Big Bear City.

Sites: 1 group site for tents or RVs that accommodates up to 40 people and 8 vehicles.

Facilities: Picnic tables, fire rings, vault toilets. No drinking water.

Fee per night: $35. Reservations required; call 800-280-CAMP. Reservation fee, $17.35.

Agency: San Bernardino National Forest, Big Bear Ranger District, 909-866-3437.

Activities: Hiking.

Finding the campground: From the intersection of California 18 and CA 38 in Big Bear City, drive west on CA 38 for half a mile, turn right onto unpaved Van Dusen Canyon Road (FR 3N09), and drive 3.5 miles. Turn right onto FR 3N16 and drive 2 miles.

About the campground: Elevation 7,400 feet. Stay limit 14 days. Open approximately May through October.

17 Holcomb Valley

Location: 4.5 miles northwest of Big Bear City.

Sites: 19 sites for tents and RVs up to 25 feet long.

Facilities: Picnic tables, fire rings, vault toilets. No drinking water.

Fee per night: $10.

Agency: San Bernardino National Forest, Big Bear Ranger District, 909-866-3437.

Activities: Hiking.

Finding the campground: From the intersection of California 18 and CA 38 in Big Bear City, drive west on CA 38 for half a mile, turn right onto unpaved Van Dusen Canyon Road (FR 3N09) and drive 3.5 miles. Turn left onto FR 3N16 and drive half a mile.

About the campground: Elevation 7,400 feet. Stay limit 14 days. Open all year.

18 Big Bear Lake Recreation Area: Serrano

Location: 3.5 miles west of Big Bear City.

Sites: 132 sites for tents and RVs up to 55 feet long, including 30 sites with full hookups.

Facilities: Picnic tables, fire rings, drinking water, showers, flush toilets, dump station.

Fee per night: $12-$24. For reservations, call 800-280-CAMP. Reservation fee, $8.65.

Agency: San Bernardino National Forest, Big Bear Ranger District, 909-866-3437.

Activities: Hiking, swimming, boating, fishing, skiing in winter.

Finding the campground: From Big Bear City, drive east on California 38 for 3.5 miles. The campground is on the north shore of Big Bear Lake.

About the campgrounds: Big Bear Lake is a popular summer and winter recreation area, offering hiking, backpacking, water sports, and snow activities. Marinas are located around the lake, offering slips, fuel, bait, and boat rentals. Public launching ramps are located on the north shore. A boat permit is required for the lake and can be obtained at most marinas. Several ski runs and lifts are located in the area. No public campgrounds are open during the winter, but some private RV parks remain open.

Serrano is the only campground in Big Bear Lake Recreation Area that offers direct access to the lake, with swimming and kayak/canoe put-in possible at Meadows Edge Picnic Area. The Pacific Crest Trail passes a mile north of the campground. Elevation 7,000 feet. Stay limit 14 days. Open approximately May through October.

19 Big Bear Lake Recreation Area: Pineknot

Location: 4 miles southwest of Big Bear City.
Sites: 52 sites for tents and RVs up to 45 feet long.
Facilities: Picnic tables, fire rings, drinking water, flush toilets.
Fee per night: $12-$24. For reservations, call 800-280-CAMP. Reservation fee, $8.65.
Agency: San Bernardino National Forest, Big Bear Ranger District, 909-866-3437.
Activities: Hiking, swimming, boating, fishing, skiing in winter.
Finding the campground: From the intersection of California 38 and CA 18 in Big Bear City, drive west on CA 18 for about 4 miles. Turn left onto Summit Boulevard.

About the campground: See Serrano Campground (No. 18 above) for more about the attractions of this recreation area. Elevation 7,000 feet. Stay limit 14 days. Open approximately May through October.

20 Big Bear Lake Recreation Area: Buttercup

Location: 4 miles southwest of Big Bear City.
Sites: 1 group site that accommodates up to 40 people and 8 vehicles.
Facilities: Picnic tables, fire rings, drinking water, chemical toilets.
Fee per night: $25-$50. Reservations required; call 800-280-CAMP. Reservation fee, $17.35.
Agency: San Bernardino National Forest, Big Bear Ranger District, 909-866-3437.
Activities: Hiking, swimming, boating, fishing, skiing in winter.
Finding the campground: From the intersection of California 38 and CA 18 in Big Bear City, drive west on CA 18 for about 4 miles. Turn left onto Summit Boulevard. Buttercup is just past the entrance to Pineknot Campground (see above).

About the campground: See Serrano Campground (No. 18 above) for more about the attractions of this recreation area. Elevation 7,000 feet. Stay limit 14 days. Open approximately May through October.

21 Big Bear Lake Recreation Area: Coldbrook

Location: 7 miles southwest of Big Bear City.
Sites: 36 sites for tents and RVs up to 25 feet long.
Facilities: Picnic tables, fire rings, drinking water, vault toilets.
Fee per night: $12-$24. For reservations, call 800-280-CAMP. Reservation fee, $8.65.
Agency: San Bernardino National Forest, Big Bear Ranger District, 909-866-3437.
Activities: Hiking, swimming, boating, fishing, skiing in winter.
Finding the campground: From the intersection of California 38 and CA 18 in Big Bear City, drive west on CA 18 for about 6 miles. Turn left onto Mill Creek Road and drive about 1 mile.

About the campground: See Serrano Campground (No. 18 above) for more about the attractions of this recreation area. Elevation 7,000 feet. Stay limit 14 days. Open approximately May through October.

22 Big Bear Lake Recreation Area: Boulder

Location: 9 miles southwest of Big Bear City.
Sites: 1 group site that accommodates up to 40 people and 8 vehicles.
Facilities: Picnic tables, fire rings, vault toilets. No drinking water.
Fee per night: $25-$50. Reservations required; call 800-280-CAMP. Reservation fee, $17.35.
Agency: San Bernardino National Forest, Big Bear Ranger District, 909-866-3437.
Activities: Hiking, swimming, boating, fishing, skiing in winter.
Finding the campground: From the intersection of California 38 and CA 18 in Big Bear City, drive west on CA 18 for about 6 miles. Turn left onto Mill Creek Road and drive about 1 mile, to where Mill Creek Road becomes FR 2N10. Continue south on FR 2N10 for about 2 miles.

About the campground: See Serrano Campground (No. 18 above) for more about the attractions of this recreation area. Elevation 7,000 feet. Stay limit 14 days. Open approximately May through October.

23 Big Bear Lake Recreation Area: Deer

Location: 9.5 miles southwest of Big Bear City.
Sites: 1 group site that accommodates up to 40 people and 8 vehicles.
Facilities: Picnic tables, fire rings, vault toilets. No drinking water.
Fee per night: $25-$50. For reservations, call 800-280-CAMP. Reservation fee, $17.35.
Agency: San Bernardino National Forest, Big Bear Ranger District, 909-866-3437.
Activities: Hiking, swimming, boating, fishing, skiing in winter.
Finding the campground: From the intersection of California 38 and CA 18 in Big Bear City, drive west on CA 18 for about 6 miles. Turn left onto Mill Creek Road and drive about 1 mile, to where Mill Creek Road becomes FR 2N10.

Continue south on FR 2N10 for about 1 mile, turn left onto FR 2N08 and drive 1 mile. Turn right onto FR 2N17 and go half a mile.

About the campground: See Serrano Campground (No. 18 above) for more about the attractions of this recreation area. Elevation 7,000 feet. Stay limit 14 days. Open approximately May through October.

24 Gray's Peak

Location: 3 miles northwest of Fawnskin.
Sites: 1 group site for tents and RVs that accommodates up to 40 people and 8 vehicles.
Facilities: Picnic tables, fire rings, vault toilets. No drinking water.
Fee per night: $25. For reservations, call 800-280-CAMP. Reservation fee, $17.35.
Agency: San Bernardino National Forest, Big Bear Ranger District, 909-866-3437.
Activities: Hiking.
Finding the campground: From California 38 in the town of Fawnskin on the north shore of Big Bear Lake, take FR 3N14 northwest and drive about 2 miles. Turn left onto FR 2N68 and drive about 1 mile.

About the campground: Elevation 7,200 feet. Stay limit 14 days. Open approximately May through October.

25 Hanna Flat

Location: 3 miles northwest of Fawnskin.
Sites: 88 sites for tents and RVs up to 40 feet long.
Facilities: Picnic tables, fire rings, drinking water, vault toilets.
Fee per night: $12. For reservations, call 800-280-CAMP. Reservation fee, $8.65.
Agency: San Bernardino National Forest, Big Bear Ranger District, 909-866-3437.
Activities: Hiking.
Finding the campground: From California 38 in the town of Fawnskin on the north shore of Big Bear Lake, take FR 3N14 northwest and drive about 3 miles. The last 2.5 miles are unpaved.

About the campground: The Pacific Crest Trail passes 1 mile north of the campground. Elevation 7,000 feet. Stay limit 14 days. Open approximately May through October.

26 Ironwood

Location: 7 miles northwest of Fawnskin.
Sites: 1 group site for tents that accommodates up to 25 people and 5 vehicles; no RVs.
Facilities: Picnic tables, fire rings, vault toilets. No drinking water.
Fee per night: $35. Reservations required; call 800-280-CAMP. Reservation fee, $17.35.

Agency: San Bernardino National Forest, Big Bear Ranger District, 909-866-3437.
Activities: Hiking.
Finding the campground: From California 38 in the town of Fawnskin on the north shore of Big Bear Lake, take FR 3N14 northwest and drive about 6 miles. Turn left onto FR 3N97 and drive about 1 mile on a rough road.

About the campground: The Pacific Crest Trail passes 1.5 miles south of the campground. Elevation 6,700 feet. Stay limit 14 days. Open approximately May through October.

27 Big Pine Horse Camp

Location: 8 miles northwest of Fawnskin.
Sites: 1 group site for tents that accommodates up to 60 people and 15 vehicles; no RVs.
Facilities: Picnic tables, fire rings, drinking water, vault toilets.
Fee per night: $35. Reservations required; call 800-280-CAMP. Reservation fee, $17.35.
Agency: San Bernardino National Forest, Big Bear Ranger District, 909-866-3437.
Activities: Horseback riding.
Finding the campground: From California 38 in the town of Fawnskin on the north shore of Big Bear Lake, take FR 3N14 northwest and drive about 7 miles. Turn left onto FR 3N16 and drive about 1 mile.

About the campground: The campground is for equestrian use only. Elevation 6,700 feet. Stay limit 14 days. Open approximately May through October.

28 Big Pine Flat

Location: 8 miles northwest of Fawnskin.
Sites: 17 sites for tents and RVs up to 30 feet long.
Facilities: Picnic tables, fire rings, drinking water, vault toilets.
Fee per night: $10.
Agency: San Bernardino National Forest, Big Bear Ranger District, 909-866-3437.
Activities: Hiking.
Finding the campground: From California 38 in the town of Fawnskin on the north shore of Big Bear Lake, take FR 3N14 northwest and drive about 7 miles. Turn left onto FR 3N16 and drive about 1 mile. Big Pine Flat is adjacent to Big Pine Horse Camp (see above).

About the campground: Elevation 6,800 feet. Stay limit 14 days. Open approximately May through October.

29 Bluff Mesa

Location: 12 miles west of Big Bear City.
Sites: 1 group site for tents or RVs that accommodates up to 40 people and 8 vehicles.

Facilities: Picnic tables, fire rings, vault toilets. No drinking water.
Fee per night: $25. For reservations, call 800-280-CAMP. Reservation fee, $17.35.
Agency: San Bernardino National Forest, Big Bear Ranger District, 909-866-3437.
Activities: Hiking.
Finding the campground: From the intersection of California 38 and CA 18 in Big Bear City, drive west on CA 18 for about 6 miles, turn left onto Mill Creek Road, and drive about 1.5 miles. Turn right onto unpaved FR 2N10 and drive about 3 miles. Then turn right onto FR 2N86 and drive about 1 mile.

About the campground: Elevation 7,600 feet. Stay limit 14 days. Open approximately May through October.

30 Shady Cove

Location: 4 miles east of Running Springs.
Sites: 1 group site for tents that accommodates up to 75 people and 15 vehicles; no RVs.
Facilities: Picnic tables, fire rings, drinking water, vault toilets.
Fee per night: $55-$100. Reservations required; call 800-280-CAMP. Reservation fee, $17.35.
Agency: San Bernardino National Forest, Arrowhead Ranger District, 909-337-2444.
Activities: Hiking.
Finding the campground: From the intersection of California 330 and CA 18 in Running Springs, drive east on CA 18 for 1 mile to the Deer Lick Fire Station. Turn right onto FR 1N96 and drive about 3 miles.

About the campground: The National Children's Forest is just east of the campground. Site of the most devastating fire in the history of the San Bernardino National Forest, the area was replanted by local children with the support of the Hunt Wesson Company. A self-guiding, 45-minute loop trail tells the story. The trail is wheelchair accessible. A key is required to enter the campground; it can be obtained by mail or from the Deer Lick Fire Station. Elevation 7,500 feet. Stay limit 14 days. Open approximately May through October.

31 Green Valley

Location: 7 miles northeast of Running Springs.
Sites: 36 sites for tents and RVs up to 22 feet long.
Facilities: Picnic tables, fire rings, drinking water, vault toilets.
Fee per night: $10. For reservations, call 800-280-CAMP. Reservation fee, $8.65.
Agency: San Bernardino National Forest, Arrowhead Ranger District, 909-337-2444.
Activities: Fishing.
Finding the campground: From the intersection of California 330 and CA 18 in Running Springs, drive east on CA 18 for about 3 miles. Turn left onto Green Valley Lake Road and drive 4 miles.

About the campground: Situated on the bank of Green Valley Creek, the campground offers trout fishing in the stream and in Green Valley Lake, 1 mile south. Elevation 7,000 feet. Stay limit 14 days. Open approximately May through October.

32 Crab Flat

Location: 10 miles north of Running Springs.
Sites: 29 sites for tents and RVs up to 15 feet long.
Facilities: Picnic tables, fire rings, drinking water, vault toilets.
Fee per night: $10.
Agency: San Bernardino National Forest, Arrowhead Ranger District, 909-337-2444.
Activities: Hiking.
Finding the campground: From the intersection of California 330 and CA 18 in Running Springs, drive east on CA 18 for about 3 miles. Turn left onto Green Valley Lake Road and drive 3 miles, then turn left onto unpaved FR 3N16 and drive 4 miles. Bear left on FR 3N34 for 0.2 mile.

About the campground: Two small streams must be forded en route to the campground. A high-clearance vehicle might be necessary if the water level is unusually high. A trail leads from the campground to the Pacific Crest Trail, a mile to the north. Elevation 6,200 feet. Stay limit 14 days. Open approximately May through October.

33 Tent Peg

Location: 11 miles north of Running Springs.
Sites: 1 group site for tents or RVs that accommodates up to 30 people and 5 vehicles.
Facilities: Picnic tables, fire rings, vault toilets. No drinking water.
Fee per night: $30. Reservations required; call 800-280-CAMP. Reservation fee, $17.35.
Agency: San Bernardino National Forest, Arrowhead Ranger District, 909-337-2444.
Activities: Hiking.
Finding the campground: From the intersection of California 330 and CA 18 in Running Springs, drive east on CA 18 for about 3 miles. Turn left onto Green Valley Lake Road and drive 3 miles, then turn left onto unpaved FR 3N16 and drive 4 miles. Bear left on FR 3N34 for 1 mile.

About the campground: Two small streams must be forded en route to the campground. A high-clearance vehicle might be necessary if the water level is unusually high. Elevation 5,400 feet. Stay limit 14 days. Open approximately May through October.

34 North Shore

Location: 11 miles northwest of Running Springs.
Sites: 27 sites for tents and RVs up to 22 feet long.
Facilities: Picnic tables, fire rings, drinking water, flush toilets.
Fee per night: $10. For reservations, call 800-280-CAMP. Reservation fee, $8.65.
Agency: San Bernardino National Forest, Arrowhead Ranger District, 909-337-2444.
Activities: Fishing, off-highway driving.
Finding the campground: From the intersection of California 330 and CA 18 in Running Springs, drive northwest on CA 18 for about 6 miles. Turn right onto CA 173 and drive about 5 miles, and then turn right onto Hospital Road. The campground is just past the hospital entrance.

About the campground: This campground is near the northeastern shore of Lake Arrowhead, which is a private lake. Public fishing is permitted from specific areas, but swimming is prohibited. There are numerous OHV trails north and east of the campground. Elevation 5,300 feet. Stay limit 14 days. Open approximately May through October.

35 Dogwood

Location: 8 miles northwest of Running Springs.
Sites: 90 sites for tents and RVs up to 22 feet long.
Facilities: Picnic tables, fire rings, drinking water, flush toilets, dump station.
Fee per night: $12-$16. For reservations, call 800-280-CAMP. Reservation fee, $8.65.
Agency: San Bernardino National Forest, Arrowhead Ranger District, 909-337-2444.
Activities: Off-highway driving.
Finding the campground: From the intersection of California 330 and CA 18 in Running Springs, drive northwest on CA 18 for about 7.5 miles. Turn right onto Daley Canyon Road and make an immediate right, then a left, to the campground entrance.

About the campground: Lake Arrowhead OHV Area is 1 mile west of the campground. See North Shore Campground (above) for information about the use of Lake Arrowhead. Elevation 5,600 feet. Stay limit 14 days. Open approximately May through October.

36 Silverwood Lake State Recreation Area

Location: 22 miles north of San Bernardino.
Sites: 128 sites for tents and RVs up to 34 feet long, plus 3 group sites.
Facilities: Picnic tables, fire grills, drinking water, showers, flush toilets, dump station, snack bar, boat launch.
Fee per night: $12-$18 individual sites, $150 group sites. For reservations, call Parknet, 800-444-7275. Reservation fee, $6.75.
Agency: California Department of Parks and Recreation, 760-389-2303.

Activities: Hiking, biking, swimming, fishing, boating, waterskiing.
Finding the campground: From the intersection of California 259 and Interstate 15, take I15 northwest for 16 miles. Exit at Cajon Junction and drive east on CA 138 for 13 miles.

About the campground: The campground is situated in an attractive wooded setting on the southwestern shore of Silverwood Lake, which offers a full range of water sports and activities. A swimming beach is located at the campground, and a boat launch is nearby. Anglers can fish for trout, catfish, bluegill, and bass. Hiking and biking trails are located throughout the park. Stay limit 10 days from June through September, 30 days from October through May. Individual sites (Mesa Campground) open all year, group site open March through October.

37 Prado Regional Park

Location: 7 miles south of Chino.
Sites: 15 tent sites; 75 sites for RVs, including 50 with full hookups and 25 with water and electricity; plus 1 group site for tents or RVs.
Facilities: Picnic tables, grills, fire rings, drinking water, flush toilets, showers, dump station, store, snack bar, bait shop, boat rentals, pony and horse rentals, playground, archery range, golf course, horseshoe pits.
Fee per night: $15, pets $1. Reservations accepted.
Agency: San Bernardino County Regional Parks Division, 909-597-4260.
Activities: Hiking, fishing, boating, horseback riding, bird watching, golf, archery.
Finding the campground: From the intersection of California 60 and CA 83 in Chino, drive 7 miles south on CA 83 (Euclid Avenue). The campground entrance is on the left.

About the campground: Prado is located on a small, stocked lake, where fishing and non-motorized boating are permitted. Swimming is prohibited. Pedal boats and row boats are available for rent, and hiking and horse trails lead from the campground to the surrounding area. Stay limit 14 days. Open all year.

38 Yucaipa Regional Park

Location: 8 miles east of Redlands.
Sites: 26 sites with full hookups for RVs, 9 group sites for tents.
Facilities: Picnic tables, grills, fire rings, flush toilets, showers, dump station, snack bar, playground, basketball court, horseshoe pits, water slides, pedal boat and aqua cycle rental.
Fee per night: $18 for RV sites, $11 for tent sites.
Agency: San Bernardino County Regional Parks Division, 909-790-3127.
Activities: Swimming, fishing, boating, bird watching.
Finding the campground: From the intersection of California 30 and Interstate 10 at Redlands, drive 3.1 miles southeast on I-10, take the Yucaipa Boulevard exit, and drive 1.9 miles. Turn left onto Oak Glen Road and drive 2.6 miles to the campground entrance on the left.

About the campground: Yucaipa is a family-oriented park centered around three small lakes. A 1-acre swimming lagoon with two 350-foot water slides is separated from the boating and fishing areas. Swimming is possible from Memorial Day to Labor Day. The lakes are stocked with trout and catfish to provide year-round fishing. The location of the park affords an excellent panoramic view of the Yucaipa Valley. Stay limit 14 days. Open all year.

RIVERSIDE COUNTY

In 1875, a small 12-room adobe inn was constructed in the town of Riverside. Over the years, the inn grew with the town, adding rooms, alcoves, stained-glass windows, and antiques. Today a major tourist attraction, the Mission Inn is the city's landmark.

South of Riverside, several scenic lakes offer complete water-sports vacations,

		Group sites	RV sites	Max. RV length	Hookups	Toilets	Showers	Drinking water	Dump station	Pets	Wheelchair	Recreation	Fee ($)	Season	Can reserve
1	Bogart County Park	•	•			F		•		•	•	H	10–12		•
2	Lake Perris SRA	•	•	31	WE	F	•	•	•	•	•	HSFBLR	8–22		•
3	Lake Elsinore Rec Area		•	40	E	F	•	•	•	•	•	SBF	14–18		
4	El Cariso North		•	22		V		•		•		H	10		
5	El Cariso South		•	17		V		•		•		H	10	Apr–Sep	
6	Upper San Juan		•	32		V		•		•		H	10	Apr–Sep	
7	Wildomar		•	22		V		•		•		O	10		
8	Boulder Basin		•			V		•		•		H	10	May–Sep	
9	Black Mountain	•	•	23		V		•		•		H	60	May–Sep	•
10	Fern Basin		•	15		V		•		•		H	10	May–Sep	
11	Marion Mountain		•	15		V		•		•		H	10	May–Sep	
12	Dark Canyon		•	23		V		•		•		H	10	May–Sep	•
13	Stone Creek		•	23		P		•		•	•	H	7–11		•
14	Idyllwild		•	23		F	•	•		•	•	H	12–17		•
15	Idyllwild County Park		•	34		F	•	•		•	•	H	10		
16	Hurkey Creek County Park		•	35		F	•	•		•		HF	12		•
17	Lake Hemet		•		WES	F	•	•	•	•	•	FB	12–15		•
18	Thomas Mountain					V				•				May–Sep	
19	Tool Box Spring					V		•		•				May–Sep	
20	Pinyon Flat		•	19		V		•		•		H	10		
21	Santa Rosa Springs					V		•		•				May–Sep	
22	Toro					V				•				May–Sep	
23	Lake Skinner Rec Area		•		WES	F	•	•	•	•	•	FB	15–18		•

Hookups: W = Water E = Electric S = Sewer
Toilets: F = Flush V = Vault P = Pit C = Chemical
Recreation: H = Hiking S = Swimming F = Fishing B = Boating L = Boat Launch O = Off-highway Driving R = Horseback Riding
Maximum Trailer/RV Length given in feet. **Stay Limit** given in days. **Fee** given in dollars.
If no entry under **Season**, campground is open all year. If no entry under **Fee**, camping is free.

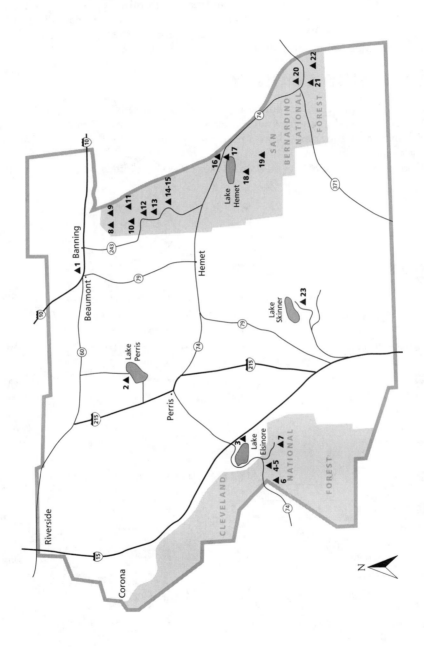

and in the southeast, the San Bernardino National Forest and Mount San Jacinto State Park offer many miles of hiking trails. The Temecula Valley boasts half a dozen wineries that produce excellent, if lesser known, wines. Most of them offer tours, tastings, and retail sales.

1 Bogart County Park

Location: 4 miles north of Beaumont.
Sites: 40 sites for tents and RVs, plus 1 group site.
Facilities: Picnic tables, fire rings, drinking water, flush toilets, playground.
Fee per night: $10-$12 for individual site, $108-$144 for group site. For reservations, call Destinet, 800-344-7275. Reservation fee, $12.
Agency: Riverside County Parks Department, 909-845-3818.
Activities: Hiking.
Finding the campground: From the intersection of Interstate 10 and Beaumont Avenue in Beaumont, take Beaumont Avenue north for 1.4 miles, turn right onto 14th Street and drive 0.8 mile to Cherry Avenue. Turn left and drive 1.8 miles to the park at 9600 Cherry Avenue.

About the campground: Stay limit 14 days. Open all year.

2 Lake Perris State Recreation Area

Location: 15 miles southeast of Riverside.
Sites: 265 sites for RVs up to 31 feet long, with water, electrical, and sink-water disposal hookups; 167 tent sites; 6 group sites; 50 primitive equestrian sites.
Facilities: Picnic tables, grills, drinking water, flush toilets, showers, dump station, playground, store, snack bar, marina, water slide.
Fee per night: $8-$22 for tent sites, $75-$100 for group sites, $20 for equestrian sites, pets $1. For reservations of individual sites, call Parknet, 800-444-7275. Reservation fee, $7.50. For group and equestrian reservations, call the number below.
Agency: California Department of Parks and Recreation, 909-940-5603.
Activities: Hiking, horseback riding, cycling, rock climbing, swimming, boating, fishing, sailboarding, waterskiing, scuba diving.
Finding the campground: From the intersection of Interstate 215 and California 60 east of Riverside, take CA 60 east for 6.6 miles, turn right at Moreno Beach Drive, drive 4.2 miles to Via del Lago, and turn left.

About the campground: Lake Perris combines a full range of water sports with lots of dryland activities. Two swimming beaches, two fishing piers, and a designated area for sailboats, sailboards, and nonmotorized boats are separated from the water-skiers. There is also a separate area for scuba diving. Fish caught in the lake include trout, bass, bluegill, and catfish. Allesandro Island, in the eastern part of the lake, has a boat-in picnic area and a trail to its cone-shaped summit. A 9-mile trail for hikers and mountain bikers circles the lake, paralleled by a trail farther inland for horses. The Ridge Top Hiking Trail provides a desert

Allesandro Island in Lake Perris is just off shore from the marina, swimming beaches, and fishing piers that attract campers to Lake Perris State Recreation Area.

backpacking trip, while a 1.4-mile climb of Terri Peak allows day hikers to share a similar experience. At the southern end of the dam, rock climbers practice on the walls of Big Rock Area. An interesting Regional Indian Museum is located on the north shore of the lake, about half a mile from the park entrance. Stay limit 15 days. Open all year.

3 Lake Elsinore Recreation Area

Location: On the northwestern shore of Lake Elsinore.
Sites: 400 sites for tents and RVs up to 40 feet long, many with electrical hookups.
Facilities: Picnic tables, grills, drinking water, flush toilets, showers, laundry, dump station, store, playground.
Fee per night: $14-$18.
Agency: City of Lake Elsinore, 909-659-4519.
Activities: Swimming, fishing, boating, waterskiing.
Finding the campground: From the intersection of Interstate 15 and California 74 in the town of Lake Elsinore, take CA 74 southwest for 3 miles.

About the campground: Formerly a state park, this lakefront campground is now operated by the nearby city of Lake Elsinore. It has an attractive beach and a small boat ramp. Stay limit 14 days. Open all year.

4 El Cariso North

Location: 7 miles southwest of Lake Elsinore.
Sites: 24 sites for tents and RVs up to 22 feet long.

Facilities: Picnic tables, fire rings, drinking water, vault toilets.
Fee per night: $10.
Agency: Cleveland National Forest, Trabuco Ranger District, 909-736-1811.
Activities: Hiking.
Finding the campground: From the intersection of Interstate 15 and California 74 in the town of Lake Elsinore, drive 7 miles southwest on CA 74.

About the campground: Stay limit 14 days. Open all year.

5 El Cariso South

Location: 7 miles southwest of Lake Elsinore.
Sites: 11 sites for tents and RVs up to 17 feet long.
Facilities: Picnic tables, fire rings, drinking water, vault toilets.
Fee per night: $10.
Agency: Cleveland National Forest, Trabuco Ranger District, 909-736-1811.
Activities: Hiking.
Finding the campground: From the intersection of Interstate 15 and California 74 in the town of Lake Elsinore, drive 7 miles southwest on CA 74.

About the campground: Stay limit 14 days. Open April through September.

6 Upper San Juan

Location: 10 miles southwest of Lake Elsinore.
Sites: 18 sites for tents and RVs up to 32 feet long.
Facilities: Picnic tables, fire rings, drinking water, vault toilets.
Fee per night: $10.
Agency: Cleveland National Forest, Trabuco Ranger District, 909-736-1811.
Activities: Hiking.
Finding the campground: From the intersection of Interstate 15 and California 74 in the town of Lake Elsinore, drive 10 miles southwest on CA 74.

About the campground: See Campground No. 6 in the Orange County section, page 177. Stay limit 14 days. Open April through September.

7 Wildomar

Location: 15 miles southeast of Lake Elsinore.
Sites: 12 sites for tents and RVs up to 22 feet long.
Facilities: Picnic tables, fire rings, drinking water, vault toilets.
Fee per night: $10.
Agency: Cleveland National Forest, Trabuco Ranger District, 909-736-1811.
Activities: Off-highway driving.
Finding the campground: From the intersection of Interstate 15 and California 74 in the town of Lake Elsinore, drive 7 miles southwest on CA 74, turn left at El Cariso Fire Station onto Killen Road, and drive 8 miles.

About the campground: Wildomar is primarily for the use of off-highway-vehicle enthusiasts. The campground provides access to 340 acres of open, hardscape riding. Stay limit 14 days. Open all year.

8 Boulder Basin

Location: 10 miles north of Idyllwild.
Sites: 34 sites for tents.
Facilities: Picnic tables, fire rings, drinking water, vault toilets.
Fee per night: $10.
Agency: San Bernardino National Forest, San Jacinto Ranger District, 909-659-2117.
Activities: Hiking.
Finding the campground: From Mount San Jacinto State Park headquarters in Idyllwild, drive north 6.7 miles on California 243. Turn right onto FR 4S01 (a narrow, unpaved road) and drive 3 miles.

About the campground: High in the Black Mountain National Scenic Area (elevation 7,300 feet), this campground provides access to several trails that lead to panoramic overlooks. Stay limit 14 days. Open May through September.

9 Black Mountain

Location: 11 miles north of Idyllwild.
Sites: 2 group sites for tents and RVs up to 23 feet long, each accommodating up to 50 people and 16 vehicles; trailers not recommended.
Facilities: Picnic tables, fire rings, drinking water, vault toilets.
Fee per night: $60. For reservations, call 800-280-CAMP. Reservation fee, $15.
Agency: San Bernardino National Forest, San Jacinto Ranger District, 909-659-2117.
Activities: Hiking.
Finding the campground: From Mount San Jacinto State Park headquarters in Idyllwild, drive north 6.7 miles on California 243. Turn right onto FR 4S01 (a narrow, unpaved road) and drive 4 miles.

About the campground: Elevation 7,500 feet. Stay limit 14 days. Open May through September.

10 Fern Basin

Location: 5 miles north of Idyllwild.
Sites: 22 sites for tents and RVs up to 15 feet long.
Facilities: Picnic tables, fire rings, drinking water, vault toilets.
Fee per night: $10.
Agency: San Bernardino National Forest, San Jacinto Ranger District, 909-659-2117.
Activities: Hiking.

Finding the campground: From Mount San Jacinto State Park headquarters in Idyllwild, drive north 3.4 miles on California 243, turn right onto FR 4S02, and drive 1.5 miles.

About the campground: Elevation 6,300 feet. Stay limit 14 days. Open May through September.

11 Marion Mountain

Location: 6 miles north of Idyllwild.
Sites: 24 sites for tents and RVs up to 15 feet long.
Facilities: Picnic tables, fire rings, drinking water, vault toilets.
Fee per night: $10.
Agency: San Bernardino National Forest, San Jacinto Ranger District, 909-659-2117.
Activities: Hiking.
Finding the campground: From Mount San Jacinto State Park headquarters in Idyllwild, drive north 3.4 miles on California 243, turn right onto FR 4S02, and drive 2.5 miles.

About the campground: Elevation 6,400 feet. Stay limit 14 days. Open May through September.

12 Dark Canyon

Location: 7 miles north of Idyllwild.
Sites: 22 sites for tents and RVs up to 23 feet long.
Facilities: Picnic tables, fire rings, drinking water, vault toilets.
Fee per night: $10. For reservations, call 800-280-CAMP. Reservation fee, $8.65.
Agency: San Bernardino National Forest, San Jacinto Ranger District, 909-659-2117.
Activities: Hiking.
Finding the campground: From Mount San Jacinto State Park headquarters in Idyllwild, drive north 3.4 miles on California 243, turn right onto FR 4S02, and drive 3.5 miles.

About the campground: Elevation 5,800 feet. Stay limit 14 days. Open May through September.

13 Mount San Jacinto State Park: Stone Creek

Location: 6 miles north of Idyllwild.
Sites: 50 sites for tents and RVs up to 23 feet long.
Facilities: Picnic tables, grills, drinking water, pit toilets.
Fee per night: $7-$11, pets $1. For reservations, call Parknet, 800-444-7275. Reservation fee, $6.75.
Agency: California Department of Parks and Recreation, 909-659-2607.
Activities: Hiking, snowshoeing, cross-country skiing.

Finding the campground: From Idyllwild, drive 6 miles north on California 243.

About the campground: See Idyllwild (No. 14 below) for more about the attractions of this state park. Elevation 5,900 feet. Stay limit 15 days from June through September, 30 days from October through May. Open all year.

14 Mount San Jacinto State Park: Idyllwild

Location: In Idyllwild.
Sites: 33 sites for tents and RVs up to 23 feet long.
Facilities: Picnic tables, grills, drinking water, showers, flush toilets.
Fee per night: $12-$17, pets $1. For reservations, call Parknet, 800-444-7275. Reservation fee, $6.75.
Agency: California Department of Parks and Recreation, 909-659-2607.
Activities: Hiking, snowshoeing, cross-country skiing.
Finding the campground: From Idyllwild, drive to the north end of town on California 243, watching for the entrance sign.

About the campground: Mount San Jacinto encompasses 13,500 acres of high-country wilderness. The park is ideal for backpackers, but day hikers can also enjoy a rewarding backcountry experience. The park can be accessed from its western border via CA 243 or from its eastern border via the Palm Springs Aerial Tramway, a 2.5-mile cable car ride that ascends more than a mile vertically.
  Hiking is the main attraction of this park. Trails connect both ends of the park and another climbs San Jacinto Peak (10,804 feet), the highest mountain in Southern California. The Pacific Crest Trail passes through the park. Since the campgrounds are open all year, snowshoeing and cross-country skiing are popular in the winter. Elevation 5,400 feet. Stay limit 15 days from June through September, 30 days from October through May. Open all year.

15 Idyllwild County Park

Location: In Idyllwild.
Sites: 90 sites for tents and RVs up to 34 feet long.
Facilities: Picnic tables, grills, drinking water, showers, flush toilets.
Fee per night: $10. For reservations, call Destinet, 800-234-7275. Reservation fee, $6.75.
Agency: Riverside County Parks Department, 909-659-2656.
Activities: Hiking.
Finding the campground: In Idyllwild, from the intersection of California 243 and Riverside County Playground Road, follow Playground Road for half a mile and watch for signs.

About the campground: Elevation 5,900 feet. Stay limit 14 days. Open all year.

16 Hurkey Creek County Park

Location: 19 miles southeast of Hemet.
Sites: 105 sites for tents and RVs up to 35 feet long.
Facilities: Picnic tables, grills, drinking water, showers, flush toilets.
Fee per night: $12. For reservations, call Destinet, 800-234-7275. Reservation fee, $6.75.
Agency: Riverside County Parks Department, 909-659-2050.
Activities: Fishing, boating at nearby Lake Hemet.
Finding the campground: From the intersection of California 79 and CA 74 in Hemet, drive east, then southeast, on CA 74 for 19 miles.

About the campground: Hurkey Creek Campground is just across the highway from Lake Hemet. It is spelled Herkey Creek on some maps. Elevation 4,300 feet. Stay limit 14 days. Open all year.

17 Lake Hemet

Location: 19 miles southeast of Hemet.
Sites: 300 sites with full hookups for tents and RVs, plus more than 700 open campsites.
Facilities: Picnic tables, grills, drinking water, showers, flush toilets, dump station, laundry, store, playground, boat ramp and rentals.
Fee per night: $12-$15.
Agency: Hemet Municipal Water District, 909-659-2680.
Activities: Fishing, boating.
Finding the campground: From the intersection of California 79 and CA 74 in Hemet, drive east, then southeast, on CA 74 for 19 miles.

About the campground: Swimming is not permitted in Lake Hemet, and boats under 10 feet long are not allowed. Elevation 4,300 feet. Stay limit 14 days. Open all year.

18 Thomas Mountain

Location: 26 miles southeast of Hemet.
Sites: 6 sites for tents.
Facilities: Picnic tables, fire rings, vault toilets. No drinking water.
Fee per night: None.
Agency: San Bernardino National Forest, San Jacinto Ranger District, 909-659-2117.
Finding the campground: From the intersection of California 79 and CA 74 in Hemet, drive east, then southeast, on CA 74 for 20 miles. Turn right onto FR 6S13 and drive 6 miles.

About the campground: Elevation 6,500 feet. Stay limit 14 days. Open May through September.

19 Tool Box Spring

Location: 28 miles southeast of Hemet.
Sites: 6 sites for tents.
Facilities: Picnic tables, fire rings, drinking water, vault toilets.
Fee per night: None.
Agency: San Bernardino National Forest, San Jacinto Ranger District, 909-659-2117.
Finding the campground: From the intersection of California 79 and CA 74 in Hemet, drive east, then southeast, on CA 74 for 20 miles. Turn right onto FR 6S13 and drive 7.8 miles, passing Thomas Mountain Campground (see above).

About the campground: Elevation 6,500 feet. Stay limit 14 days. Open May through September.

20 Pinyon Flat

Location: 12 miles south of Palm Desert.
Sites: 18 sites for tents and RVs up to 19 feet long.
Facilities: Picnic tables, fire grills, drinking water, vault toilets.
Fee per night: $10.
Agency: San Bernardino National Forest, San Jacinto Ranger District, 909-659-2117.
Activities: Hiking.
Finding the campground: From the intersection of California 111 and CA 74 in Palm Desert, take CA 74 south for about 12 miles.

About the campground: About 2 miles before reaching the campground, Cahuilla Tewanet Vista Point offers fine views of the Santa Rosa Wilderness. A trail (FR 5E01) leads east into the wilderness from the campground, and another leads west half a mile past the campground on CA 74. Stay limit 14 days. Open all year.

21 Santa Rosa Springs

Location: 22 miles south of Palm Desert.
Sites: 3 sites for tents.
Facilities: Picnic tables, fire rings, drinking water, vault toilets.
Fee per night: None.
Agency: San Bernardino National Forest, San Jacinto Ranger District, 909-659-2117.
Finding the campground: From Palm Desert, drive 16 miles south on California 74, turn left onto FR 7S02, and drive 6 miles.

About the campground: Elevation 6,000 feet. Stay limit 14 days. Open May through September.

22 Toro

Location: 23 miles south of Palm Desert.
Sites: 5 sites for tents.
Facilities: Picnic tables, grills, vault toilets. No water.
Fee per night: None.
Agency: San Bernardino National Forest, San Jacinto Ranger District, 909-659-2117.
Finding the campground: From Palm Desert, drive 16 miles south on California 74, turn left onto FR 7S02, and drive 7.5 miles.

About the campground: Elevation 6,200 feet. Stay limit 14 days. Open May through September.

23 Lake Skinner Recreation Area

Location: 10 miles northeast of Temecula.
Sites: 257 sites for tents and RVs, many with full hookups.
Facilities: Picnic tables, grills, drinking water, showers, flush toilets, dump station, store, playground, boat ramp and rentals.
Fee per night: $15-$18. Reservations suggested; call Destinet, 800-234-7275. Reservation fee, $6.75.
Agency: Riverside County Parks Department, 909-926-1541.
Activities: Fishing, boating.
Finding the campground: From the intersection of Interstate 15 and Rancho California Road in Temecula, drive northeast on Rancho California for 10 miles.

About the campground: No swimming or waterskiing is permitted on Lake Skinner, nor are nonmotorized boats under 10 feet long. Five wineries line Rancho California Road en route to the campground, providing touring, tasting, picnicking, and retail sales opportunities. Stay limit 14 days. Open all year.

SAN DIEGO COUNTY

San Diego is considered the birthplace of California. In 1769, the Franciscan priest Father Junipero Serra founded the Mission San Diego de Alcala, the first European settlement not only in California, but on the west coast of what what would eventually become the United States. Since then, the city has become one of the nation's most popular places to visit and live. Tourists and

SAN DIEGO COUNTY AREA MAP

residents alike are drawn by the climate—usually dry, warm, and sunny—and by an enviable array of cultural and recreational attractions. Two of these—Balboa Park, with its museums and world-famous zoo, and Mission Bay, with miles of public beach and grassy fields offering water sports of every description—would alone be enough to satisfy most residents and visitors.

But San Diego County offers much more than the features of its largest city. From San Onofre to the Mexican border stretch 76 miles of some of the finest beaches on the West Coast. Inland, the hills, streams, and woodlands of the Cleveland National Forest offer a different outdoor perspective. And the vast Anza Borrego Desert State Park devotes almost a quarter of the land in the county to providing visitors a fascinating and unusual desert experience.

Many who live in San Diego claim that it has the finest weather in the nation, and it is difficult to disagree. Average maximum/minimum temperatures range in summer from 75 to 64 degrees Farenheit and in winter from 66 to 49 degrees F. Spring brings temperatures from 67 to 55 degrees F, and fall 74 to 60 degrees F. The percentage of average days of sunshine is 65 percent in summer, 70 in fall, 72 in winter, and 65 in spring.

This book divides San Diego County into three areas: the Coastal Plain, Cleveland National Forest, and Anza Borrego Desert State Park.

THE COASTAL PLAIN

On Presidio Hill in the city of San Diego stands the Mission San Diego de Alcala, the birthplace of the city and of California. A short distance down the hill, Old Town provides another sense of the state's early settlement. Downtown, the Gaslamp Quarter, a national historic district, contains fine examples of Victorian architecture. San Diego Harbor hosts one of the largest naval bases in the world, yet the waterfront is a showcase. The Embarcadero, a landscaped boardwalk, leads past the Maritime Museum to Seaport Village, a replica of an early California seaport.

San Diego boasts what is probably the finest water-oriented park in the nation, Mission Bay. Encompassing 4,600 acres and 27 miles of sandy beaches, the park offers every conceivable water activity, as well as picnic areas, playgrounds, tennis and volleyball courts, cycling/skating/jogging paths, restaurants, shops, and two huge campgrounds. In addition, Seaworld, the world's largest oceanarium, provides education and entertainment to flocks of visitors. Not far from Mission Bay is Balboa Park, home to the famed San Diego Zoo, where 3,800 animals occupy 150 acres. The park also features nine museums, three art galleries, several theaters, and a golf course.

Outside the city, 76 miles of some of California's finest beaches extend from San Onofre in the north to Imperial Beach near the Mexican border. Inland, the restored Mission San Luis Rey, east of Oceanside, and the Mission San Antonio de Pala are well worth a visit. The San Diego Wild Animal Park, near Escondido, houses more than 2,500 animals, many of which roam free on 1,800 acres. Also near Escondido are several wineries, the southernmost in the state.

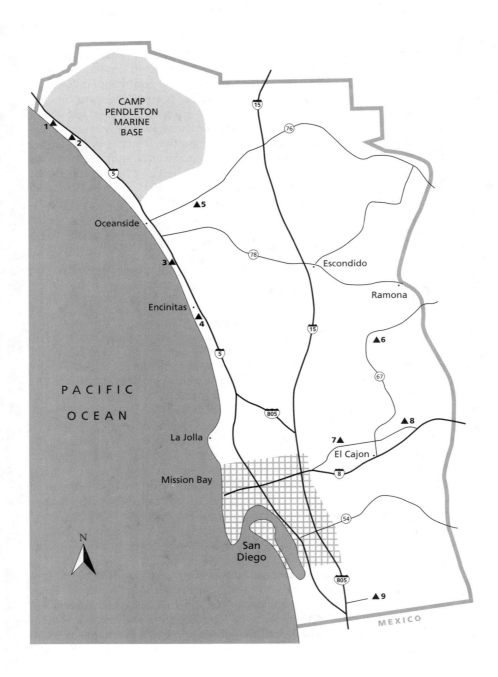

	Group sites	RV sites	Max. RV length	Hookups	Toilets	Showers	Drinking water	Dump station	Pets	Wheelchair	Recreation	Fee ($)	Season	Can reserve
1 Bluffs		•	30		F	•	•		•	•	SF	14–18		•
2 San Mateo		•	36	WE	F	•	•	•	•	•	H	14–24		•
3 South Carlsbad State Beach		•	35		F		•	•	•	•	SF	14–23		•
4 San Elijo State Beach		•	35		F	•	•	•	•	•	SF	14–23		•
5 Guajome Regional Park		•		WE	F	•	•	•	•	•	FR	14		•
6 Dos Picos Regional Park		•		WE	F	•	•		•	•	HF	10–14		•
7 Santee Lakes Regional Park		•	40	WES	F	•	•	•	•	•	SFB	14–20		•
8 Lake Jennings Regional Park		•		WES	F	•	•	•	•	•	H	10–16		•
9 Sweetwater Summit Park		•		WE	F	•	•	•	•	•	HR	12–16		•

Hookups: W = Water E = Electric S = Sewer
Toilets: F = Flush V = Vault P = Pit C = Chemical
Recreation: H = Hiking S = Swimming F = Fishing B = Boating L = Boat Launch O = Off-highway Driving R = Horseback Riding
Maximum Trailer/RV Length given in feet. **Stay Limit** given in days. **Fee** given in dollars.
If no entry under **Season**, campground is open all year. If no entry under **Fee**, camping is free.

1 San Onofre State Beach: Bluffs

Location: 6 miles south of San Clemente.
Sites: 221 sites for tents and RVs up to 30 feet long.
Facilities: Picnic tables, fire rings, drinking water, outdoor cold showers, flush toilets.
Fee per night: $14-$18, pets $1. For reservations, call Parknet, 800-444-7275. Reservation fee, $7.50.
Agency: California Department of Parks and Recreation, 714-492-4872.
Activities: Surfing, swimming, fishing, biking.
Finding the campground: From San Clemente, drive 3 miles south on Interstate 5, take the Basilone Road exit, and drive southeast for 2.8 miles.

About the campground: The Bluffs is the focal point of a 3-mile stretch of pristine beach, famous nationwide as a prime year-round surfing location. The campground lies atop the bluff on a paved strip that was once the coastal highway, and sites are spread along the pavement in a line almost 2 miles long. There is no shade. Several short trails lead down the bluffs to the beach. A paved, 16-mile bike path runs from the south end of the campground to Oceanside. Stay limit 15 days from June through September, 30 days from October through May. Open all year.

2 San Onofre State Beach: San Mateo

Location: 3 miles south of San Clemente.
Sites: 150 sites for tents and RVs up to 36 feet long, including 70 with water and electrical hookups.
Facilities: Picnic tables, fire rings, flush toilets, hot showers, drinking water, dump station.

Fee per night: $14-$24, pets $1. For reservations, call Parknet, 800-444-7275. Reservation fee, $7.50.
Agency: California Department of Parks and Recreation, 714-361-2531.
Activities: Hiking, cycling.
Finding the campground: From San Clemente, drive 2 miles south on Interstate 5, take the Christianitos Road exit, and drive east for 1 mile.

About the campground: Situated off the inland side of the highway, San Mateo affords limited shade at some sites. A 1.5-mile trail leads from the campground to Trestle's Beach, one of the three beaches that comprise San Onofre State Beach. About halfway down this trail, a spur trail leads to San Mateo Creek Natural Preserve, a riparian habitat. Stay limit 15 days from June through September, 30 days from October through May. Open all year.

3 South Carlsbad State Beach

Location: 4 miles south of Carlsbad.
Sites: 222 sites for tents and RVs up to 35 feet long.
Facilities: Picnic tables, fire rings, flush toilets, drinking water, dump station.
Fee per night: $14-$23, pets $1. For reservations, call Parknet, 800-444-7275. Reservation fee, $7.50.
Agency: California Department of Parks and Recreation, 619-438-3143.
Activities: Surfing, swimming, fishing, scuba diving.
Finding the campground: From Carlsbad, drive 4 miles south on County Road S21 (Carlsbad Boulevard).

About the campground: South Carlsbad is one of six beaches that provide access to a 9-mile stretch of ocean between Carlsbad and Cardiff. A mix of sand and cobblestones comprises most of the shoreline. Situated on a bluff above the beach, parts of the campground are exposed to traffic noise. About half the sites have a view of the ocean. Open all year.

4 San Elijo State Beach

Location: Cardiff-by-the-Sea.
Sites: 171 sites for tents and RVs up to 35 feet long.
Facilities: Picnic tables, fire rings, drinking water, flush toilets, showers, dump station.
Fee per night: $14-$23, pets $1. For reservations, call Parknet, 800-444-7275. Reservation fee, $7.50.
Agency: California Department of Parks and Recreation, 619-753-5091.
Activities: Surfing, swimming, fishing, scuba diving.
Finding the campground: From Cardiff, drive north on County Road S21 (Old Highway 101) to its intersection with Chesterfield Drive, where the campground entrance is located.

About the campground: Situated on a rugged bluff overlooking the long beach, the campsites are attractive but afford no shade, despite planted palms and cypress trees. A long wooden staircase descends to the beach. A reef just offshore attracts scuba divers. Stay limit 7 days from June through September, 15 days from October through May. Open all year.

5 Guajome Regional Park

Location: 7 miles east of Oceanside.
Sites: 17 sites with water and electrical hookups for RVs.
Facilities: Picnic tables, fire rings, drinking water, flush toilets, showers, dump station, playground.
Fee per night: $14, pets $1. For reservations, call 760-565-3600. Reservation fee, $3.
Agency: San Diego County Department of Parks and Recreation, 760-694-3049.
Activities: Fishing, hiking, horseback riding.
Finding the campground: From the intersection of Interstate 5 and California 76 in Oceanside, take CA 76 east for 7 miles, turn right onto Santa Fe Avenue, and proceed to the campground entrance on the right.

About the campground: The park was named for a large adobe ranch house. Still standing, the house is now a National Historic Landmark. The Antique Gas and Steam Engine Museum is nearby. Stay limit 14 days. Open all year.

6 Dos Picos Regional Park

Location: 20 miles north of El Cajon.
Sites: 50 sites with water and electrical hookups for RVs, 14 sites for tents.
Facilities: Picnic tables, fire rings, drinking water, flush toilets, showers, playground.
Fee per night: $10-$14, pets $1. For reservations, call 760-565-3600. Reservation fee, $3.
Agency: San Diego County Department of Parks and Recreation, 760-694-3049.
Activities: Fishing, hiking.
Finding the campground: From the intersection of Interstate 8 and California 67 in El Cajon, drive 18 miles north on CA 67, turn right onto Mussey Grade Road, and drive 2 miles.

About the campground: The park is attractively situated in a stand of mature oak trees near San Diego's famous Wild Animal Park. Stay limit 14 days. Open all year.

7 Santee Lakes Regional Park

Location: 5 miles northwest of El Cajon.
Sites: 152 sites with full hookups for RVs up to 40 feet long, including 18 sites with pull-thrus and 61 sites also for tents.
Facilities: Picnic tables, barbecue grills, drinking water, flush toilets, showers, dump station, laundry, store, playground, pool, Jacuzzi, recreation hall, boat rentals.

Fee per night: $14 for tents, $20 for RVs, pets $1. Good Sam discount. Reservations accepted.

Agency: Padre Dam Municipal Water District, 619-448-2482.

Activities: Fishing, boating, swimming (pool only), volleyball and shuffleboard courts, horseshoe pits.

Finding the campground: From the intersection of Interstate 8 and California 67 in El Cajon, drive north 2.2 miles on CA 67, turn left onto Magnolia, and drive 1 mile. Turn left onto Mission Gorge Road and drive 1.7 miles. Turn right onto Carleton Hills Boulevard and drive half a mile, then turn left onto Carleton Oaks Drive and follow it to the campground entrance.

About the campground: A series of seven small lakes is the centerpiece of this attractive campground, which offers all the facilities of a first-rate commercial RV park in a lush, natural setting. The lakes are stocked seasonally with rainbow trout, channel catfish, largemouth bass, and bluegill, and fishing in two lakes is reserved exclusively for campers. Stay limit 15 days. Open all year.

8 Lake Jennings Regional Park

Location: 8 miles northeast of El Cajon.

Sites: 63 sites with full hookups for RVs, 13 sites with no hookups for tents and RVs, 35 sites for tents.

Facilities: Picnic tables, fire rings, drinking water, flush toilets, showers, playground, dump station.

Fee per night: $10-$16, pets $1. For reservations, call 760-565-3600. Reservation fee, $3.

Agency: San Diego County Department of Parks and Recreation, 760-694-3049.

Activities: Hiking.

Finding the campground: From the intersection of California 67 and Interstate 8 in El Cajon, drive east on I-8 for 7 miles to Jennings Park Road. Turn left and drive 1.2 miles.

About the campground: The camping area is on a ridge high above the lake, with scenic views in all directions. The lake is noted for trophy-size catfish and bass. Boat rentals are available nearby. Miles of trails meander across chaparral-covered hillsides. Stay limit 14 days. Open all year.

9 Sweetwater Summit Regional Park

Location: 10 miles southeast of San Diego.

Sites: 60 sites with water and electrical hookups for tents and RVs, including 22 sites with horse corrals.

Facilities: Picnic tables, fire rings, drinking water, showers, flush toilets, dump station.

Fee per night: $12-$16, pets $1. For reservations, call 760-565-3600. Reservation fee, $3.

Agency: San Diego County Department of Parks and Recreation, 760-694-3049.

Activities: Hiking, horseback riding.

Finding the campground: From the intersection of Interstate 805 and County Road S17 (Bonita Road) in south San Diego, drive 4 miles east on CA S17, bear right on San Miguel Road, and drive 6 miles to the park entrance on Summit Meadow Road.

About the campground: Situated high enough to offer views of the blue Pacific, San Diego Bay, and rugged backcountry mountains, the campground also offers miles of trails for hikers and equestrians. Fishing is possible in nearby Sweetwater Reservoir. Stay limit 14 days. Open all year.

CLEVELAND NATIONAL FOREST

Cleveland National Forest occupies most of the central third of San Diego County. Its 567,000 acres stretch from the northern county line to within a few miles

	Group sites	RV sites	Max. RV length	Hookups	Toilets	Showers	Drinking water	Dump station	Pets	Wheelchair	Recreation	Fee ($)	Season	Can reserve
1 Dripping Springs		•	22		V		•		•		HR	8–16		
2 Oak Grove		•	27		F		•		•		H	8		
3 Crestline	•				V		•		•	•		50	May–Nov	•
4 Observatory		•	27		V		•		•		H	8	May–Nov	
5 Fry Creek		•	15		V		•		•		H	8	May–Nov	
6 Palomar Mountain State Park	•	•	21		F	•	•		•	•	HF	12–18		•
7 Indian Flats	•	•	15		V		•		•	•	H	7		
8 William Heise Regional Park	•				F	•	•	•	•	•	HR	11		•
9 Paso Picacho		•	30		F	•	•		•	•	HFR	12–16		•
10 Green Valley		•	30		F	•	•		•		HFR	12–16		•
11 Los Caballos		•	30		F	•	•				HFR	19–20		•
12 Wooded Hill	•	•	40		V		•				HR	30–80	May–Oct	•
13 Burnt Rancheria		•	27		F		•				HR	12	May–Oct	•
14 Horse Heaven	•				V		•				HR	30–80	May–Oct	•
15 Laguna		•	27		F		•				HR	12		•
16 El Prado	•				V		•				HR	30–80	May–Oct	•
17 Cibbets Flat		•	27		V		•		•		H	8		
18 Boulder Oaks		•	27		V		•		•		HR	8		•
19 Lake Morena Regional Park		•	30	WE	F	•	•		•		HFB	10–12		•
20 Bobcat		•	27		V				•		O			
21 Corral Canyon		•	27		V				•		O			
22 Potrero Regional Park		•	35	WE	F	•	•	•	•	•		10–12		•

H2okups: W = Water   E = Electric   S = Sewer
Toilets: F = Flush   V = Vault   P = Pit   C = Chemical
Recreation: H = Hiking   S = Swimming   F = Fishing   B = Boating   L = Boat Launch   O = Off-highway driving   R = Horseback Riding
Maximum Trailer/RV Length given in feet.   **Stay Limit** given in days.   **Fee** given in dollars.
If no entry under **Season**, campground is open all year. If no entry under **Fee**, camping is free.

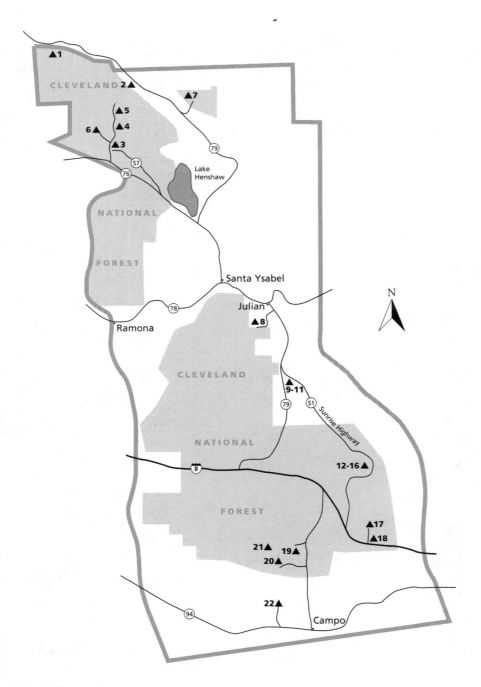

of the Mexican border. The forest vegetation is mostly chaparral, but fine stands of oak can be found in meadows and along streams, and forests of Coulter and Jeffrey pine grow at the higher altitudes. Four designated wilderness areas protect the most primitive sections of the forest. The use of vehicles and bicycles in these areas is prohibited, but hikers, campers, and equestrians are allowed. A free permit is required for overnight wilderness camping.

A warm, dry climate prevails over most of the area, with hot summers and mild winters. Elevations range from 460 to 6,271 feet. The primary activities in the forest are hiking, horseback riding, picnicking, and sightseeing. There are 26 developed campgrounds that can be reached by vehicle, most of them under national forest jurisdiction. They are described below.

1 Dripping Springs

Location: 12 miles east of Temecula.
Sites: 34 sites for tents and RVs up to 22 feet long, plus 9 equestrian sites.
Facilities: Picnic tables, fire rings, drinking water, vault toilets, corrals.
Fee per night: $8, equestrian sites $16.
Agency: Cleveland National Forest, Palomar Ranger District, 760-788-0250.
Activities: Hiking, horseback riding.
Finding the campground: From the intersection of Interstate 15 and California 79 near Temecula, drive 12 miles east on CA 79.

About the campground: Although actually 2 miles north of the San Diego County line, Dripping Springs is integrally a part of the Cleveland National Forest. It is also the gateway to the Agua Tibia Wilderness, most of which lies in San Diego County. The Dripping Springs Trail (13 miles) leads into the wilderness, beginning in open chaparral country and climbing to oak woodland and finally a forest of mixed conifers. Stay limit 14 days. Open all year.

2 Oak Grove

Location: 6 miles southeast of Aguanga.
Sites: 81 sites for tents and RVs up to 27 feet long.
Facilities: Picnic tables, fire rings, drinking water, flush toilets.
Fee per night: $8.
Agency: Cleveland National Forest, Palomar Ranger District, 760-788-0250.
Activities: Hiking.
Finding the campground: From Aguanga, drive southeast on California 79 for 6 miles.

About the campground: Elevation 2,800 feet. Stay limit 14 days. Open all year.

3 Crestline

Location: 27 miles northeast of Escondido.
Sites: 1 large group site for tents.
Facilities: Picnic tables, fire rings, drinking water, vault toilets.
Fee per night: $50. Reservations required; call 800-280-CAMP. Reservation

fee, $17.35.

Agency: Cleveland National Forest, Palomar Ranger District, 760-788-0250.

Activities: Stargazing.

Finding the campground: From the intersection of Interstate 15 and County Road S6, drive 27 miles northeast on CR S6. For travelers approaching from the east, and for those with long or heavy rigs, a less steep approach with fewer curves may be made from the intersection of California Highway 76 and CR S7 at Lake Henshaw. Take CR S7 for 10 miles, turn right onto CR 56, and drive 2 miles.

About the campground: The campground is 4 miles south of Palomar Observatory (see Observatory Campground below). Elevation 4,800 feet. Stay limit 14 days. Open May 1 to November 30.

4 Observatory

Location: 29 miles northeast of Escondido.

Sites: 42 sites for tents and RVs up to 27 feet long.

Facilities: Picnic tables, fire rings, drinking water, vault toilets.

Fee per night: $8.

Agency: Cleveland National Forest, Palomar Ranger District, 760-788-0250.

Activities: Hiking, stargazing.

Finding the campground: From the intersection of Interstate 15 and County Road S6, drive 29 miles northeast on CR S6. For travelers approaching from the east, and for those with long or heavy rigs, a less steep approach with fewer curves may be made from the intersection of California 76 and CR S7 at Lake Henshaw. Take CR S7 for 10 miles, turn right onto CR S6, and drive 2 miles.

About the campground: An excellent 2.2-mile trail leads from the campground to Palomar Observatory (2 miles by road), which houses four astronomical telescopes, including one of the world's largest, the 200-inch Hale telescope. The observatory museum and the telescope viewing area are open to the public daily from 9 A.M. to 4 P.M. Elevation 4,800 feet. Stay limit 14 days. Open May 1 to November 30.

5 Fry Creek

Location: 30 miles northeast of Escondido.

Sites: 20 sites for tents and RVs up to 15 feet long; trailers not recommended.

Facilities: Picnic tables, fire rings, drinking water, vault toilets.

Fee per night: $8.

Agency: Cleveland National Forest, Palomar Ranger District, 760-788-0250.

Activities: Hiking, stargazing.

Finding the campground: From Observatory Campground (see No. 4 above), continue north half a mile on County Road S6. For travelers approaching from the east, and for those with long or heavy rigs, a less steep approach with fewer curves may be made from the intersection of California 76 and

CR S7 at Lake Henshaw. Take CR S7 for 10 miles, turn right onto CR S6, and drive 1.5 miles.

About the campground: See Observatory Campground (above). Elevation 4,900 feet. Stay limit 14 days. Open May 1 to November 30.

6 Palomar Mountain State Park

Location: 28 miles northeast of Escondido.
Sites: 30 sites for tents and RVs up to 27 feet long, 2 group sites for tents, 1 group site for RVs up to 21 feet long.
Facilities: Picnic tables, fire rings, drinking water, showers, flush toilets.
Fee per night: $12-$18 individual sites, $30-$38 group sites, pets $1. For reservations, call Parknet, 800-444-7275. Reservation fee, $7.50.
Agency: California Department of Parks and Recreation, 760-765-0755.
Activities: Hiking, fishing, stargazing.
Finding the campground: From the intersection of Interstate 15 and County Road S6 in Escondido, drive northeast 25 miles on CR 56, turn left (west) onto CR S7 and drive 2.5 miles. For those coming from the east, or with long or heavy rigs, an easier grade approach with fewer curves may be made from the intersection of California 76 and CR S7 at Lake Henshaw. Take CR S7 northwest for 10 miles, turn right onto CR S6 and drive 2 miles.

About the campground: Located on the west slope of Palomar Mountain at an altitude of 4,700 feet, the park is a blend of forest and meadow. Doane Trail leads 2 miles to a magnificent stand of old oak trees, many of them 10 feet in diameter. The Upper Doane Valley Loop Trail (3.5 miles) gains more than 700 feet as it winds through meadows and into the forest. Doane Pond is stocked twice annually with trout, and anglers can also fish for bluegill and catfish. The park is 6.5 miles from Palomar Observatory and one of the world's largest telescopes (see Observatory Campground, No. 4, above). Elevation 4,700 feet. Stay limit 30 days. Open all year.

7 Indian Flats

Location: 8 miles north of Warner Springs.
Sites: 17 sites for tents and RVs up to 15 feet long, plus 2 group sites.
Facilities: Picnic tables, fire rings, drinking water, vault toilets.
Fee per night: $7.
Agency: Cleveland National Forest, Palomar Ranger District, 760-788-0250.
Activities: Hiking.
Finding the campground: From Warner Springs, drive 2 miles west on CA 79, turn right onto Indian Flats Road (FR 9S05), and drive 6 miles.

About the campground: The Pacific Crest Trail passes less than 2 miles east of the campground. Elevation 3,600 feet. Stay limit 14 days. Open all year.

8 William Heise Regional Park

Location: 5 miles south of Julian.
Sites: 86 sites for tents and RVs.
Facilities: Picnic tables, grills, drinking water, showers, flush toilets, laundry, playground, dump station.
Fee per night: $11, pets $1. Reservations accepted; call 760-565-3600. Reservation fee, $3.
Agency: San Diego County Department of Parks and Recreation, 760-694-3049.
Activities: Hiking, horseback riding.
Finding the campground: From Julian, drive west on California 79 for 1 mile, turn left onto Pine Hills Road, and drive south 2 miles. Turn left onto Frisius Road and drive 2 more miles.

About the campground: William Heise Regional Park has been listed by *Sunset* as one of the 100 best camping sites in the western United States. The park consists of 700 acres of oak, cedar, and pine forest in combination with mountain meadows. Because of its 4,200-foot altitude, it enjoys four distinct seasons. Miles of hiking and equestrian trails include the Kelly Ditch Trail, which connects the park to Lake Cuyamaca. Stay limit 14 days. Open all year.

9 Cuyamaca Rancho State Park: Paso Picacho

Location: 14 miles south of Julian.
Sites: 85 sites for tents and RVs up to 30 feet long.
Facilities: Picnic tables, grills, drinking water, showers, flush toilets, dump station.
Fee per night: $12-$16, pets $1. For reservations, call Parknet, 800-444-7275. Reservation fee, $7.50.
Agency: California Department of Parks and Recreation, 760-765-0755.
Activities: Hiking, mountain biking, horseback riding, fishing.
Finding the campground: From Julian, drive 14 miles south on California 79. For travelers approaching from the south, take Interstate 8 to the CA 79 exit and drive north 11 miles. Paso Picacho is just north of park headquarters.

About the campground: Cuyamaca's 25,000 acres extend from 3,000 to 6,000 feet in elevation. Forests of oak, yellow pine, and chaparral are interspersed with stony mesas, rock outcroppings, and rugged peaks. Several trails are located in the park, including two that ascend local peaks, Cuyamaca (6,512 feet) and Stonewall (5,730 feet). Fishing is permitted seasonally in Lake Cuyamaca and the Sweetwater River, but results are usually mediocre. A Native American museum and a nature trail are located at the park headquarters. Paso Picacho is on *Sunset's* list of 100 best campgrounds in the western United States. Stay limit 30 days. Open all year.

10 Cuyamaca Rancho State Park: Green Valley

Location: 18 miles south of Julian.
Sites: 81 sites for tents and RVs up to 30 feet long.
Facilities: Picnic tables, grills, drinking water, showers, flush toilets.
Fee per night: $12-$16, pets $1. For reservations, call Parknet, 800-444-7275. Reservation fee, $7.50.
Agency: California Department of Parks and Recreation, 760-765-0755.
Activities: Hiking, mountain biking, horseback riding, fishing.
Finding the campground: From Julian, drive 18 miles south on California 79. For travelers approaching from the south, take Interstate 8 to the CA 79 exit and drive north 6 miles.

About the campground: See Paso Picacho Campground (above) for information about the attractions of this state park. Stay limit 30 days. Open all year.

11 Cuyamacha Rancho State Park: Los Caballos

Location: 13 miles south of Julian.
Sites: 15 equestrian sites for tents and RVs up to 30 feet long.
Facilities: Picnic tables, grills, drinking water, showers, flush toilets, corrals.
Fee per night: $19-$20. For reservations, call Parknet, 800-444-7275. Reservation fee, $7.50.
Agency: California Department of Parks and Recreation, 760-765-0755.
Activities: Hiking, mountain biking, horseback riding, fishing.
Finding the campground: From Julian, drive 14 miles south on California 79. For travelers approaching from the south, take Interstate 8 to the CA 79 exit and drive north 10 miles. Los Caballos is a mile north of park headquarters.

About the campground: Los Caballos is intended for campers with horses. See Paso Picacho Campground (No. 9 above) for information about the attractions of the state park. Stay limit 30 days. Open all year.

12 Laguna Recreation Area: Wooded Hill

Location: 22 miles northeast of Alpine.
Sites: 1 group site for RVs up to 40 feet long.
Facilities: Picnic tables, fire rings, drinking water, vault toilets.
Fee per night: $30-$80. For reservations, call 800-280-CAMP. Reservation fee, $8.25.
Agency: Cleveland National Forest, Descanso Ranger District, 760-445-1753.
Activities: Hiking, horseback riding, scenic driving.
Finding the campground: From Alpine, drive east on Interstate 8 for 15 miles, turn left onto County Road S1 (Sunrise National Scenic Byway), and drive 7 miles.

About the campground: The Sunrise National Scenic Byway extends 24 miles from Interstate 8 near the town of Pine Valley to California 79 at the north end of

Cuyamaca Reservoir. From it, travelers have changing views of oak and pine forests, mountain meadows, and chaparral-covered hillsides. A spectacular panorama of Anza Borrego Desert State Park unfolds as the road climbs to 6,000 feet. Campgrounds, trailheads, picnic areas, and information centers line the route. Several nature loops are found near the campgrounds, and longer trails lead to small lakes, wooded ravines, and scenic overlooks. Stay limit 14 days. Open May through October.

13 Laguna Recreation Area: Burnt Rancheria

Location: 23 miles northeast of Alpine.
Sites: 110 sites for tents and RVs up to 27 feet long (55 sites by reservation only).
Facilities: Picnic tables, fire rings, drinking water, flush toilets.
Fee per night: $12. For reservations, call 800-280-CAMP. Reservation fee, $8.25.
Agency: Cleveland National Forest, Descanso Ranger District, 760-445-1753.
Activities: Hiking, horseback riding, scenic driving.
Finding the campground: From Alpine, drive east on Interstate 8 for 15 miles, turn left onto County Road S1 (Sunrise National Scenic Byway), and drive 8 miles.

About the campground: *Sunset* named Burnt Rancheria as one of the 100 best campgrounds in the western United States. See Wooded Hill (No. 12 above) for more about the attractions of this recreation area. Stay limit 14 days. Open May through October.

14 Laguna Recreation Area: Horse Heaven

Location: 26 miles northeast of Alpine.
Sites: 3 group sites for tents.
Facilities: Picnic tables, fire rings, drinking water, vault toilets.
Fee per night: $30-$80. Reservations required; call 800-280-CAMP. Reservation fee, $8.25.
Agency: Cleveland National Forest, Descanso Ranger District, 760-445-1753.
Activities: Hiking, horseback riding, scenic driving.
Finding the campground: From Alpine, drive east on Interstate 8 for 15 miles, turn left onto County Road S1 (Sunrise National Scenic Byway), and drive about 11 miles.

About the campground: See Wooded Hill (No. 12 above) for more about the attractions of this recreation area. Despite its name, Horse Heaven Campground has no equestrian facilities. Rental horses are available near Burnt Rancheria Campground (see No. 13 above). Stay limit 14 days. Open May through October.

15 Laguna Recreation Area: Laguna

Location: 26 miles northeast of Alpine.
Sites: 104 sites for tents and RVs up to 27 feet long (52 sites by reservation only).
Facilities: Picnic tables, fire rings, drinking water, flush toilets.

Fee per night: $12. For reservations, call 800-280-CAMP. Reservation fee, $8.25.
Agency: Cleveland National Forest, Descanso Ranger District, 760-445-1753.
Activities: Hiking, horseback riding, scenic driving.
Finding the campground: From Alpine, drive east on Interstate 8 for 15 miles, turn left onto County Road S1 (Sunrise National Scenic Byway), and drive about 11 miles.

About the campground: See Wooded Hill (No. 12 above) for more about the attractions of this recreation area. Stay limit 14 days. Open all year.

16 Laguna Recreation Area: El Prado

Location: 26 miles northeast of Alpine.
Sites: 5 group sites for tents.
Facilities: Picnic tables, fire rings, drinking water, vault toilets.
Fee per night: $30-$80. For reservations, call 800-280-CAMP. Reservation fee, $8.25.
Agency: Cleveland National Forest, Descanso Ranger District, 760-445-1753.
Activities: Hiking, horseback riding, scenic driving.
Finding the campground: From Alpine, drive east on Interstate 8 for 15 miles, turn left onto County Road S1 (Sunrise National Scenic Byway), and drive about 11 miles.

About the campground: See Wooded Hill (No. 12 above) for more about the attractions of this recreation area. Stay limit 14 days. Open May through October.

17 Cibbets Flat

Location: 14 miles southeast of Pine Valley.
Sites: 24 sites for tents and RVs up to 27 feet long.
Facilities: Picnic tables, fire rings, drinking water, vault toilets.
Fee per night: $8.
Agency: Cleveland National Forest, Descanso Ranger District, 760-445-1753.
Activities: Hiking.
Finding the campground: From Pine Valley, drive south 9 miles on Interstate 8 to the Kitchen Creek/Cameron Station exit. Turn north onto Kitchen Creek Road and drive 4.6 miles.

About the campground: The Pacific Crest Trail passes less than a mile east of the campground. Elevation 4,200 feet. Stay limit 14 days. Open all year.

18 Boulder Oaks

Location: 11 miles south of Pine Valley.
Sites: 36 sites for tents and RVs up to 27 feet long, including 17 sites for equestrian use.
Facilities: Picnic tables, fire rings, drinking water, vault toilets.

Fee per night: $8. Reservations required for equestrian sites; call 800-280-CAMP. Reservation fee, $8.65.
Agency: Cleveland National Forest, Descanso Ranger District, 760-445-1753.
Activities: Hiking, horseback riding.
Finding the campground: From Pine Valley, drive 9 miles south on Interstate 8 to the Kitchen Creek/Cameron Station exit. Turn right onto the frontage road and drive northwest for 1.6 miles.

About the campground: The Pacific Crest Trail passes less than a mile north of the campground. Elevation 3,300 feet. Stay limit 14 days. Open all year.

19 Lake Morena Regional Park

Location: 11 miles south of Pine Valley.
Sites: 100 sites for tents and RVs up to 30 feet long, some with water and electrical hookups.
Facilities: Picnic tables, fire rings, drinking water, showers, flush toilets, playground.
Fee per night: $10-$12, pets $1. For reservations, call 760-565-3600. Reservation fee, $3.
Agency: San Diego County Department of Parks and Recreation, 760-694-3049.
Activities: Hiking, fishing, boating.
Finding the campground: From Pine Valley, drive about 4 miles south on Interstate 8 to Buckman Springs Road. Drive 4 miles south on Buckman Springs Road, turn right onto Oak Drive, and go 3 miles to Lake Morena Road. Turn right to the park entrance.

About the campground: The campground lies along the south shore of Lake Morena, which boasts good fishing for trout in winter and bass in spring. The lake record is a 19-pound, 3-ounce largemouth bass. Boat rentals are available. For hikers, the Pacific Crest Trail passes through the park. Elevation 3,000 feet. Stay limit 14 days. Open all year.

20 Corral Canyon OHV Area: Bobcat

Location: 15 miles south of Pine Valley.
Sites: 20 sites for tents and RVs up to 27 feet long.
Facilities: Vault toilets. No water.
Fee per night: None.
Agency: Cleveland National Forest, Descanso Ranger District, 760-445-1753.
Activities: Off-highway driving.
Finding the campground: From Pine Valley, drive about 4 miles south on Interstate 8 to Buckman Springs Road. Drive 4 miles south on Buckman Springs Road, turn right onto unpaved FR 17S04 (just south of Cottonwood Fire Station), and drive about 6 miles to where FR 17S06 forks to the left. Take the left fork and drive 1 mile.

About the campground: The campground offers access to the trails of the Corral Canyon OHV Area. Stay limit 14 days. Open all year.

21 Corral Canyon OHV Area: Corral Canyon

Location: 15 miles south of Pine Valley.
Sites: 24 sites for tents and RVs up to 27 feet long.
Facilities: Vault toilets. No water.
Fee per night: None.
Agency: Cleveland National Forest, Descanso Ranger District, 760-445-1753.
Activities: Off-highway driving.
Finding the campground: From Pine Valley, drive about 4 miles south on Interstate 8 to Buckman Springs Road. Drive 4 miles south on Buckman Springs Road, turn right onto unpaved FR 17S04 (just south of Cottonwood Fire Station), and drive about 7 miles.

About the campground: The campground offers access to the trails of the Corral Canyon OHV Area. Stay limit 14 days. Open all year.

22 Potrero Regional Park

Location: 10 miles west of Campo.
Sites: 39 sites for tents and RVs up to 35 feet long, including 32 sites with water and electrical hookups.
Facilities: Picnic tables, fire rings, drinking water, showers, flush toilets, dump station, playground.
Fee per night: $10-$12, pets $1. For reservations, call 760-565-3600. Reservation fee, $3.
Agency: San Diego County Department of Parks and Recreation, 760-694-3049.
Activities: Car touring, visiting Mexico.
Finding the campground: From Campo, drive 8 miles west on California 94 to Potrero, turn right onto Potrero Valley Road, and drive 1 mile. Turn right onto Potrero Park Road and drive 1 mile.

About the campground: Potrero is set in an attractive oak grove only 5 miles from the Mexican town of Tecate, with its well-known brewery. Stay limit 14 days. Open all year.

ANZA BORREGO DESERT STATE PARK

Anza Borrego easily ranks with the finest desert parks in the nation. Only its status as a state park keeps it from achieving the popularity of Death Valley and Joshua Tree National Parks. Even so, it receives more than 1 million visitors a year, many of them in the early spring when the park is carpeted in a blaze of colorful wildflowers. The visitor center alone is worth a visit to the park. Partially buried in a desert hillside and landscaped with cactus and other desert plants, it contains exhibits of the desert environment, a theater, and a bookstore. It also provides maps, brochures, and trail guides.

The park's more than 600,000 acres offer miles of trails for hiking, biking,

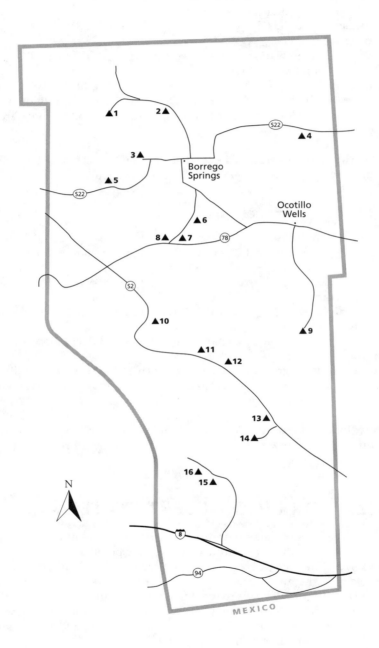

horseback riding, and exploring by four-wheel-drive. But Anza Borrego is also unusually accessible by ordinary vehicle. Excellent desert views, nature exhibits, and points of interest can be enjoyed from the roadside or after short hikes. And for those willing to leave the road behind, the views will include seldom-seen oases of fan palms, stands of elephant trees, and eroded canyons.

There are 16 developed campgrounds in the park or its environs. Stay limits are 30 days in any one year unless otherwise noted. Of particular interest to the adventurous owner of a self-contained RV is the fact that open camping is permitted virtually anywhere in the park except near the visitor center, in the vicinity of the developed campgrounds, or where posted. For those who want to get away from it all, this option can provide a sense of solitude unequaled almost anywhere else. Even drivers of the largest rigs can leave the main road, roam around on backcountry dirt roads, and select a camping spot out of sight of another vehicle or human being.

The park charges a daily user fee of $5 per vehicle ($20 per week, $75 per year) for any backcountry use of the park, including camping, hiking, biking, etc. The fee is not required for car tours through the park or stops at the visitor center. It also is not charged on top of a fee to stay in an established campground, but campers at no-fee campgrounds must pay the $5 daily user fee.

	Group sites	RV sites	Max. RV length	Hookups	Toilets	Showers	Drinking water	Dump station	Pets	Wheelchair	Recreation	Fee ($)	Season	Can reserve
1 Sheep Canyon	•				P				•		HR			
2 Vernon Whitaker Horse Camp		•	24		F	•	•				R	16		•
3 Borrego Palm Canyon	•	•	35	WES	F	•	•		•	•	H	16–22		•
4 Arroyo Salado	•								•		H			
5 Culp Valley	•								•		HR			
6 Yaqui Pass	•								•		H			
7 Tamarisk Grove		•	21		F	•	•		•	•	HR	10–16		•
8 Yaqui Well	•				P				•		H			
9 Fish Creek	•								•		H			
10 Blair Valley	•								•		H			
11 Vallecito Regional Park	•				F	•			•	•		8	Oct–June	•
12 Agua Caliente Regional Park	•			WES	F	•	•		•		HS	10–14	Sep–May	•
13 Mountain Palm Springs	•				C				•		H			
14 Bow Willow		•	24		C	•			•		H	7–9		
15 Lark Canyon	•				P		•		•		HRO	6		
16 Cottonwood	•				P		•		•		HRO	6		

Hookups: W = Water   E = Electric   S = Sewer
Toilets: F = Flush   V = Vault   P = Pit   C = Chemical
Recreation: H = Hiking   S = Swimming   F = Fishing   B = Boating   L = Boat Launch   O = Off-highway Driving   R = Horseback Riding
Maximum Trailer/RV Length given in feet.   **Stay Limit** given in days.   **Fee** given in dollars.
If no entry under **Season,** campground is open all year. If no entry under **Fee,** camping is free.

1 Anza Borrego Desert State Park: Sheep Canyon

Location: 17 miles northwest of the visitor center in Borrego Springs.
Sites: 5 sites for tents and RVs.
Facilities: Picnic tables, shade ramadas, pit toilets.
Fee per night: None.
Agency: Anza Borrego Desert State Park, 619-767-5311.
Activities: Hiking, horseback riding, four-wheel-drive exploring.
Finding the campground: A high-clearance or four-wheel-drive vehicle is recommended to reach the campground. From the park visitor center in Borrego Springs, drive 2 miles east on Palm Canyon Drive and turn left (north) onto Di Giorgio Road. After 4.5 miles, the pavement ends. Continue on the unpaved road for about 10 more miles, passing Desert Gardens Picnic Area (2.3 miles) and Santa Catarina Spring (6.4 miles).

About the campground: A small palm oasis lies just south of the campground. Coyote Canyon, 1.5 miles east (along the entry road) contains a year-round stream and features hiking and riding trails and rough four-wheel-drive roads. The historic Anza Trail runs through the canyon in a northeasterly direction, from Borrego Springs to the town of Anza. Stay limit 30 days. Open all year.

2 Anza Borrego Desert State Park: Vernon V. Whitaker Horse Camp

Location: 8 miles north of the visitor center in Borrego Springs.
Sites: 10 sites for tents and RVs up to 24 feet long, exclusively for campers with horses.
Facilities: Fire rings, drinking water, flush toilets, solar-heated showers, 40 corrals.
Fee per night: $16. For reservations, call Parknet, 800-444-7275. Reservation fee, $7.50.
Agency: Anza Borrego Desert State Park, 619-767-5311.
Activities: Horseback riding.
Finding the campground: From the park visitor center in Borrego Springs, drive 1.3 miles east on Palm Canyon Drive and turn left (north) onto Borrego Springs Road. After the road makes a sharp curve to the right (about 3 miles), take the first unpaved road to the left (about 0.3 mile) and drive 3.3 miles north.

About the campground: Each of the ten campsites can hold up to eight people and four horses. Good riding trails run from the campground through Coyote Canyon to the northwest, inviting exploration of backcountry palm canyons and this historic section of the Anza Trail. Stay limit 30 days. Open all year.

3 Anza Borrego Desert State Park: Borrego Palm Canyon

Location: 1 mile north of the visitor center in Borrego Springs.
Sites: 117 sites for tents and RVs up to 35 feet long, including 52 with full hookups, plus 5 group sites for tents.

Facilities: Picnic tables, fire rings, drinking water, showers, flush toilets, public phone.

Fee per night: $16-$22 for individual sites, $36 for group sites. Reservations required 6 months in advance for group sites. For reservations, call Parknet, 800-444-7275. Reservation fee, $7.50.

Agency: Anza Borrego Desert State Park, 619-767-5311.

Activities: Hiking.

Finding the campground: From the park visitor center, take the first left turn and drive 1 mile north.

About the campground: Borrego Palm Canyon, the most popular palm oasis in the park, lies 1.5 miles northwest of the campground and is accessible via an easy nature trail. Self-guiding brochures are available. The campground receives heavy use, and reservations are recommended any time of the year. Stay limit 30 days. Open all year.

4 Anza Borrego Desert State Park: Arroyo Salado

Location: 16 miles east of the visitor center in Borrego Springs.

Sites: Open camping.

Facilities: None. Best suited for tents and pickup campers.

Fee per night: None.

Agency: Anza Borrego Desert State Park, 619-767-5311.

Activities: Hiking, mountain biking, four-wheel-drive exploring.

Spring brings out the best in the many species of cactus that burst into bloom in Anza Borrego Desert State Park.

Finding the campground: From the park visitor center, drive east on Palm Canyon Drive (County Road S22) for 5.2 miles. Turn left (north) with CR S22 onto Pegleg Road, and drive 2.3 miles, to where the highway makes a right turn. Continue to follow S22 for about 8 miles, watching for an unpaved road to the right posted with a very small sign to Arroyo Salado.

About the campground: Three separate palm oases lie about 2 miles southeast of the campground. They can be reached by continuing east along the unpaved entry road. Stay limit 30 days. Open all year.

5 Anza Borrego Desert State Park: Culp Valley

Location: 7 miles southwest of the visitor center in Borrego Springs.
Sites: Open camping for trailers and motor homes.
Facilities: None.
Fee per night: None.
Agency: Anza Borrego Desert State Park, 619-767-5311.
Activities: Hiking, mountain biking, horseback riding.
Finding the campground: From the park visitor center in Borrego Springs, drive southwest on Montezuma Valley Road (County Road S22) for 7 miles.

About the campground: A hiking and equestrian trail leads east and west from the campground. Lookout Point and Pena Spring are nearby. Elevation 3,400 feet. Stay limit 30 days. Open all year.

6 Anza Borrego Desert State Park: Yaqui Pass

Location: 10 miles southeast of the visitor center in Borrego Springs.
Sites: Open camping for trailers and motor homes.
Facilities: None.
Fee per night: None.
Agency: Anza Borrego Desert State Park, 619-767-5311.
Activities: Hiking.
Finding the campground: From the park visitor center in Borrego Springs, drive 1.3 miles east on Palm Canyon Drive, turn right (south) onto County Road S3, and drive 9 miles to the campground on the left.

About the campground: The Kenyon Overlook Trail (0.6 mile) begins at the campground, offering panoramic vistas and a variety of desert vegetation. Stay limit 30 days. Open all year.

7 Anza Borrego Desert State Park: Tamarisk Grove

Location: 11 miles southeast of the visitor center in Borrego Springs.
Sites: 27 sites for tents and RVs up to 21 feet long.
Facilities: Picnic tables, fire rings, drinking water, showers, flush toilets, shade ramadas.

Fee per night: $10-$16. For reservations, call Parknet, 800-444-7275. Reservation fee, $7.50.

Agency: Anza Borrego Desert State Park, 619-767-5311.

Activities: Hiking, horseback riding.

Finding the campground: From the park visitor center in Borrego Springs, drive 1.3 miles east on Palm Canyon Drive, turn right (south) onto County Road S3, and drive 10 miles to the campground at the intersection of California 78 and CR S3.

About the campground: The Cactus Loop Trail (0.7 mile) begins across the road from the campground entrance. It features examples of seven different types of cactus. Stay limit 30 days. Open all year.

8 Anza Borrego Desert State Park: Yaqui Well

Location: 11 miles southeast of the visitor center in Borrego Springs.

Sites: 10 sites for tents and RVs, plus open camping area with no facilities (best suited for tents and pickup campers).

Facilities: Pit toilets.

Fee per night: None.

Agency: Anza Borrego Desert State Park, 619-767-5311.

Activities: Hiking.

Finding the campground: From the park visitor center in Borrego Springs, drive 1.3 miles east on Palm Canyon Drive, turn right (south) onto County Road S3, and drive 10 miles to the campground at the intersection of California 78 and CR S3 (across from the entrance to Tamarisk Grove Campground, No. 7 above).

About the campground: The mile-long Yaqui Well Trail begins at the campground and climbs to a small seep that smells of sulphur. Stay limit 30 days. Open all year.

9 Anza Borrego Desert State Park: Fish Creek

Location: 9 miles south of Ocotillo Wells.

Sites: 8 sites for tents and pickup campers.

Facilities: Picnic tables, fire rings.

Fee per night: None.

Agency: Anza Borrego Desert State Park, 619-767-5311.

Activities: Hiking, four-wheel-drive exploring.

Finding the campground: From Ocotillo Wells, drive south 7.5 miles on Split Mountain Road, turn right (west) onto Fish Creek Wash Road, and drive 1 mile.

About the campground: The park service offers four-wheel-drive tours from the campground through Split Mountain's rugged geological fault. Participants must have their own vehicles and must sign up at the visitor center in Borrego Springs. Stay limit 30 days. Open all year.

10 Anza Borrego Desert State Park: Blair Valley

Location: 16 miles east of Julian.
Sites: Open camping for trailers and motor homes.
Facilities: None.
Fee per night: None.
Agency: Anza Borrego Desert State Park, 619-767-5311.
Activities: Hiking, mountain biking, four-wheel-drive exploring.
Finding the campground: From the town of Julian, drive east 10 miles on California 78. Turn right (south) onto County Road S2 and drive 6 miles to the unpaved road to Blair Valley on the left.

About the campground: Camping is permitted over a large area, which allows maximum privacy for those seeking it. The Ghost Mountain Trail (2 miles), Morteros Trail (0.3 mile), and Pictograph Trail (2 miles) are all accessed from the campground, as is the Marshal South Home. Maps and trail guides are available at the visitor center. Stay limit 30 days. Open all year.

11 Vallecito Regional Park

Location: 25 miles southeast of Julian.
Sites: 44 sites for tents and RVs.
Facilities: Picnic tables, fire rings, drinking water, flush toilets, playground.
Fee per night: $8, pets $1. For reservations, call 760-565-3600. Reservation fee, $3.
Agency: San Diego County Department of Parks and Recreation, 760-694-3049.
Finding the campground: From the town of Julian, drive east 10 miles on California 78. Turn right (south) onto County Road S2 and drive 15 miles.

About the campground: A centerpiece of the park is a restored sod stagecoach station of the Butterfield Overland Stage Line, which established the first regular transportation between California and the East Coast. Stay limit 14 days. Open October 1 to June 1.

12 Agua Caliente Regional Park

Location: 29 miles southeast of Julian.
Sites: 104 sites with full and partial hookups for RVs, 36 dry sites for tents and RVs.
Facilities: Picnic tables, fire grills, drinking water, showers, flush toilets, swimming pool, therapy pool, playground.
Fee per night: $10-$14. For reservations, call 760-565-3600. Reservation fee, $3.
Agency: San Diego County Department of Parks and Recreation, 760-694-3049.
Activities: Swimming, hiking, shuffleboard, horseshoes.
Finding the campground: From the town of Julian, drive east 10 miles on California 78. Turn right (south) onto County Road S2 and drive 19 miles.

About the campground: Agua Caliente's geothermal pools attract wildlife and promote lush vegetation in an otherwise arid environment. A large outdoor pool and a smaller (and hotter) indoor one attract tourists. No pets are allowed. Stay limit 14 days. Open Labor Day weekend through Memorial Day weekend.

13 Anza Borrego Desert State Park: Mountain Palm Springs

Location: 15 miles northwest of Ocotillo.
Sites: Open camping for trailers and motor homes.
Facilities: Chemical toilets. No drinking water.
Fee per night: None.
Agency: Anza Borrego Desert State Park, 619-767-5311.
Activities: Hiking.
Finding the campground: From the intersection of Interstate 8 and County Road S2 at Ocotillo, drive 15 miles northwest on CR S2.

About the campground: The North Fork Trail leads 0.6 mile from the campground to Mountain Palm Springs Oasis, which features two separate stands of fan palms. Also starting at the campground is the South Fork Trail, which leads 1.4 miles through stands of palms and elephant trees to Torote Bowl Overlook. Stay limit 30 days. Open all year.

14 Anza Borrego Desert State Park: Bow Willow

Location: 13 miles northwest of Ocotillo.
Sites: 16 sites for tents and RVs up to 24 feet long.
Facilities: Picnic tables, fire rings, drinking water, shade ramadas, chemical toilets.
Fee per night: $7-$9.
Agency: Anza Borrego Desert State Park, 619-767-5311.
Activities: Hiking.
Finding the campground: From the intersection of Interstate 8 and County Road S2 at Ocotillo, drive 13.4 miles northwest on CR S2.

About the campground: A trail leading north from the campground intersects the trail to Torote Bowl Overlook (see Mountain Palm Springs Campground above). Stay limit 30 days. Open all year.

15 McCain Valley Resource Conservation Area: Lark Canyon

Location: 27 miles east of Pine Valley.
Sites: 20 sites for tents and RVs.
Facilities: Picnic tables, fire rings, drinking water, pit toilets.
Fee per night: $6.
Agency: Bureau of Land Management, 760-337-4400.
Activities: Hiking, horseback riding, off-highway driving.
Finding the campground: From Pine Valley, drive east 18 miles on Interstate 8, take the Boulevard exit, and drive 2 miles east of Boulevard on Old Highway 80. Turn left onto McCain Valley Road and drive 7 miles.

About the campground: The scenic In-Ko-Pah Mountains provide a boulder-garden setting for the two campgrounds in the conservation area (see also Cottonwood below). Both are nestled among oak trees in an area where bighorn sheep are sometimes seen. Lark Canyon is near a popular OHV driving area. An elevation of 3,500 feet makes for pleasant desert camping, even in summer. Stay limit 14 days. Open all year.

16 McCain Valley Resource Conservation Area: Cottonwood

Location: 33 miles east of Pine Valley.
Sites: 25 sites for tents and RVs.
Facilities: Picnic tables, fire rings, drinking water, pit toilets.
Fee per night: $6.
Agency: Bureau of Land Management, 760-337-4400.
Activities: Hiking, horseback riding, off-highway driving.
Finding the campground: From Pine Valley, drive east 18 miles on Interstate 8, take the Boulevard exit, and drive 2 miles east of Boulevard on Old Highway 80. Turn left onto McCain Valley Road and drive 13 miles.

About the campground: The Pepperwood Trail starts at Cottonwood and accommodates hikers and equestrians. See Lark Canyon (No. 15 above) for more about the attractions of this area. Stay limit 14 days. Open all year.

DESERTS

It may come as a surprise to some, but a quarter of California is desert. Even more of the state would fall into that category if it were not for the extensive water reclamation and irrigation projects that have turned hundreds of thou-

DESERTS AREA MAP

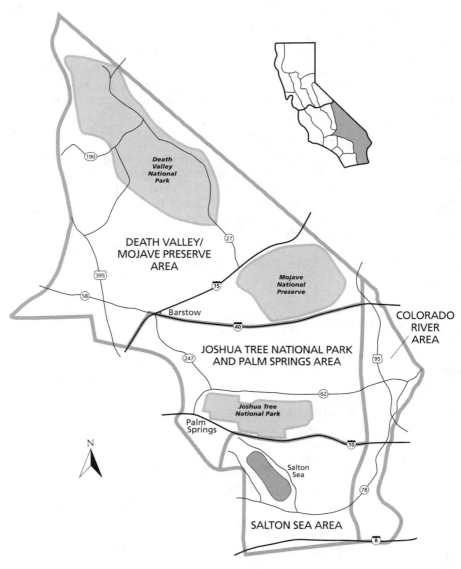

sands of arid acres into fertile farmland. And just as the irrigated acres have been made fruitful, the unchanged acreage has become equally bountiful, producing a bumper crop of thousands of tourists fleeing winter storms and snow to bask in the desert's warmth and sun.

Probably nowhere in the world is it easier to explore the desert environment than in southeastern California, where some of the continent's major deserts come together. Two national parks, a national preserve, and an immense state park (in adjacent San Diego County) provide visitor centers, trail networks, interpretive displays, guided activities, and developed and primitive campgrounds, all of which combine to offer an unequaled opportunity to enjoy a intimate and rewarding desert experience.

Although the desert is seen by many as a bleak, barren landscape, those who have traveled there know that the desert teems with life and color. Dozens of plants can be seen at any time of year, and in the spring the desert bursts forth in a riot of wildflowers—a carpet of bright yellows, blues, whites, reds, and lavenders. It is not even necessary to leave the highway to enjoy these sights. But those willing to abandon their cars for the trail will be rewarded with hidden palm oases, narrow canyons, eroded cliffs, majestic sand dunes, and other sights hidden from the road-bound.

Average summer temperatures in the Deserts Region range from a high of 106 degrees F to a low of 70 degrees F, while winter brings highs of 71 degrees F and lows of 41 degrees F. Spring sees readings between 86 and 52 degrees F, and in the fall temperatures reach highs of 91 degrees F and lows of 56 degrees F. It is important to keep in mind that these are *averages*. In places such as Death Valley and the Salton Sea, daily temperatures can get much hotter. The sun shines almost all the time in the desert. The number of average days of sunshine is 93 percent in summer, 91 percent in fall, 81 percent in winter, and 91 percent in spring.

This book subdivides the Deserts Region into four areas: Death Valley National Park & Mojave National Preserve and Vicinity, Joshua Tree National Park & Palm Springs Vicinity, Salton Sea & Vicinity, and the Colorado River.

DEATH VALLEY/MOJAVE PRESERVE & VICINITY

Death Valley. Named by Forty-niners who struggled across this virtually waterless furnace on the way to seek their fortunes in the California gold rush, Death Valley is both the hottest spot in North America and the lowest point in the Western Hemisphere—282 feet below sea level. Visitors expecting a barren, arid landscape will certainly find it. But they will also find dramatic snowcapped mountains, golden sand dunes, and colorful wildflowers. Scenic driving, hiking, climbing, and backpacking all reward the traveler with glimpses of a world apart.

Summer visitors must be prepared for some of the hottest, driest conditions encountered anywhere. Normal daily temperatures in July range from a high of 116 degrees F to a low of 88 degrees F, and temperatures have been recorded as high as 126 degrees F. Not surprisingly, some park facilities close during the summer, and services are reduced. January temperatures range from an average daily high of 64 degrees F to a low of 40 degrees F, making winter a good time to visit. Monthly precipitation for July averages 0.2 inch, while January is only

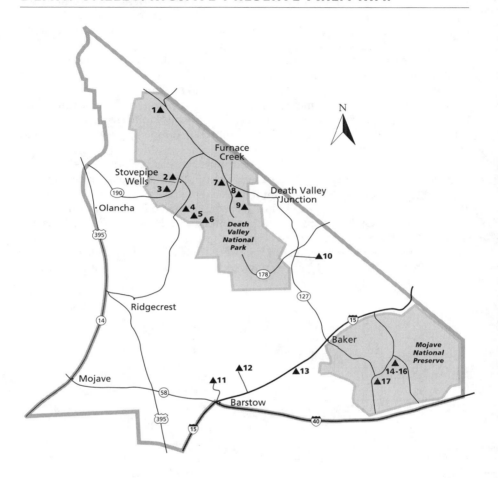

slightly better at 0.4 inch.

Despite Death Valley's foreboding name and harsh environment, life manages to exist and even flourish. More than 900 kinds of plants live within the park, and many animals roam the desert at night, escaping from the heat of day in underground burrows. Abandoned mines and other forsaken structures stand as monuments to man's attempts to wrest economic treasures from the desert.

There are nine public campgrounds in Death Valley National Park, with a total of more than 1,500 campsites. All public campgrounds are available on a first-come, first-served basis except for family sites at Furnace Creek (page 242) and group sites at Texas Spring (page 243), both of which which may be reserved from October through April. Camping is not permitted along roadsides, in parking lots, or in day-use areas.

Mojave National Preserve. Desert landscapes, volcanic cinder cones, pinyon-juniper woodlands, abandoned mines, Native American rock art, and California's second highest sand dunes provide almost limitless opportunities for exploration in this 1.4 million-acre preserve. Three of North America's major deserts—the Mojave, Great Basin, and Sonoran—come together in the preserve to form a huge transition zone.

As in Death Valley to the north, wildlife is abundant if not always visible. Nearly 330 species make their homes here, including coyotes, mule deer, desert bighorn sheep, and tortoises. Quail, doves, chukar, and larger birds, such as hawks and golden eagles, manage to survive and prosper in the washes and canyons of the preserve. In the spring, the desert hosts a rainbow of wildflowers, while cacti, yuccas, creosote bushes, sagebrush, junipers, pinyon pines, and Joshua trees provide year-round vegetation.

The high desert climate tends to the extreme: there is an 85-degree difference between summer highs and winter lows. Daytime summer temperatures range from 70 to 115 degrees F, while winter days average between 40 and 60 degrees F, with temperatures falling to below freezing at night. Precipitation is sparse, with much of what does occur falling as winter snow. However, flash floods can occur at any time of year.

The main information center for the preserve is the Mojave Desert Information Center, off Interstate 15 in the town of Baker (72157 Baker Boulevard, Bak-

		Group sites	RV sites	Max. RV length	Hookups	Toilets	Showers	Drinking water	Dump station	Pets	Wheelchair	Recreation	Fee ($)	Season	Can reserve
1	Mesquite Spring	•	•			F		•	•	•	•	H	10		
2	Stovepipe Wells		•			F		•	•	•	•	H	10	Oct–Apr	
3	Emigrant		•			F		•		•		H		Apr–Oct	
4	Wildrose		•			P				•		H			
5	Thorndike		•			P				•		H		Apr–Oct	
6	Mahogany Flat		•			P				•		H		Mar–Oct	
7	Furnace Creek		•			F		•	•	•	•	H	16		•
8	Sunset		•			F		•	•	•	•	H	10	Oct–Apr	
9	Texas Spring	•	•			F		•	•	•		H	10	Oct–Apr	
10	Tecopa Hot Springs Park		•		E	F	•		•	•	•	HS	6.50–8		
11	Owl Canyon		•			V				•		H	6		
12	Calico Ghost Town		•		WES	F	•	•	•	•	•	O	18–22		
13	Afton Canyon		•			P				•		H	6		
14	Hole-in-the-Wall		•			V	•			•		H	10		
15	Black Canyon	•	•			P				•		HR	20		•
16	Mid Hills		•			V				•		H	10		
17	Providence Mountain SRA		•	32		F	•			•	•	H	14		

Hookups: W = Water E = Electric S = Sewer
Toilets: F = Flush V = Vault P = Pit C = Chemical
Recreation: H = Hiking S = Swimming F = Fishing B = Boating L = Boat Launch O = Off-highway Driving R = Horseback Riding
Maximum Trailer/RV Length given in feet. **Stay Limit** given in days. **Fee** given in dollars.
If no entry under **Season,** campground is open all year. If no entry under **Fee,** camping is free.

238

er, CA 92309; phone: 760-733-4040), which is open all year. However, the more popular features of the park, including the campgrounds, are more easily accessible from the Hole-in-the-Wall area, where there is another information center, open seasonally (spring and fall, some weekends at other times). To reach this information center from Barstow, drive east on Interstate 40 for 98 miles and take the Essex Road exit. Drive 10 miles north to Black Canyon Road. Turn right and drive 12 miles.

There are several roadside sites in Mojave that have traditionally been used for car and RV camping. They have no facilities of any kind. The most popular of these are Kelso Dunes, Black Canyon Road, Sunrise Rock, and Powerline. More information about them and other roadside sites may be obtained at either of the two information centers listed above.

1 Death Valley: Mesquite Spring

Location: 49 miles northwest of Furnace Creek Visitor Center.
Sites: 30 sites for tents and RVs, plus some group sites.
Facilities: Picnic tables, fireplaces, drinking water, flush toilets, dump station.
Fee per night: $10 for individual sites; check with park headquarters for group fees.
Agency: Death Valley National Park, 760-786-2331.
Activities: Hiking, cycling.
Finding the campground: From the Furnace Creek Visitor Center, drive north on California 190 (North Highway) about 17 miles to where CA 190 turns left (southwest). Turn right (northwest) and continue on North Highway for about 32 miles. The access road to the campground lies just south of the intersection with CA 267 and 3 miles south of Scotty's Castle.

Scotty's Castle, an elaborate mansion built in 1922 by a Chicago millionaire, offers daily tours to Death Valley visitors.

About the campground: Scotty's Castle, an elaborate Spanish-style mansion built in 1922 by a Chicago millionaire, lies 3 miles north of the campground. For many years, it was the home of local legend "Death Valley Scotty," a con man who convinced several wealthy investors that he owned a gold mine in Death Valley. Although Scotty (Walter Scott) was actually the mansion's caretaker, he liked to claim that the "castle" was his. Tours are offered daily. Windy Point Trail (0.75 mile) and Tie Canyon Trail (0.7 mile) also begin at the castle. Also nearby is Ubehebe Crater, a 500-foot-deep volcanic crater formed more than 2,000 years ago. Elevation 1,800 feet. Stay limit 30 days. Open all year.

2 Death Valley: Stovepipe Wells

Location: 24 miles northwest of Furnace Creek.
Sites: 210 sites for tents and RVs.
Facilities: Drinking water, flush toilets, dump station. Pay showers available at Stovepipe Wells Motel.
Fee per night: $10.
Agency: Death Valley National Park, 760-786-2331.
Activities: Hiking, cycling, four-wheel-drive exploring.
Finding the campground: From the Furnace Creek Visitor Center, drive about 24 miles northwest on California 190 to Stovepipe Wells Village.

About the campground: The campground is a large gravel parking lot with no trees or other vegetation but a good view of the distant mountains. An adjacent private campground offers hookups. Across CA 190, a short drive leads to the trail into Mosaic Canyon, a twisting canyon featuring polished marble and mosaic-like patterns in its narrow rock walls. Elevation sea level. Stay limit 30 days. Open October through April.

3 Death Valley: Emigrant

Location: 9 miles southwest of Stovepipe Wells.
Sites: 10 sites for tents and RVs.
Facilities: Picnic tables, drinking water, flush toilets.
Fee per night: None.
Agency: Death Valley National Park, 760-786-2331.
Activities: Hiking, cycling.
Finding the campground: From Stovepipe Wells Village, drive 9 miles southwest on California 190.

About the campground: Emigrant is a small gravel pad unsuitable for trailers or large RVs. Although a sign at the entrance says "Tents Only," officials at the visitor center confirm that small RVs are permitted. Elevation 2,100 feet. Stay limit 30 days. Open April through October.

4 Death Valley: Wildrose

Location: 29 miles south of Stovepipe Wells.
Sites: 30 sites for tents and RVs.
Facilities: Picnic tables, fireplaces, pit toilets, drinking water April through November only.
Fee per night: None.
Agency: Death Valley National Park, 760-786-2331.
Activities: Hiking.
Finding the campground: From Stovepipe Wells Village, drive south on California 190 for 8 miles. Just past the Emigrant Ranger Station, take Emigrant Canyon Road, which forks left off CA 190. Continue for 21 more miles. The road is steep, winding, and narrow, and not recommended for vehicles longer than 25 feet.

About the campground: A wild, lonely beauty surrounds Wildrose, which may explain why, despite its lack of amenities, *Sunset* lists it as one of the 100 best campgrounds in the western United States. An 8.2 mile round-trip hiking trail at the end of Wildrose Canyon Road, 7 miles east of the campground at Charcoal Kilns, leads to Wildrose Peak (9,054 feet). Elevation 4,100 feet. Stay limit 30 days. Open all year.

5 Death Valley: Thorndike

Location: 37 miles south of Stovepipe Wells.
Sites: 10 sites for tents.
Facilities: Picnic tables, fireplaces, pit toilets. No water.
Fee per night: None.

Visitors willing to abandon their vehicles for the hiking trails of Death Valley will be rewarded with palm oases, narrow canyons, eroded cliffs, majestic sand dunes, and other sights hidden from the road-bound.

Agency: Death Valley National Park, 760-786-2331.
Activities: Hiking.
Finding the campground: From Wildrose Campground (see above), drive 7.5 miles east on Wildrose Canyon Road. After about 5 miles, the road is no longer paved and is not passable to trailers or RVs. A four-wheel-drive or high-clearance vehicle may be required.

About the campground: Elevation 7,400 feet. Stay limit 30 days. Open April through October.

6 Death Valley: Mahogany Flat

Location: 38 miles south of Stovepipe Wells.
Sites: 10 sites for tents.
Facilities: Picnic tables, fireplaces, pit toilets. No water.
Fee per night: None.
Agency: Death Valley National Park, 760-786-2331.
Activities: Hiking.
Finding the campground: From Wildrose Campground (see No. 4 above), drive about 9 miles east on Wildrose Canyon Road. The road is passable to high-clearance vehicles only; four-wheel-drive may be required.

About the campground: A trail leads 7 miles from the campground to Telescope Peak (11,049 feet), the highest point in the park. Elevation 8,200 feet. Stay limit 30 days. Open March through October.

7 Death Valley: Furnace Creek

Location: Furnace Creek.
Sites: 136 sites for tents and RVs.
Facilities: Picnic tables, fireplaces, drinking water, flush toilets, pit toilets, dump station. Pay showers, laundry, and swimming pool available at nearby Furnace Creek Ranch.
Fee per night: $16. For reservations (October through April), call 800-365-CAMP.
Agency: Death Valley National Park, 760-786-2331.
Activities: Hiking, cycling, four-wheel-drive exploring.
Finding the campground: From the Furnace Creek Visitor Center, drive 1 mile north on California 190.

About the campground: Furnace Creek is the only campground in Death Valley with trees large enough to shade some of its campsites—an important consideration in summer. Its campsites are spaced along several loops, offering an alternative to the parking-lot style of Stovepipe Wells (No. 2 above) and Sunset (see No. 8 below) campgrounds. There are good views of the mountains from many of the sites. The Death Valley Museum and the Borax Museum are located close to the campground, as are two interpretive trails, the Harmony Borax Works Trail and the Golden Canyon Trail. Elevation 196 feet below sea level. Stay limit 14 days. Open all year.

8 Death Valley: Sunset

Location: 3.5 miles south of Furnace Creek Visitor Center.
Sites: 1,000 sites, primarily for RVs, but some tent sites available.
Facilities: Drinking water, flush toilets, pit toilets, dump station. Pay showers, laundry, and swimming pool available at nearby Furnace Creek Ranch.
Fee per night: $10.
Agency: Death Valley National Park, 760-786-2331.
Activities: Hiking, bicycling.
Finding the campground: From the Furnace Creek Visitor Center, drive about 3.5 miles south on California 190.

About the campground: Sunset is a large gravel parking lot without trees or other vegetation, but it has a good view of the distant mountains. The Death Valley Museum and the Borax Museum are located close to the campground, as are two interpretive trails, the Harmony Borax Works, and the Golden Canyon Trails. Elevation 190 feet below sea level. Stay limit 30 days. Open October through April.

9 Death Valley: Texas Spring

Location: 4.5 miles southeast of the Furnace Creek Visitor Center.
Sites: 92 sites for tents and RVs, plus some group sites.
Facilities: Picnic tables, fireplaces, drinking water, flush toilets, pit toilets, dump station. Pay showers, laundry, and swimming pool available at nearby Furnace Creek Ranch.
Fee per night: $10. For group reservations (October through April), call 800-365-CAMP.
Agency: Death Valley National Park, 760-786-2331.
Activities: Hiking, bicycling.
Finding the campground: From Sunset Campground (see above), drive 1 mile east.

About the campground: Texas Spring is spread out over several small loops. Small trees and shrubs are interspersed among some of its campsites. The Death Valley Museum and the Borax Museum are located close to the campground, as are two interpretive trails: the Harmony Borax Works and the Golden Canyon Trails. Elevation sea level. Stay limit 30 days. Open October through April.

10 Tecopa Hot Springs Park

Location: 38 miles south of Death Valley Junction.
Sites: 365 sites for tents and RVs, including 15 with pull-thrus and 80 with electrical hookups.
Facilities: Picnic tables, grills, flush toilets, showers, dump station, horseshoes, community center, bathhouses, hot mineral pools. No drinking water.
Fee per night: $6.50-$8.

Amargosa Canyon Natural Area, near Tecopa Hot Springs, features an easy and fascinating hike through a river canyon.

Agency: Inyo County Parks and Recreation Department, 760-852-4264.
Activities: Hiking, rock hounding, swimming.
Finding the campground: From Death Valley Junction, drive south on California 127 for about 35 miles (about 5 miles south of Shoshone). Turn left onto Furnace Creek Road and drive 3 miles.

About the campground: Tecopa Hot Springs was discovered by the Paiute Indians, who brought their lame and ill relatives to soak in the healing mineral baths. Today, three bathhouses with pools are located at the campground: one for men, one for women, and a private pool for invalids. There are two pools in each of the main bathhouses; each measures about 10 by 18 feet and holds up to 8 people. Nude bathing is required, and coed bathing is not permitted. Several private campgrounds nearby have their own baths, where mixed bathing is allowed.

Fed by a hot mineral spring, the pools have an average temperature of 108 degrees F. They are free and open to the public seven days a week, all year long. The area attracts geologists and rock hounds interested in the high-quality amethysts and opals that can be found east and south of the town. Amargosa Canyon Natural Area, beginning near the town of Tecopa, provides an interesting hike through a river canyon. The trail is easy, level, and hikers can go as far as they like. For those wanting full hookups, there are private campgrounds adjacent to the county facility. Stay limit 9 months. Open all year.

11 Owl Canyon

Location: 8 miles north of Barstow.
Sites: 31 sites for tents and RVs.
Facilities: Picnic tables, fire rings, vault toilets. Drinking water sometimes available from a hand-pumped well, but supply is limited and erratic.
Fee per night: $6.
Agency: Bureau of Land Management, 760-256-3591.
Activities: Hiking, fossil exploring.
Finding the campground: From the intersection of California 58 and Irwin Road in Barstow, drive north on Irwin for 5.5 miles to Fossil Bed Road. Turn left and drive 3 miles northwest.

About the campground: Owl Canyon is situated in Rainbow Basin Natural Area. While hiking or horseback riding, it is possible to find the exposed fossils of ancient mammals, but their removal is prohibited. Colorful rock formations and badlands topography add to the camping experience. Stay limit 14 days. Open all year.

12 Calico Ghost Town Regional Park

Location: 11 miles northeast of Barstow.
Sites: 268 sites for tents and RVs, including 47 with full hookups.
Facilities: Picnic tables, barbecue grills, drinking water, flush toilets, showers, dump station.
Fee per night: $18-$22, which includes admission to the park ($6 per person if not camping).
Agency: San Bernardino County Regional Parks Department, 760-254-2122.
Activities: Sightseeing, off-highway driving.
Finding the campground: From the intersection of Interstate 15 and California 247 (Barstow Road) in Barstow, take I-15 east for about 8 miles to Ghost Town Road exit. Drive north on Ghost Town Road for 3 miles.

About the campground: Calico is not much of a ghost town these days. Shops and a bar, restaurant, and other tourist attractions have revived this once prosperous and then abandoned silver-mining town. Walter Knott, of Knott's Berry Farm fame, reconstructed the town and then donated it to the County of San Bernardino. A ride on a narrow-gauge railway and a self-guided tour of a silver mine are the main offerings. Both are inexpensive and worthwhile. Stay limit 14 days. Open all year.

13 Afton Canyon

Location: 45 miles northeast of Barstow.
Sites: 22 sites for tents and RVs.
Facilities: Picnic tables, fire pits, barbecue grills, pit toilets. Drinking water sometimes available from a hand-pumped well, but supply is limited and erratic.

Fee per night: $6.

Agency: Bureau of Land Management. For information call California Desert Information Center, 760-255-8760.

Activities: Hiking.

Finding the campground: From the intersection of Interstate 15 and California 247 (Barstow Road) in Barstow, take I-15 east for about 42 miles to Afton Canyon Road. Turn right onto Afton and drive for 3 miles.

About the campground: Known as the "Grand Canyon of the Mojave," Afton Canyon is as beautiful as its Arizona cousin, but on a much smaller scale. The Mojave River has carved a chasm 300 feet deep through red rock, creating sheer walls and striking formations. A trail from the campground leads into Afton Canyon and one of its side canyons, Pyramid. The latter is as narrow and claustrophobic as can be expected of a typical slot canyon. Afton also serves as a gateway to the Mojave National Preserve, which lies only 12 miles to the east. Stay limit 14 days. Open all year.

14 Mojave National Preserve: Hole-in-the-Wall

Location: 62 miles west of Needles.

Sites: 35 sites for tents and RVs.

Facilities: Picnic tables, fire rings, vault toilets, drinking water (usually).

Fee per night: $10.

Agency: Mojave National Preserve, 760-733-4040.

Activities: Hiking.

Finding the campground: From Needles, drive west on Interstate 40 for 41 miles, turn right onto Essex Road, and drive 10 miles. Turn right onto Black Canyon Road and drive 11 miles (1 mile past the visitor center.)

About the campground: *Sunset* includes Hole-in-the-Wall on its list of the 100 best campgrounds in the western United States. The campground is situated at an elevation of 4,500 feet and is backed by dramatic walls and towers of volcanic rock. Two scenic hikes begin nearby. The first starts at the picnic ground and travels west through a rocky, volcanic area. It requires a descent that involves the use of metal rings. The second hike leads 7 miles through Wild Horse Canyon and ends at Mid Hills Campground (see below). Drinking water is trucked into Hole-in-the-Wall and is usually available, but visitors should not count on it. Stay limit 14 days. Open all year.

15 Mojave National Preserve: Black Canyon

Location: 62 miles west of Needles.

Sites: 2 sites for groups and campers with horses.

Facilities: Picnic tables, fire rings, pit toilets, corrals. Drinking water usually available at Hole-in-the-Wall Campground (see above) across the road.

Fee per night: $20 for groups of up to 25 people, $20 corral fee for groups with horses. Reservations required; call 760-733-4040.

Agency: Mojave National Preserve, 760-733-4040.
Activities: Hiking, horseback riding.
Finding the campground: Across the road from the Hole-in-the-Wall Campground (see above).

About the campground: Stay limit 14 days. Open all year.

16 Mojave National Preserve: Mid Hills

Location: 74 miles west of Needles.
Sites: 26 sites for tents and RVs.
Facilities: Picnic tables, fire rings, vault toilets. No drinking water.
Fee per night: $10.
Agency: Mojave National Preserve, 760-733-4040.
Activities: Hiking.
Finding the campground: From the Hole-in-the-Wall Campground (see No. 14 above), drive north for 12 miles. The road is rough and not recommended for large RVs or trailers.

About the campground: Situated in an attractive pinyon and juniper forest at an elevation of 5,600 feet, Mid Hills is a pleasant spot for summer camping. A trail leads from this campground to Hole-in-the-Wall Campground (see No. 14 above). Stay limit 14 days. Open all year.

17 Providence Mountain State Recreation Area

Location: 57 miles west of Needles.
Sites: 6 sites for tents and RVs up to 32 feet long.
Facilities: Picnic tables, fire rings, drinking water, flush toilets.
Fee per night: $14, pets $1.
Agency: California Department of Parks and Recreation, 805-942-0662.
Activities: Hiking, cave exploring.
Finding the campground: From Needles, drive west on Interstate 40 for 41 miles and take the Essex Road exit. Drive north on Essex for 16 miles.

About the campground: The main attraction here is a guided tour of Mitchell Caverns. It is offered from mid-September through mid-June. The tour traverses two caves, Tecopa and El Pakiva, that are connected by a tunnel. It leads past some unique limestone formations. A separate, self-guided nature trail introduces hikers to high-desert flora, and Crystal Springs Trail offers fine views of the Providence Mountains. Stay limit 15 days. Open all year.

JOSHUA TREE NATIONAL PARK & PALM SPRINGS

Joshua Tree, one of the nation's newest national parks, encompasses an area of more than 558,000 acres of desert, rugged mountains, winding arroyos, and strangely shaped granite monoliths. Two major North American deserts come together at Joshua Tree. The Colorado, occupying the eastern half of the park below 3,000 feet, is vegetated mainly by creosote bushes, with sprinklings of ocotillo and cholla cactus. The Mojave, at a higher and cooler elevation, is the province of the park's namesake, the Joshua tree.

Huge, twisted rock formations are as representative of the park as the Joshua tree, and rock climbing is a popular activity. More than 25 hiking trails of varying lengths lead to lovely fan-palm oases, abandoned mines and ranches, and high overlooks (ten peaks in the park are over 5,000 feet high). Mountain bikers are welcome in the park, and many dirt roads are open to bike tours of scenic, geologic, and historic interest. In the spring, the entire desert ignites in a blaze of wildflowers, many of which can be enjoyed from roadside pullouts and during short nature walks. Two visitor centers are located in the park, Oasis Visitor

JOSHUA TREE N.P. & PALM SPRINGS AREA MAP

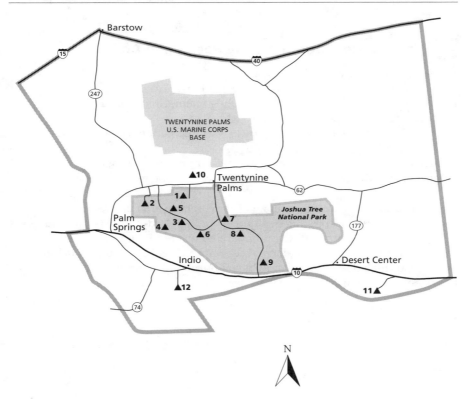

	Group sites	RV sites	Max. RV length	Hookups	Toilets	Showers	Drinking water	Dump station	Pets	Wheelchair	Recreation	Fee ($)	Season	Can reserve
1 Indian Cove	•	•	32		P				•		H			•
2 Black Rock Canyon		•	32		F	•	•	•	•		H	10	Sep–May	•
3 Sheep Pass	•				P				•		H	13		•
4 Ryan		•	29		P				•		H			
5 Hidden Valley		•	29		P				•		H			
6 Jumbo Rocks		•			P				•	•	H			
7 Belle		•	29		P				•		H			
8 White Tank		•	29		P				•		H		Sep–May	
9 Cottonwood	•	•	29		F		•			•	H	8		
10 Knott Sky Park		•		WES	F	•	•	•	•		H	10–16		•
11 Corn Springs		•			P		•		•		H	6		
12 Lake Cahuilla County Park		•		WE	F	•	•	•	•	•	SFBR	12–16		

Hookups: W = Water E = Electric S = Sewer
Toilets: F = Flush V = Vault P = Pit C = Chemical
Recreation: H = Hiking S = Swimming F = Fishing B = Boating L = Boat Launch O = Off-highway Driving R = Horseback Riding
Maximum Trailer/RV Length given in feet. **Stay Limit** given in days. **Fee** given in dollars.
If no entry under **Season,** campground is open all year. If no entry under **Fee,** camping is free.

Center at the north entrance at Twentynine Palms, and Cottonwood, at the park's south entrance near Cottonwood Springs.

Palm Springs, along with its associated communities of Desert Hot Springs, Cathedral City, and Indio, is the golf capital of the United States. More than 90 courses bloom like green oases in an otherwise arid desert. Even more astonishing in this normally parched environment is the presence of 30,000 swimming pools, public and private. And for those seeking a more vigorous workout, 600 tennis courts will provide it.

Created by visionary Hollywood personalities and sustained by retirees and snowbirds from all over the country, Palm Springs has been transformed from an inhospitable tract of desert into a winter warm-weather playground.

The climate is typical of medium-altitude desert locations. Normal daily temperatures in July range from a high of 104 degrees F to a low of 75 degrees F. January temperatures range from a high of 64 degrees F to a low of 37 degrees F. Precipitation is minimal year-round, ranging from none at all in May and June to a high of 0.4 inch in January.

1 Joshua Tree National Park: Indian Cove

Location: 6 miles southwest of Twentynine Palms.
Sites: 107 sites for tents and RVs up to 32 feet long, plus 13 group sites for tents.
Facilities: Picnic tables, fire rings, pit toilets. Drinking water available at Indian Cove Ranger Station.
Fee per night: None for individual sites, $15-$30 for group sites. For group

A visitor to Joshua Tree National Park takes a close but cautious look at a bristly cholla cactus.

reservations, call 800-365-CAMP.
Agency: Joshua Tree National Park, 760-367-7511.
Activities: Hiking.
Finding the campground: From the intersection of Larrea Avenue and California 62 in Twentynine Palms, drive west on CA 62 for 3.2 miles to Indian Cove Road. Turn left onto Indian Cove Road and drive south 3 miles.

About the campground: Stay limit 14 days from October through May, 30 days from June through September. Open all year.

2 Joshua Tree National Park: Black Rock Canyon

Location: 25 miles southwest of Twentynine Palms.
Sites: 100 sites for tents and RVs up to 32 feet long.
Facilities: Picnic tables, fire grills, drinking water, flush toilets, dump station.
Fee per night: $10. For reservations, call 800-365-CAMP.

Agency: Joshua Tree National Park, 760-367-7511.
Activities: Hiking.
Finding the campground: From the intersection of Larrea Avenue and California 62 in Twentynine Palms, drive west on CA 62 for about 20 miles to Joshua Lane, in the town of Yucca Valley. Turn left onto Joshua Lane and drive south about 5 miles.

About the campground: Stay limit 14 days. Open September through May.

3 Joshua Tree National Park: Sheep Pass

Location: 15 miles south of Twentynine Palms.
Sites: 6 group sites for tents.
Facilities: Picnic tables, fire grills, pit toilets. No drinking water.
Fee per night: $13. For reservations, call 800-365-CAMP.
Agency: Joshua Tree National Park, 760-367-7511.
Activities: Hiking, rock climbing.
Finding the campground: From the intersection of California 62 and Utah Trail in Twentynine Palms, drive south on Utah Trail (which becomes Loop Road) for about 15 miles.

About the campground: Stay limit 14 days from October through May, 30 days from June through September. Open all year.

4 Joshua Tree National Park: Ryan

Location: 18 miles south of Twentynine Palms.
Sites: 29 sites for tents and RVs up to 29 feet long.
Facilities: Picnic tables, fire grills, pit toilets. No water.
Fee per night: None.
Agency: Joshua Tree National Park, 760-367-7511.
Activities: Hiking, rock climbing.
Finding the campground: From the intersection of California 62 and Utah Trail in Twentynine Palms, drive south on Utah Trail (which becomes Loop Road) for about 18 miles.

About the campground: Stay limit 14 days from October through May, 30 days from June through September. Open all year.

5 Joshua Tree National Park: Hidden Valley

Location: 12 miles southeast of the town of Joshua Tree.
Sites: 39 sites for tents and RVs up to 29 feet long.
Facilities: Picnic tables, fire grills, pit toilets. No water.
Fee per night: None.
Agency: Joshua Tree National Park, 760-367-7511.
Activities: Hiking.

Finding the campground: From the intersection of California 62 and Park Boulevard in Joshua Tree, drive southeast on Park Boulevard (which becomes Quail Springs Road) for about 12 miles.

About the campground: Hidden Valley Trail, a 1-mile loop, begins across the road from the campground. Stay limit 14 days from October through May, 30 days from June through September. Open all year.

6 Joshua Tree National Park: Jumbo Rocks

Location: 12.5 miles south of Twentynine Palms.
Sites: 125 sites for tents and RVs.
Facilities: Picnic tables, fire grills, pit toilets. No water.
Fee per night: None.
Agency: Joshua Tree National Park, 760-367-7511.
Activities: Hiking, rock climbing.
Finding the campground: From the intersection of California 62 and Utah Trail in Twentynine Palms, drive south on Utah Trail (which becomes Loop Road) for 12.5 miles.

About the campground: A 1.7-mile loop trail leads from the campground through Jumbo Rocks to Skull Rock. Stay limit 14 days from October through May, 30 days from June through September. Open all year.

Huge, bizarre rock formations are common in Joshua Tree National Park, and many campsites, such as this one at Belle Campground, butt right up against them.

7 | Joshua Tree National Park: Belle

Location: 10 miles south of Twentynine Palms.
Sites: 17 sites for tents and RVs up to 29 feet long.
Facilities: Picnic tables, fire grills, pit toilets. No water.
Fee per night: None.
Agency: Joshua Tree National Park, 760-367-7511.
Activities: Hiking, rock climbing.
Finding the campground: From the intersection of California 62 and Utah Trail in Twentynine Palms, drive south on Utah Trail for 8.5 miles to Cottonwood Springs Road, which bears left. Take Cottonwood Springs Road for 1.5 miles.

About the campground: Stay limit 14 days from October through May, 30 days from June through September. Open all year.

8 | Joshua Tree National Park: White Tank

Location: 11 miles south of Twentynine Palms.
Sites: 15 sites for tents and RVs up to 29 feet long.
Facilities: Picnic tables, fire grills, pit toilets. No water.
Fee per night: None.
Agency: Joshua Tree National Park, 760-367-7511.
Activities: Hiking, rock climbing.
Finding the campground: From the intersection of California 62 and Utah Trail in Twentynine Palms, drive south on Utah Trail for 8.5 miles to Cottonwood Springs Road, which bears left. Take Cottonwood Springs Road for 2.3 miles.

About the campground: Stay limit 14 days. Open September through May.

9 | Joshua Tree National Park: Cottonwood

Location: 29 miles east of Indio.
Sites: 62 sites for tents and RVs up to 29 feet long, plus 3 group sites that accommodate up to 30 people each.
Facilities: Picnic tables, fireplaces, drinking water, flush toilets.
Fee per night: $8 for individual sites, $15 for group sites. For group reservations, call 800-365-CAMP.
Agency: Joshua Tree National Park, 760-367-7511.
Activities: Hiking.
Finding the campground: From the Dillon Road entrance to Interstate 10 in Indio, take I-10 east for 22 miles to Cottonwood Springs Road. Drive north for about 7 miles to the park's Cottonwood Visitor Center and then the campground.

About the campground: Three trails start at the campground: Mastodon Peak (4 miles round trip) affords fine views of the desert landscape and the Salton Sea, Lost Palms Oasis (8 miles round trip) leads to one of the most beautiful fan-palm oases in California, and a mile-long nature trail leads from the campground to Cottonwood Spring. Check at the Cottonwood Visitor Center for additional hikes in the area. Stay limit 14 days from October through May, 30 days from June through September.

10 Knott Sky Park

Location: 1 mile southwest of Twentynine Palms.
Sites: 42 sites for RVs, all with pull-thrus, some with full hookups and some with water and electrical hookups, plus some tent sites.
Facilities: Picnic tables, grills, drinking water, flush toilets, showers, dump station, playground, ball field, hiking trails.
Fee per night: $10-$16 for RVs, $7 for tents. Reservations accepted. Good Sam Club discount.
Agency: Twentynine Palms Parks and Recreation District, 760-367-7562.
Activities: Hiking, visiting Joshua Tree National Park.
Finding the campground: From the intersection of California 62 and El Sol Drive in Twentynine Palms, drive 1 mile southwest on El Sol Drive.

About the campground: The campground is close to the entrance to Joshua Tree National Park and is a good option for park visitors who want more amenities than can be found in the park. Stay limit 14 days. Open all year.

11 Corn Springs

Location: 63 miles east of Indio.
Sites: 10 sites for tents and RVs.
Facilities: Picnic tables, fire rings, drinking water, pit toilets.
Fee per night: $6.
Agency: Bureau of Land Management, 760-251-0812.
Activities: Hiking.
Finding the campground: From the Dillon Road entrance to Interstate 10 in Indio, take I-10 east for 56 miles to Corn Springs Road. Drive 7 miles south on Corn Springs Road.

About the campground: Situated in an isolated fan-palm oasis, the campground features an interpretive trail that explains the flora, fauna, and culture of the area. Corn Springs also provides a place to stay to explore the south part of Joshua Tree National Park if Cottonwood Campground (No. 9 above) is full. Stay limit 14 days. Open all year.

12 Lake Cahuilla County Park

Location: 8 miles south of Indio.
Sites: 60 sites for RVs, including 50 with water and electrical hookups, plus additional undesignated sites for tents and RVs.
Facilities: Picnic tables, barbecue grills, drinking water, flush toilets, showers, dump station, boat ramp, playground, swimming pool, corrals.

Visitors to Joshua Tree National Park camp right among the trees for which the park is named at Black Rock Canyon Campground.

Fee per night: $12-$16, pets $2.
Agency: Riverside County Parks Department, 760-564-4712.
Activities: Fishing, boating, horseback riding.
Finding the campground: From the intersection of California 111 and Monroe Street in Indio, take Monroe south for 6 miles to 58th Avenue. Turn right (west) onto 58th and drive about 2 miles.

About the campground: Fishing and boating are permitted on the lake, but swimming is restricted to the pool. Stay limit 14 days. Open all year.

SALTON SEA & VICINITY

The Salton Sea, sometimes referred to as California's Dead Sea, is the state's largest lake, covering about 360 square miles. It was created accidentally in 1905 when diversion controls on the Colorado River gave way, sending floodwaters rushing into a wide depression in the desert. The lake is about 17 miles wide and 40 miles long, and it has an average depth of 10 to 20 feet. It lies 228 feet below sea level. Its salinity closely matches that of the Gulf of California to the south, and in 1950 the lake was successfully stocked with several species of fish from that sea. Excellent fishing exists year-round, primarily for corvina, a fish similar to the white sea bass.

The biggest attraction of this area is fishing, but swimming, boating, and waterskiing are popular, too. Because outboard motors operate more efficiently below sea level, many boat racing events are held on the lake. Hiking is possible along the shores of the lake, and the area features several nature trails. The area is a paradise for bird watching, as it lies within the North American Flyway. More than 380 species of birds can be seen around the lake.

SALTON SEA AREA MAP

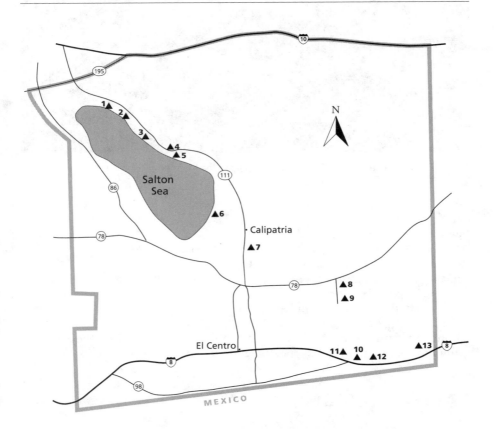

	Group sites	RV sites	Max. RV length	Hookups	Toilets	Showers	Drinking water	Dump station	Pets	Wheelchair	Recreation	Fee ($)	Season	Can reserve
1 Headquarters		•		WES	F	•	•	•	•	•	HSFBL	12-16		•
2 Mecca Beach		•			F	•	•		•	•	HSFB	12		
3 Corvina Beach		•			C		•		•	•	HSFBL	7		
4 Salt Creek		•			C				•	•	HSFB	7		
5 Bombay Beach		•			C		•		•	•	HSFB	7		
6 Red Hill Marina County Park		•		E	F	•	•		•	•	SFB	7–12		
7 Wiest Lake County Park		•		WES	F	•	•	•	•	•	FBL	7–12		
8 Gecko		•			P						HO			
9 Roadrunner		•			P				•		HO			
10 Midway		•			P						HO			
11 Hot Spring LTVA		•									HO	See entry	Sep-Apr	
12 Tamarisk LTVA		•									HO	See entry	Sep-Apr	
13 Dunes Vista LTVA		•									HO	See entry	Sep-Apr	

Hookups: W = Water E = Electric S = Sewer
Toilets: F = Flush V = Vault P = Pit C = Chemical
Recreation: H = Hiking S = Swimming F = Fishing B = Boating L = Boat Launch O = Off-highway Driving R = Horseback Riding
Maximum Trailer/RV Length given in feet. **Stay Limit** given in days. **Fee** given in dollars.
If no entry under **Season,** campground is open all year. If no entry under **Fee,** camping is free.

1 Salton Sea State Recreation Area: Headquarters

Location: 10 miles southeast of Mecca.
Sites: 40 sites for tents and RVs, including 15 with full hookups.
Facilities: Picnic tables, barbecue grills, drinking water, flush toilets, showers, dump station, boat launch.
Fee per night: $12-$16, pets $1. For reservations, call Parknet, 800-444-7275. Reservation fee, $7.50.
Agency: California Department of Parks and Recreation, 760-393-3059.
Activities: Swimming, fishing, boating, waterskiing, hiking.
Finding the campground: From Mecca, drive 10 miles southeast on California 111 to the campground entrance on the right.

About the campground: The Salton Sea State Recreation Area encompasses 17,913 acres along the northeastern shore of the lake. A visitor center is located here at Headquarters Campground, and a mile-long, self-guided nature trail follows the shoreline from Headquarters to Mecca Beach Campground (see No. 2 below). Stay limit 30 days. Open all year.

2 Salton Sea State Recreation Area: Mecca Beach

Location: 11.5 miles southeast of Mecca.
Sites: 110 sites for tents and RVs.

Facilities: Picnic tables, fire rings, drinking water, flush toilets, showers.
Fee per night: $12, pets $1.
Agency: California Department of Parks and Recreation, 760-393-3059.
Activities: Swimming, fishing, boating, waterskiing, hiking.
Finding the campground: From Mecca, drive 11.5 miles southeast on California 111 to the campground entrance on the northeastern side of the lake.

About the campground: See Headquarters Campground (No. 1 above) for more about the attractions of this area. Stay limit 30 days. Open all year.

3 Salton Sea State Recreation Area: Corvina Beach

Location: 14 miles southeast of Mecca.
Sites: 500 sites for tents and RVs.
Facilities: Drinking water, chemical toilets, boat ramp.
Fee per night: $7, pets $1.
Agency: California Department of Parks and Recreation, 760-393-3059.
Activities: Swimming, fishing, boating, waterskiing, hiking.
Finding the campground: From Mecca, drive 14 miles southeast on California 111 to the campground entrance on the lake side of the highway. Stay limit 30 days. Open all year.

About the campground: See Headquarters Campground (No. 1 above) for more about the attractions of this area. Stay limit 30 days. Open all year.

4 Salton Sea State Recreation Area: Salt Creek

Location: 17 miles southeast of Mecca.
Sites: 150 sites for tents and RVs.
Facilities: Drinking water, chemical toilets.
Fee per night: $7, pets $1.
Agency: California Department of Parks and Recreation, 760-393-3059.
Activities: Swimming, fishing, boating, waterskiing, hiking.
Finding the campground: From Mecca, drive 17 miles southeast on California 111.

About the campground: See Headquarters Campground (No. 1 above) for more about the attractions of this area. Stay limit 30 days. Open all year.

5 Salton Sea State Recreation Area: Bombay Beach

Location: 27 miles southeast of Mecca.
Sites: 200 sites for tents and RVs.
Facilities: Drinking water, chemical toilets.
Fee per night: $7, pets $1.
Agency: California Department of Parks and Recreation, 760-393-3059.
Activities: Swimming, fishing, boating, waterskiing, hiking.

Finding the campground: From Mecca, drive 27 miles southeast on California 111.

About the campground: See Headquarters Campground (No. 1 above) for more about the attractions of this area. Stay limit 30 days. Open all year.

6 Red Hill Marina County Park

Location: 11 miles southwest of Niland.
Sites: 400 sites for tents and RVs, some with electrical hookups, most dry.
Facilities: Picnic tables, barbecue grills, drinking water, flush toilets, showers, boat ramp, loading dock.
Fee per night: $7-$12.
Agency: Imperial County Parks Department, 760-348-2310.
Activities: Swimming, fishing, boating, bird watching.
Finding the campground: From the intersection of Noffsinger Road and California 111 in Niland, take CA 111 south for 5 miles and turn right onto Sinclair Road. Continue for 4.5 miles to Garst Road, turn right, and drive 1.5 miles to Red Hill Road. Turn left and follow Red Hill Road to the campground.

About the campground: Red Hill is situated on a grassy spit of land on the southeastern shore of the Salton Sea. It is 3.6 miles northwest of the Salton Sea National Wildlife Refuge. Stay limit 14 days. Open all year.

7 Wiest Lake County Park

Location: 7 miles north of Brawley.
Sites: 24 sites with full hookups for RVs, 20 sites for tents.
Facilities: Picnic tables, barbecue grills, drinking water, flush toilets, showers, dump station, boat ramp.
Fee per night: $7-$12.
Agency: Imperial County Parks Department, 760-344-3712.
Activities: Fishing, boating, bird watching.
Finding the campground: From the intersection of Main Street and California 111 in Brawley, drive north on CA 111 for 5 miles, turn right (east) onto Rutherford Road, and drive 2 miles.

About the campground: Situated on a small lake 14 miles south of the Salton Sea, the campground is just south of the Imperial State Wildlife Area. Stay limit 14 days. Open all year.

8 Imperial Sand Dunes Recreation Area: Gecko

Location: 22 miles east of Brawley.
Sites: Paved open area that accommodates 120 vehicles, including RVs.
Facilities: Pit toilets. No drinking water.
Fee per night: None.

Agency: Bureau of Land Management, 760-337-4400.
Activities: Off-highway driving, hiking.
Finding the campground: From Brawley, drive 18 miles east on California 78 to where it crosses the Coachella Canal. Continue on CA 78 for less than a mile, watching for Gecko Road on the right. Turn right onto Gecko and drive about 3 miles.

About the campground: The Imperial Dunes, the largest sand dunes in California, cover an area 40 miles long and 5 miles wide along the eastern border of Imperial Valley. Shifting sands continually build and topple dunes rising more than 300 feet high over an area of 180,000 acres. Summer temperatures can reach 110 degrees F, and annual rainfall is less than 2 inches.

The most popular activity in the dunes is OHV driving, and two-thirds of the recreation area permits this use. Most of the OHV area is south of CA 78, extending from the highway to the Mexican border. Vehicles are prohibited from the Algodones Outstanding Natural Area, which is reserved for hiking. In addition to the campgrounds, camping is permitted in all areas open to vehicle use in the recreation area. Stay limit 14 days. Open all year.

9 Imperial Sand Dunes Recreation Area: Roadrunner

Location: 25 miles east of Brawley.
Sites: Paved open area that accommodates 120 vehicles, including RVs.
Facilities: Pit toilets. No drinking water.
Fee per night: None.
Agency: Bureau of Land Management, 760-337-4400.
Activities: Off-highway driving, hiking.
Finding the campground: From Brawley, drive 18 miles east on California 78 to where it crosses the Coachella Canal. Continue on CA 78 for less than a mile, watching for Gecko Road on the right. Turn right onto Gecko and drive about 6 miles.

About the campground: See Gecko Campground (No. 8 above) for more about the attractions of this recreation area. Stay limit 14 days. Open all year.

10 Imperial Sand Dunes Recreation Area: Midway

Location: 17 miles west of Yuma.
Sites: Paved open area that accommodates 120 vehicles, including RVs.
Facilities: Pit toilets. No drinking water.
Fee per night: None.
Agency: Bureau of Land Management, 760-337-4400.
Activities: Off-highway driving, hiking.
Finding the campground: From Yuma on the California-Arizona border, drive about 17 miles west on Interstate 8 to the Sand Hills exit. Drive south to Gray's Hill Road and then west less than a mile to the campground.

About the campground: See Gecko Campground (No. 8 above) for more about the attractions of this recreation area. Stay limit 14 days. Open all year.

11 Hot Spring Long-Term Visitor Area

Location: 19 miles east of El Centro.
Sites: Open camping for self-contained RVs.
Facilities: None.
Fee: $20 per week, $100 per season (September 15 to April 15) for use of all campgrounds in the program (see "About the campground").
Agency: Bureau of Land Management, 760-337-4400.
Activities: Hiking, off-highway driving, water sports.
Finding the campground: From El Centro, drive east on Interstate 8 for 17 miles to the California 115 exit. Turn north and drive to Old Highway 80, then drive east about 2 miles, watching for signs.

About the campground: Hot Spring is one of the campgrounds in the California Long-Term Visitor Areas Program, established by the BLM for the benefit of campers who wish to spend all or part of the winter season in the deserts of southeastern California. Once paid, the weekly or seasonal fee entitles the participant to camp at any of eight campgrounds in California and two in Arizona, and to move around freely among them for the duration of the permit. The program is explained more fully on page 4.

Accessible from this campground are the Imperial Dunes, where hiking and off-highway driving are popular, and the Colorado River, which presents opportunities for water sports.

12 Tamarisk Long Term-Visitor Area

Location: 32 miles east of El Centro.
Sites: Open camping for self-contained RVs.
Facilities: None.
Fee: $20 per week, $100 per season (September 15 to April 15) for use of all campgrounds in the program (see Hot Spring Campground above).
Agency: Bureau of Land Management, 760-337-4400.
Activities: Hiking, off-highway driving, water sports.
Finding the campground: From the intersection of Interstate 8 and California 98 about 30 miles east of El Centro, take CA 98 west for about 2 miles, watching for signs.

About the campground: See Hot Spring Campground (No. 11 above).

13 Dunes Vista Long-Term Visitor Area

Location: 11 miles west of Winterhaven.
Sites: Open camping for self-contained RVs.
Facilities: None.

Fee: $20 per week, $100 per season (September 15 to April 15) for use of all campgrounds in the program (see Hot Spring Campground above).
Agency: Bureau of Land Management, 760-337-4400.
Activities: Hiking, off-highway driving, water sports.
Finding the campground: From Winterhaven, drive west about 11 miles on Interstate 8 to the Ogilby Road exit. Drive north on Ogilby Road (County Road S34) for 0.3 mile, watching for signs.

About the campground: See Hot Spring Campground (above).

COLORADO RIVER

The Colorado River forms the border between southeastern California and Arizona. In recent years, this sparsely populated region has become a popular winter tourist destination, as well as a retirement location for those seeking year-round sunshine and warm weather. The area's popularity is due in large part to the combination of desert sunshine and the water-sports opportunities afforded by Lake Havasu and the Colorado.

From Needles in the north to Winterhaven in the south, 200 miles of the river water the desert and provide recreational opportunities. Houseboats, cabin cruisers, and nonmotorized craft ply the river, while residents and visitors fish, water-ski, or simply enjoy the scenery of such places as the Topock Gorge.

The region is also rich in history and cultural heritage. Examples include the historic train depot and Harvey House Hotel in the former frontier town of Needles as well as the giant figures south of Blythe, carved in the earth centuries ago by Native Americans.

	Group sites	RV sites	Max. RV length	Hookups	Toilets	Showers	Drinking water	Dump station	Pets	Wheelchair	Recreation	Fee ($)	Season	Can reserve
1 Moabi Regional Park		•		WES	F	•	•	•	•	•	HSFBRO	12–20		•
2 Midland LTVA		•						•				See entry	Sep–Apr	
3 Mayflower County Park		•		WE	F	•	•	•	•	•	SFBL	15–16		
4 Wiley's Well (LTVA)		•			P		•				H	See entry	Sep–Apr	
5 Coon Hollow (LTVA)		•			P						H	See entry	Sep-Apr	
6 Palo Verde County Park		•			F	•								
7 Picacho State Rec Area	•	•	35		P	•	•		•	•	HFBL	9–12		
8 Senator Wash Rec Area		•			P				•		FBL			
9 Squaw Lake		•			F	•			•	•	FBL	Call		
10 Imperial Dam LTVA		•			P	•	•	•			HO	See entry		
11 Pilot Knob LTVA		•									HO	See entry		

Hookups: W = Water E = Electric S = Sewer
Toilets: F = Flush V = Vault P = Pit C = Chemical
Recreation: H = Hiking S = Swimming F = Fishing B = Boating L = Boat Launch O = Off-highway Driving R = Horseback Riding
Maximum Trailer/RV Length given in feet. **Stay Limit** given in days. **Fee** given in dollars.
If no entry under **Season**, campground is open all year. If no entry under **Fee**, camping is free.

Colorado River Area Map

1 Moabi Regional Park

Location: 10 miles south of Needles.
Sites: 647 sites for tents and RVs, including 131 with full hookups.
Facilities: Picnic tables, grills, fire rings, drinking water, showers, flush toilets, laundry, dump station, store, snack bar, bait shop, playground, ball field, basketball and volleyball courts, horseshoe pits, marina, boat ramp.
Fee per night: $12-$20, pets $1. Reservations accepted.
Agency: San Bernardino County Regional Parks, 760-326-9222.
Activities: Swimming, fishing, boating, waterskiing, hiking, horseback riding, bird watching, off-highway driving.
Finding the campground: From Needles, drive 10 miles south on Interstate 40 to Park Moabi Road. Turn left and drive half a mile.

About the campground: Moabi occupies over 1,000 acres on the banks of the Colorado River and offers a full range of water sports. Some campsites have shoreline frontage on an attractive peninsula. Houseboats and power boats are available for rent. Stay limit 14 days. Open all year.

2 Midland Long-Term Visitor Area

Location: 10 miles northeast of Blythe.
Sites: Open camping for self-contained RVs.
Facilities: Dump station. No drinking water.
Fee: $20 per week, $100 per season (September 15 to April 15) for use of all campgrounds in the LTVA program (see "About the campground").
Agency: Bureau of Land Management, 760-337-4400.
Activities: Water sports on Colorado River.
Finding the campground: From Interstate 10 in Blythe, take the Lovekin Boulevard exit and drive north for 6 miles. Turn left (northwest) onto Midland Road and drive about 4 miles.

About the campground: Midland is one of the campgrounds in the California Long-Term Visitor Area Program, established by the BLM for the benefit of campers who wish to spend all or part of the winter season in the deserts of southeastern California. Payment of the weekly or seasonal fee entitles the visitor to camp at any of eight campgrounds in California and two in Arizona, and to move around freely among them for the duration of the permit. See page 4 for more information about this program.

The Colorado River is only 15 miles away, providing an opportunity to engage in a variety of water sports.

3 Mayflower County Park

Location: 6 miles north of Blythe.
Sites: 28 sites for tents, 152 sites with water and electrical hookups for RVs.
Facilities: Picnic tables, barbecue grills, drinking water, flush toilets, showers,

dump station, boat ramp.
Fee per night: $15-$16, pets $2.
Agency: Riverside County Parks Department, 760-922-4665.
Activities: Swimming, fishing, boating, waterskiing.
Finding the campground: From the intersection of Interstate 10 and U.S. Highway 95 just east of Blythe, take US 95 north for 3.7 miles to 6th Avenue. Turn right and drive 2.5 miles.

About the campground: The campground is located on the banks of the Colorado River, with opportunities for a variety of water sports. Stay limit 14 days. Open all year.

4 Mule Mountain Long-Term Visitor Area: Wiley's Well

Location: 23 miles southwest of Blythe.
Sites: 13 sites for tents and RVs.
Facilities: Pit toilets, dump station. No water.
Fee: $20 per week, $100 per season for use of all campgrounds in the program (see Midland LTVA above).
Agency: Bureau of Land Management, 760-337-4400.
Activities: Hiking, four-wheel-drive exploring, water sports on Colorado River.
Finding the campground: From Blythe, drive west 15 miles on Interstate 10, turn left onto Wiley's Well Road, and drive south about 8 miles.

About the campground: The Colorado River is only 25 miles away, affording an opportunity to engage in a variety of water sports. See Midland LTVA (above).

5 Mule Mountain Long-Term Visitor Area: Coon Hollow

Location: 27 miles southwest of Blythe.
Sites: 27 sites for tents and RVs.
Facilities: Pit toilets. No water.
Fee: $20 per week, $100 per season (September 15 to April 15) for use of all campgrounds in the program (see Midland LTVA above).
Agency: Bureau of Land Management, 760-337-4400.
Activities: Hiking, four-wheel-drive exploring, water sports on Colorado River.
Finding the campground: From Blythe, drive west 15 miles on Interstate 10, turn left onto Wiley's Well Road, and drive south about 12 miles.

About the campground: The Colorado River is 25 miles away, affording an opportunity to engage in a variety of water sports. See Midland LTVA (above).

6 Palo Verde County Park

Location: 3 miles south of Palo Verde.
Sites: Undesignated sites for tents and RVs.
Facilities: Drinking water, flush toilets, playground.

Fee per night: None.
Agency: Imperial County Department of Parks, 760-339-4384.
Finding the campground: From Palo Verde, drive 3 miles south on California 78. Watch for the campground sign on the east side of the highway.

About the campground: Located close to the Cibola National Wildlife Refuge, the campground has no access to the Colorado River. The nearest boat launch is about 5 miles away. Stay limit 14 days. Open all year.

7 Picacho State Recreation Area

Location: 25 miles north of Winterhaven.
Sites: 59 sites for tents, RVs up to 35 feet long, and trailers up to 30 feet long, plus group sites and boat-in sites.
Facilities: Picnic tables, fire grills, drinking water, solar showers, pit toilets, boat ramp.
Fee per night: $9-$12.
Agency: California Department of Parks and Recreation, 760-339-1360.
Activities: Hiking, swimming, fishing, boating, waterskiing, four-wheel-drive exploring.
Finding the campground: From Winterhaven, take Picacho Road north for 25 miles. Once it crosses the All American Canal, the road is unpaved and winding, with frequent potholes and washboarding. Drivers of large trailers and RVs should use caution. Picacho Road ends at the campground.

About the campground: This 7,000-acre recreation area features 8 miles of frontage along a 76-mile stretch of the Colorado River, from Blythe to the Imperial Dam, which has been designated for recreational activity. A nature trail and several longer trails begin in the campground area. Those with four-wheel-drive vehicles can drive to the Little Grand Canyon Trailhead. Stay limit 14 days. Open all year.

8 Senator Wash Recreation Area

Location: 19 miles northeast of Winterhaven.
Sites: Undesignated sites for tents and RVs.
Facilities: Pit toilets, boat ramp.
Fee per night: None.
Agency: Bureau of Land Management, 602-726-6300.
Activities: Fishing, boating.
Finding the campground: From Winterhaven, drive northeast on County Road S24 for about 15 miles to Senator Wash Road. Turn left and drive 4 miles.

About the campground: Stay limit 14 days. Open all year.

9 Squaw Lake

Location: 20 miles northeast of Winterhaven.
Sites: 80 sites for tents and RVs.
Facilities: Picnic tables, fire rings, drinking water, flush toilets, boat ramp.
Fee per night: Call BLM.
Agency: Bureau of Land Management, 602-726-6300.
Activities: Fishing, boating.
Finding the campground: From Winterhaven, drive northeast on County Road S24 for about 15 miles to Senator Wash Road. Turn left and drive 4.5 miles.

About the campground: Stay limit 14 days. Open all year.

10 Imperial Dam Long-Term Visitor Area

Location: 12 miles northeast of Winterhaven.
Sites: Open camping for RVs.
Facilities: Drinking water, pit toilets, dump station, public phone.
Fee: $20 per week, $100 per season for use of all campgrounds in the program (see Midland LTVA above).
Agency: Bureau of Land Management, 760-337-4400.
Activities: Hiking, off-highway driving, water sports.
Finding the campground: From Interstate 8 in Winterhaven, take the 4th Street exit and drive north to County Road S24. Turn right and drive northeast on CR S24 for about 12 miles.

About the campground: The nearby Imperial Sand Dunes offer hiking and OHV driving opportunities, while the Colorado River is readily accessible for water sports. See Midland LTVA (above).

11 Pilot Knob Long Term Visitor Area

Location: 5 miles west of Winterhaven.
Sites: Open camping for self-contained RVs.
Facilities: None.
Fee: $20 per week, $100 per season for use of all campgrounds in the program (see Midland LTVA above).
Agency: Bureau of Land Management, 760-337-4400.
Activities: Hiking, off-highway driving, water sports.
Finding the campground: From Winterhaven, drive west on Interstate 8 for 5 miles to the Sidewinder Road exit, turn south onto Sidewinder Road, and drive 0.3 mile.

About the campground: The nearby Imperial Sand Dunes offer hiking and OHV driving opportunities, while the Colorado River is readily accessible for water sports. See Midland LTVA (above).

INDEX

ABOUT THE AUTHOR

Richard McMahon lives in Kahuku, Hawaii, but spends his summers in an RV traveling California. He has written numerous articles for magazines and newspapers and writes a weekly outdoor column for *The Advertiser*, Honolulu's largest daily paper. After retiring from the U.S. Army, he led hiking and backpacking trips worldwide for Mountain Travel and REI Adventures. In addition to this book, he is the author of *Adventuring in Hawaii, Camping Hawaii,* and *Scenic Driving Hawaii.*

FALCON GUIDES® Leading the Way™

FALCON GUIDES® are available for where-to-go hiking, mountain biking, rock climbing, walking, scenic driving, fishing, rockhounding, paddling, birding, wildlife viewing, and camping. We also have FalconGuides on essential outdoor skills and subjects and field identification. The following titles are currently available, but this list grows every year. For a free catalog with a complete list of titles, call FALCON toll-free at 1-800-582-2665.

HIKING GUIDES

Hiking Alaska
Hiking Arizona
Hiking Arizona's Cactus Country
Hiking the Beartooths
Hiking Big Bend National Park
Hiking the Bob Marshall Country
Hiking California
Hiking California's Desert Parks
Hiking Carlsbad Caverns
   and Guadalupe Mtns. National Parks
Hiking Colorado
Hiking Colorado, Vol.II
Hiking Colorado's Summits
Hiking Colorado's Weminuche Wilderness
Hiking the Columbia River Gorge
Hiking Florida
Hiking Georgia
Hiking Glacier & Waterton Lakes National Parks
Hiking Grand Canyon National Park
Hiking Grand Staircase-Escalante/Glen Canyon
Hiking Grand Teton National Park
Hiking Great Basin National Park
Hiking Hot Springs in the Pacific Northwest
Hiking Idaho
Hiking Maine
Hiking Michigan
Hiking Minnesota
Hiking Montana
Hiking Mount Rainier National Park
Hiking Mount St. Helens
Hiking Nevada
Hiking New Hampshire

Hiking New Mexico
Hiking New York
Hiking North Carolina
Hiking the North Cascades
Hiking Northern Arizona
Hiking Olympic National Park
Hiking Oregon
Hiking Oregon's Eagle Cap Wilderness
Hiking Oregon's Mount Hood/Badger Creek
Hiking Oregon's Three Sisters Country
Hiking Pennsylvania
Hiking Shenandoah National Park
Hiking the Sierra Nevada
Hiking South Carolina
Hiking South Dakota's Black Hills Country
Hiking Southern New England
Hiking Tennessee
Hiking Texas
Hiking Utah
Hiking Utah's Summits
Hiking Vermont
Hiking Virginia
Hiking Washington
Hiking Wyoming
Hiking Wyoming's Cloud Peak Wilderness
Hiking Wyoming's Wind River Range
Hiking Yellowstone National Park
Hiking Zion & Bryce Canyon National Parks
The Trail Guide to Bob Marshall Country
Wild Country Companion
Wild Montana
Wild Utah

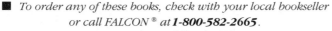
*To order any of these books, check with your local bookseller
or call FALCON ® at **1-800-582-2665**.*
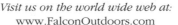
Visit us on the world wide web at:
www.FalconOutdoors.com

FALCON®

FALCON GUIDES ® Leading the Way

FIELD GUIDES

Bitterroot: Montana State Flower
Canyon Country Wildflowers
Central Rocky Mountains
  Wildflowers
Great Lakes Berry Book
New England Berry Book
Ozark Wildflowers
Pacific Northwest Berry Book
Plants of Arizona
Rare Plants of Colorado
Rocky Mountain Berry Book
Scats & Tracks of the Pacific
  Coast States
Scats & Tracks of the
  Rocky Mountains
Southern Rocky Mountain
  Wildflowers
Tallgrass Prairie Wildflowers
Western Trees
Wildflowers of Southwestern
  Utah
Willow Bark and Rosehips

FISHING GUIDES

Fishing Alaska
Fishing the Beartooths
Fishing Florida
Fishing Glacier National Park
Fishing Maine
Fishing Montana
Fishing Wyoming
Fishing Yellowstone
  National Park

ROCKHOUNDING GUIDES

Rockhounding Arizona
Rockhounding California
Rockhounding Colorado
Rockhounding Montana
Rockhounding Nevada
Rockhound's Guide to New
  Mexico
Rockhounding Texas
Rockhounding Utah
Rockhounding Wyoming

MORE GUIDEBOOKS

Backcountry Horseman's
  Guide to Washington
Camping California's
  National Forests
Exploring Canyonlands &
  Arches National Parks
Exploring Hawaii's Parklands
Exploring Mount Helena
Exploring Southern California
  Beaches
Recreation Guide to WA
  National Forests
Touring California & Nevada
  Hot Springs
Touring Colorado Hot Springs
Touring Montana & Wyoming
  Hot Springs
Trail Riding Western
  Montana
Wild Country Companion
Wilderness Directory
Wild Montana
Wild Utah

BIRDING GUIDES

Birding Minnesota
Birding Montana
Birding Northern California
Birding Texas
Birding Utah

PADDLING GUIDES

Floater's Guide to Colorado
Paddling Minnesota
Paddling Montana
Paddling Okefenokee
Paddling Oregon
Paddling Yellowstone & Grand
  Teton National Parks

HOW-TO GUIDES

Avalanche Aware
Backpacking Tips
Bear Aware
Desert Hiking Tips
Hiking with Dogs
Leave No Trace
Mountain Lion Alert
Reading Weather
Route Finding
Using GPS
Wilderness First Aid
Wilderness Survival

WALKING

Walking Colorado Springs
Walking Denver
Walking Portland
Walking St. Louis
Walking Virginia Beach

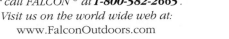

■ *To order any of these books, check with your local bookseller*
or call FALCON ® *at 1-800-582-2665 .*
Visit us on the world wide web at:
www.FalconOutdoors.com

FALCON®

Going Somewhere?

Insiders' Guides offer 60 current and upcoming titles to some of the country's most popular vacation destinations (including the ones listed below), and we're adding many more. Written by local authors and averaging 400 pages, our guides provide the information you need quickly and easily—whether searching for savory local cuisine, unique regional wares, amusements for the kids, a picturesque hiking spot, off-the-beaten-track attractions, new environs or a room with a view.

Explore America and experience the joy of travel with the Insiders' Guide® books.

Adirondacks	Montana's Glacier Country
Atlanta, GA	Monterey Peninsula
Austin, TX	Myrtle Beach
Baltimore	Nashville
Bend & Central Oregon	New Hampshire
Bermuda	North Carolina's Central Coast & New Bern
Boca Raton & the Palm Beaches	North Carolina's Southern Coast & Wilmington
Boise & Sun Valley	North Carolina's Mountains
Boulder & the Rocky Mountain National Park	North Carolina's Outer Banks
Branson & the Ozark Mountains	Phoenix
California's Wine Country	The Pocono Mountains
Cape Cod, Nantucket and Martha's Vineyard	Portland
Charleston, SC	Relocation
Cincinnati	Richmond
Civil War Sites in the Eastern Theater	Salt Lake City
Colorado's Mountains	San Diego
Denver	Santa Barbara
The Florida Keys & Key West	Santa Fe
Florida's Great Northwest	Sarasota & Bradenton
Golf in the Carolinas	Savannah
Indianapolis	Southwestern Utah
The Lake Superior Region	Tampa & St. Petersburg
Las Vegas	Texas Coastal Bend
Lexington, KY	Tucson
Louisville, KY	Twin Cities
Madison, WI	Virginia's Blue Ridge
Maine's Mid-Coast	Virginia's Chesapeake Bay
Maine's Southern Coast	Washington, D.C.
Michigan's Traverse Bay Region	Williamsburg
Mississippi	Yellowstone

Insiders' Guide® books retail between $14.95 and $17.95. To order, go to your local bookstore, call Falcon Publishing at 800-582-2665 or visit our website at www.insiders.com.

The Insiders' Guides are an imprint of Falcon Publishing, P.O. Box 1718, Helena, MT 59624
Fax 800-968-3550
www.FalconOutdoors.com

FALCONGUIDES ® Leading the Way™

More Birding Books From FALCON

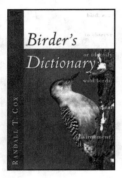

Birder's Dictionary
By Randall T. Cox, Illustrated by Todd Telander

A unique pocket reference for birders of all levels, or for anyone who needs quick reference to ornithological terms. For editors, writers, students, and avid birders.

Softcover, 4 1/2 x 7 1/2", illustrated.
Only $8.95 plus shipping

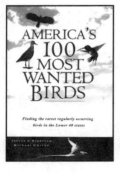

America's 100 Most Wanted Birds
By Stephen G. Mlodinow and Michael O'Brien

A guide to finding and seeing 100 of the rarest regularly occurring birds in the continental United States.

Softcover, 6 x 9", 40-page color section.
Only $24.95 plus shipping.

■ *To order any of these books, check with your local bookseller or call FALCON at* **1-800-582-2665**.

Visit us on the world wide web at:
www.FalconOutdoors.com

FALCON®

FALCONGUIDES ®Leading the Way™

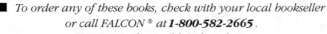

■ *To order any of these books, check with your local bookseller
or call FALCON ® at **1-800-582-2665**.
Visit us on the world wide web at:*
www.FalconOutdoors.com

FALCON®